Umberto Eco

is Professor of Semiotics at the University of Bologna and contributes a regular column to the newspaper *L'Espresso*. He has been a broadcaster both on radio and on television since the mid-50s and he is an editor for the Italian publisher Bompiani.

He is the bestselling author of *The Name of the Rose* and *Foucault's Pendulum* as well as a renowned semiologist and medievalist whose *Faith in Fakes (Travels in Hyperreality)* is a masterpiece of contemporary cultural studies.

Robert Lumley

is Lecturer in Italian Studies at University College, London. His books include *States of Emergency — Cultures of Revolt in Italy 1968–1978* and he has also translated Gianni Celati's *Voices from the Plains*.

D1048656

UMBERTO ECO

Apocalypse Postponed

Edited by Robert Lumley

Flamingo
An Imprint of HarperCollinsPublishers

Flamingo
An Imprint of HarperCollins*Publishers*
77–85 Fulham Palace Road,
Hammersmith, London W6 8JB

Published by Flamingo 1995
9 8 7 6 5 4 3 2 1

First published in Great Britain by
British Film Institute 1994

Author photograph by John Foley

ISBN 0 00 654851 2

Set in Linotron Galliard by
Rowland Phototypesetting Ltd
Bury St Edmunds, Suffolk

Printed in Great Britain by
HarperCollinsManufacturing Glasgow

CONTENTS

ACKNOWLEDGMENTS

Details of original place of publication and (where necessary) the name of the translator: 'Apocalyptic and Integrated Intellectuals' (*Apocalittici e integrati*, Milan, 1964; trans. Jenny Condie); 'The World of Charlie Brown' (*Apocalittici e integrati*; trans. William Weaver; first published in translation for exhibition catalogue 'The Graphic Art of Charles Schulz'); 'Reactions of Apocalyptic and Integrated Intellectuals: Then' and 'Reactions of the Author: Now' (*Apocalittici e integrati*, 1977; trans. Jenny Condie); 'Orwell, or Concerning Visionary Power' (preface to Mondadori edition of *1984*; trans. Jenny Condie); 'The Future of Literacy' (International Conference: 'Books and Literacy: A Response to New Developments', Amsterdam 1987); 'Political Language: The use and abuse of rhetoric' (G. L. Beccaria [ed.], *I linguaggi settoriali in Italia*, Milan, 1973; trans. Robert Lumley); 'Does the Audience have Bad Effects on Television?' (*Dalla periferia dell'impero*, Milan, 1977; trans. Robert Lumley); 'Event as *mise-en-scène* and Life as Scene-setting' (G. F. Bettetini [ed.], *Forme scenografiche della televisione*, Milan, 1982; trans. Robert Lumley); 'The Phantom of Neo-TV: The debate on Fellini's *Ginger and Fred*' (*L'Espresso*, 2 February 1986; trans. Jenny Condie); 'Does Counter-culture Exist?' (*Sette anni di desiderio*, Milan, 1983; trans. Jenny Condie); 'The New Forms of Expression' (*Atti dell'VIII congresso dell'associazione internazionale per gli studi di lingua e letteratura italiana*, April 1973; trans. Jenny Condie); 'On Chinese Comic Strips: Counter-information and alternative information' (*V. S.*, 1, September 1971; trans. [from French] Liz Heron); 'Independent Radio in Italy' (*Cultures*, 1, 1978); 'Striking at the Heart of the State?' (*Sette anni di desiderio*; trans. Geoffrey Nowell-Smith); 'Phenomena of This Sort Must Also be Included . . . ' (P. Sartogo [ed.], *Italian Re-evolution: Design in Italy in the 1980s*; La Jolla Museum of Contemporary Art, La Jolla, CA, 1982); 'A Dollar for a Deputy: La

Cicciolina' (*L'Espresso*, 5 July 1987; trans. Robert Lumley); 'For Grace Received' (*L'Espresso* supplement, 19 April 1970; trans. Robert Lumley); 'The Italian Genius Industry' (*Il costume di casa*, Milan, 1973; trans. Jenny Condie).

INTRODUCTION

Robert Lumley

UMBERTO ECO is mainly known outside Italy as the writer of *The Name of the Rose* and *Foucault's Pendulum*, novels that became international bestsellers in the 1980s. In Italy, Eco's name was well established some thirty years ago with *Opera aperta* (1962),[1] widely seen as a manifesto of the Italian neo-avantgarde; *Diario minimo* (1963),[2] a brilliant exercise in stylistic pastiche; and *Apocalittici e integrati* (1964), whose explorations of mass culture became a touchstone for cultural commentators. It is the last book that provides the springboard for this collection of Eco's writings on cultural questions in the period from the mid-1960s to the late 1980s. This introduction will therefore take it as a starting-point, before going on to discuss Eco's role as an intellectual in relation to Italian debates about culture, society and politics.

Apocalittici e integrati came out at a critical moment in post-war history in the wake of the 'economic miracle', and its distinction between 'apocalyptic' and 'integrated' responses to the accompanying cultural transformation has entered the language. Today the book's basic arguments about the need to analyse and understand the workings of mass cultural products before passing judgment, and about the subsequent importance of discriminating rather than accepting or rejecting them wholesale, have become commonplace (even if phantom battles between 'high' and 'low' culture continue to be re-enacted).[3] To appreciate the impact and consequences of a book like *Apocalittici e integrati* one has to reconstruct a context in which Europe was struggling to come to terms with a rise of commercial culture to which the United States had become habituated.

A review in the *Times Literary Supplement* (which, interestingly, examines Eco's book alongside Stuart Hall and Paddy Whannel's *The Popular Arts*) is symptomatic. The situation of the arts in the twentieth century is compared to that of the horse: 'Outside a few underdeveloped countries it has been entirely replaced by the automobile, which runs faster, and the tractor, which pulls heavier loads. It survives entirely as a luxury.' The review continues: 'The professional writer of books is in the position of the handloom weaver after the invention of the power-loom . . . As every advertising agent and editor knows, it is the photographer and not the "artist" who today commands the high fees.' The new reality might be undesirable, and 'no class of people is enthusiastic about writing its own obituary'. But there were intellectuals coming to terms with 'industrial culture' in different countries, forming three main currents: 'The Americans have discovered, described and measured, the Continentals – especially the French and Italians – have theorized, and the British have moralized.'[4]

However, the moralizing that might here be associated with Richard Hoggart's classic *The Uses of Literacy* was not exclusive to Britain.[5] There was a widespread hostility on the part of European intellectuals towards what was seen as an American-led invasion of 'mass culture' and a consequent standardization and homologization of cultural forms at the expense of rich and variegated national ones. In Italy this saw an unholy alliance of Left and Right: for the idealist tradition of neo-Crocean thought (influential also among Gramscians) Art was the expression of the Spirit and was embodied in the works of the masters; for the Marxist tradition of the Frankfurt School, successfully imported into Italy from the late 1950s, Art was the antithesis of industry. In addition, there was the antipathy of Catholic culture to the emergent 'threat'.[6] And if this picture is somewhat oversimplified (overlooking Croce's notes on popular song on the one hand, and the non-Adornian positions within the Frankfurt School on the other), it reflects the polemical thrust of Eco's critique. He felt himself to be somewhat isolated, occupying a narrow strip between the great 'churches' of Italian postwar culture. Yet, as a glance at his overview 'Reactions of Apocalyptic and Integrated Intellectuals' shows, the book's reception was more favourable than had been anticipated. Not least because, as its regular republication suggests, its detailed and persuasive readings of texts of mass culture from comics to television made it not only timely but a model of how to approach a new cultural order.

At the same time, when reading the essay 'Apocalyptic and Integrated Intellectuals', one is struck by what Eco recalls as his '"Enlightenment" belief that desirable cultural action would bring about an improvement in messages'. Eco seems to identify with the figure of the 'uomo colto' or 'man of culture', someone 'aware of his surroundings, who knows how to discriminate within a hierarchy of values continually undergoing revision, and who is able to develop coherent proposals for action to bring about changes'.[7] There is an underlying assumption that while mass culture needs to be understood whatever the subsequent value-judgments, the real provocation, and pleasure, lies in rescuing works like Schulz's cartoons (see 'The World of Charlie Brown'), and elevating them to the status of 'Art'.[8]

Eco is very much of a generation that has not grown up from the cradle with mass culture, and for whom it has the slightly exotic aura of forbidden fruit (an idea reinforced by its largely American provenance). His citation of Leonardo da Vinci ('Truth is so excellent that, if it praises but small things, they become noble') serves as a high cultural justification of an exploration into barbarian lands. Significantly, Eco dedicates his book to the apocalyptics 'without whose unjust, biased, neurotic, desperate censure I could never have elaborated three-quarters of the ideas I want to share here'. But no, Eco isn't one of their company (or only for twelve hours in the day, as he says in 'The Future of Literacy'). Rather it is the vision of the outsider (the anthropologist looking at his own society?), or of the artist who makes us see by making things strange, that inspires him. By contrast, the integrated intellectual tends to be ignored, dismissed or, in the case of Marshall McLuhan, mercilessly taken apart.[9]

Yet Eco has never lived on the margins, and his refutation of Adornian pessimism concerning the 'culture industry' has been sustained by his own involvement in that industry. From 1955 he worked on cultural programmes for RAI television, from 1959 he started a lifelong collaboration with Bompiani as editor (later consultant and author), and in 1965 he began writing for the weekly magazine *L'Espresso*, for which he now contributes a regular column. His academic post at the University of Bologna perhaps represents his most consistent activity – teacher and researcher in the field of semiotics (a discipline he helped to found) – but he has maintained a multiplicity of roles. It is difficult without examining this 'practical' side to understand Eco's cultural contribution, and too often commentators focus entirely on his writings as if they existed independently of other realities.

Eco's involvement with the world of publishing illustrates this well. Firstly, in relation to the 'modernization' of Italian culture in the 1960s, Eco was one of a generation of intellectuals determined to open up Italy to international currents, breaking down the cultural autarchy identified with Croce,[10] and producing cultural forms better adapted to conditions of modernity. It was an exciting time when American sociology and later French structuralism served to attack the citadels of orthodoxy. In literature the Italian *neo-avanguardia* represented a radical challenge to the poetics of neo-realism and an attempt to make language itself a cultural battleground.[11] One might perhaps expect the poetry of the *novissimi* to have been printed on an artisanal basis. But no. The new literature was published by companies such as Feltrinelli and Bompiani. As Eco observes of the avant-garde Gruppo 63, of which he was a leading light: '[It] was born because certain people, working inside established institutions, had made a different choice, both on the front of cultural politics and on that of culture as a political act. On the former, the project consisted of blowing up the invisible structures of the "tiny clique" which governed culture. [. . .] On the second front, the goal was to proceed, by way of a criticism of the *miniature system* of official culture, to a critique of the *grand system* of bourgeois society.'[12] It was precisely by acceding to (or wresting) control of decision-making in cultural institutions that 'men of culture' forced much needed changes, making themselves, in turn, into the new clique at the top.

Secondly, this involvement had consequences for how 'culture' came to be defined. In Eco it is visible in his interest in the whole cycle of cultural activity from production, on which he focused in his earlier works, through to distribution and consumption, which has concerned him especially in relation to television. His recent warnings about the dangers of using acid paper for books signals an appreciation of the material conditions governing the very (im)permanence of cultural products and their communication to later generations: 'We should start by thinking of ecological books. When, in the last century, the book industry stopped making books from rags and started to make them from trees, it not only menaced our survival, it jeopardized the civilization of the book' ('Books and Literacy').

Few other cultural commentators can rival Eco in his knowledge and love of books and book-making, an area of expertise he puts to good use in his portrait of the publisher, Garamond, in *Foucault's Pendulum*. Emblematic of this familiarity with the inside of the publishing world is his appreciation of the art of inventing titles.[13] The technology also fascinates Eco, whether it is the quills and inks of the medieval *scriptorium* or the computer of today. Above all, he attaches great importance to the hidden arts of 'technique'. His admiration of artifice and virtuosity – the display of technique – inform his championing of cultural phenomena as diverse as the Baroque, rhetoric and hyperrealism. His own version of Raymond Queneau's *Exercices de style* affirms the Frenchman's hymn to rhetorical techniques and is in itself a virtuoso translation[14] (that underestimated 'craft' without which books like this one would not exist). And Eco's 'occasional writings' are likewise characterized by 'the Baroque taste for the excessive, the hyperbolic, the defamiliarising, the fake and the apocryphal'.[15]

But there is a more mundane aspect of Eco's interest in technique that calls for comment, namely his concern for use, or use-value. Culture, for Eco, is about 'making things' and the verb *fare* ('to make' and 'to do') recurs in his writings, along with the figure of the 'producer'. His essay on design, for instance, insists on the importance of anonymous, as opposed to 'signed', design, and on the diffuse and collective rather than exclusively individual nature of creativity ('Phenomena of this sort must also be included . . . '). In Italy his manual on how to write a dissertation is on every university student's bookshelf.[16] Above all, it is *useful* – a cultural guide explaining how to use libraries, how to file information etc. Culture is not the monopoly of Art and Artists but is, in Raymond Williams's word, 'ordinary'. And this has implications for *what* constitutes culture and *how* to analyse it. If a predominantly 'aesthetic' or 'ethical' conception of culture persists in Italy, as evidenced by the entries in standard dictionaries, Eco prefers an anthropological definition as answering the 'requirements of a scientific approach – scientific in the sense of allowing a cautious structural descriptiveness' ('Does Counter-culture exist?').

Eco the enlightened reformer of the early and mid-1960s shared in the widespread hopes in cultural modernization from above producing the conditions for the growth of a participatory democracy from below. However, it took the student and worker rebellions of 1968–9 to dispel such illusions, even though these had already been tarnished by the failures of the Centre-Left government (whose verbal vacillations are brilliantly dissected in 'Political Language: the use and abuse of rhetoric'). For some, including the Socialist thinker Norberto Bobbio, the protest, at least initially, seemed to presage a new barbarism.[17] Eco, however, was one of those who welcomed the challenge to the *ancien régime* from the very start. Speaking to *Newsweek* in 1987, he still put a positive gloss on events: 'Even though all visible traces of 1968 are gone, it profoundly changed the way all of us, at least in Europe, behave and relate to one another. Relations between bosses and workers, students and teachers, even children and parents, have opened up. They'll never be the same again.'[18]

To some extent Eco felt vindicated. He notes in 'Reactions of the Author' that he had predicted that 'a quantitative growth in information, no matter how muddled and oppressive it appears, can produce unforeseen results.' The conflict between apocalyptics and optimists continued even if political affiliations had changed, with the Left now leading denunciations of mass culture as capitalist. For Eco, redefining his role was facilitated by his close association with the artistic avant-garde from the foundation of Gruppo 63 to the demise of the journal *Quindici*. For all their differences over what was to be done, there was a common antipathy to the values and culture that went by the name 'neo-capitalism'. Nor should the role of friendship and mutual respect be forgotten. Eco did not follow Nanni Balestrini down the path of revolutionary politics but, as seen in the essay 'New Forms of Expression', he continued to follow and appreciate his work.

Eco's position was both strategically vital (at the intersection of democratic and revolutionary politics) and difficult if not invidious, being vulnerable to moral blackmail by those to his left. Between 1968 and 1977 (the year of a second wave of youth protest) Eco engaged in a continuing dialogue with the protagonists of the social movements, searching to understand them as producers of new cultural meanings and to make sense of messages (slogans, graffiti, demonstrations etc.) often seen as 'senseless', 'irrational' or plain 'nonsense'.[19] Clearly Eco's sympathies are with those who subvert convention, whether it is the situationist provocations of Gruppo Ufo (see the questionnaire attached to 'New Forms of Expression') or the experiments of Radio Alice (an independent radio station named after *Alice in Wonderland*). He is even prepared in the early 1970s to read Mao's *Little Red Book* as a lesson in openness: 'Thanks to its aphoristic structure and encyclopedic accessibility it offers itself as a tool for application and interpretation in any circumstance . . . It is a tool with a thousand possible uses rather than a one-way track like the railway timetable.'[20] Consistent with the idea first enunciated in *Open Work*, Eco favours forms of communication that are open: ' "Openness" for Eco,' writes David Robey, 'results from the artist's decision to leave the production of the work's meaning to the public or to chance; the consequent multiplicity of interpretations is peculiarly suited to the present, because it corresponds to the feelings of disorder and senselessness produced in us by the world in which we live'.[21]

On the other hand, Eco is suspicious and critical of what he sees as attempts to impose order by suppressing complexity and polyvalency in the name of some ideological mission, whether that of the Cold War hero 'Superman' or of the dogmatic Marxist theorist. While Eco too was swayed by the 'wind from the East', which swept along so many left-wing intellectuals in Italy (Pasolini, Bertolucci, Moravia), he still kept his distance just as he had consistently done in relation to the powerful Communist Party, more attracted as he was to radical and libertarian ideas (heresies) than to party orthodoxies.[22] The political culture of the Red Brigade is but the most extreme manifestation of ideological closure, and represents 'not the enemy of the great systems but their natural, accepted and taken for granted counterpart' ('Striking at the Heart of the State?'). In fact Eco's novels, *The Name of the Rose* and *Foucault's Pendulum*, can be interpreted as political allegories of a country described by one historian as a victim of a 'torbid and bloody game consisting of massacres, cover-ups and blackmail'[23] with political forces manipulating secret services and vice versa. Obscurantism, dogma and recourse to violence are all enemies of the reason and openness of which Eco is a champion.

The decline of the social movements and the dramatic episodes of terrorism in the years 1978–9 marked the end of a decade of turbulent change in Italy during which intellectuals felt impelled to intervene in political debates. Workers continued to exist but somehow the working class was declared to have disappeared. Talk of post-modernism, post-industrial or information societies quickly displaced the metaphors of Marxist discourse so current in the writings of the 1960s and 1970s even among non-Marxists like Eco. In Italy the cultural arena was flooded with the images of the newly deregulated television channels, provoking a reprise of the mass culture debate of the mid-1960s.[24] But this time many of the former apocalyptics of the social movements had become the ideologues and professionals of the media revolution.

Italy had changed between the early 1960s and the 1980s from a country with major areas of poverty and illiteracy into a customer society with a literate population. Throughout the course of this transformation television acted both as a motor of and a metaphor for change, introducing new forms of cultural production and consumption and symbolizing all that was modern and innovatory (or, in the eyes of the apocalyptics, all that reduced cultural life to the lowest common denominator). It is not surprising, therefore, that Eco followed the development of the medium closely, focusing particularly on television's language and forms (the live broadcast, the vocabulary of the quiz-master, TV genres) and carrying out pioneering joint research on audience reception of TV messages using a semiotic approach ('Does the Audience have Bad Effects on Television?'). Until the advent of private channels in the late 1970s, the state broadcasting company, RAI, had a monopoly and produced programmes according to the public service trinity of 'inform, educate and entertain'. Then the rules were overturned as the pursuit of ratings made entertainment ('spettacolo') sovereign and made many genre distinctions redundant. Eco, with his flair for neologism, announced the arrival of 'Neo-TV' in the place of the television of a paleolithic age ('Paleo-TV'). With Neo-TV, he writes, there is 'the cancerous proliferation of the same programme endlessly repeated . . . the ultimate impossibility of making distinctions, discerning and choosing' ('The Phantom of Neo-TV'). The triumph of phatic communication and of self-referentiality also brings the abolition of reference to an outside world ('the referent'), or the end of a reality that is not fabricated for television's *mise en scène* ('Event as *mise en scène*').

The world of Neo-TV is depicted with 'ill-concealed hatred and loathing' in *Fred and Ginger* by that old apocalyptic Federico Fellini. Eco sympathizes but insists, 'First you have to understand, with cool detachment, its inner workings.' Likewise with La Cicciolina, a character of Fellinian inspiration, the 'porno-star' who caused outrage – and amusement – by standing (successfully) for parliament. To be condemned? But wait, says Eco, consider the arguments in turn, don't presume that her job, intellectual competence or morals disqualify her. Look at the other parliamentarians! And using *paradox*, a favourite figure in an extensive rhetorical repertoire, Eco assumes the role of the devil's advocate in reverse, only finally to come down against Ms Staller's candidature.

Eco does not renounce the need to make value judgments and choices but he dispels any impression of moralism through the distancing effect of humour. Somehow Eco is 'above' a certain kind of *engagement* and his viewpoint is well illustrated by his reply to Stuart Hall's question: 'Isn't it extremely convenient when intellectuals impose on themselves this partial retirement from engagement?' 'Well,' says Eco, 'there's a book

I like by Italo Calvino called *The Baron in the Trees*, which is the story of an 18th-century aristocrat who decides to spend all his life on the top of a tree without stepping down. But in doing so he still takes part in the French Revolution . . . He is a metaphor, an allegory. There is a way to stay up a tree and to change life on the ground.'[25]

Is there something 'Italian' about this answer? The easy reference to a work of fiction to explain a contemporary situation? Its freedom from a certain moral discourse more ingrained in Protestant cultures? There is no simple answer. Anyway it helps lead on to a further question with which to conclude this Introduction, namely 'Just how "Italian" is Umberto Eco?'

National identity, paradoxically, is often most acutely perceived by the cosmopolitan. Travel, speaking other languages, living and working abroad, all invite reflection on one's own cultural formation and identity. They can make a person feel intensely 'Italian' or 'American' when away but not fully integrated when at home. This seems very much to be the case with Eco: conversant in several languages, a translator, an academic who has taught regularly in North and South America, a member, *de facto*, of the 'jet set'. Furthermore, his business as a scholar is concerned with developing and applying a 'science of signs' which with Eco entails the whole dimension of what Teresa de Lauretis calls his 'semiotic imagination'. What better way to investigate the problems of communication and culture than by moving between different cultures, contemporary and historical. Imagine our hero: 'For Eco, John Ford of the semiological frontier, Europe and America, the Middle Ages and the Future are the times and the places of a personal and political fiction, his ever present temptation: the Middle Ages of the scholar wandering among the ruins of a knowledge still useful, and the Extraterrestrial Future of the Martian avant-gardes that is already ours.'[26]

A gatekeeper between the cultural worlds of the United States and Italy (the US of 'mass culture' and the Italy of 'high culture'), Eco has become in Omar Calabrese's words 'a sort of unofficial representative of Italian culture abroad' while he has long been an importer and interpreter of foreign cultural goods 'on the periphery of the Empire'. In the process he has frequently reflected on the cultural configurations of national character. Asked in an interview in 1985 about what for him constituted *italianità*, he gave a reply that has some application to himself: 'An Italian character does exist. The first is a transhistorical characteristic which relates to *genialità* and *inventività* . . . and consists in our ability to marry humanist tradition and technological development. What has undoubtedly acted as a brake on our culture, the predominance of the humanistic over the technological, has also permitted certain fusions, eruptions of fantasy within technology and the technologization of fantasy. Secondly, Italy is a country that has known enormous crises, foreign domination, massacres. And yet (or for this reason) has produced Raphael and Michelangelo . . . What often fascinates foreigners is that in Italy economic crises, uneven development, terrorism accompany great inventiveness.'[27]

It might well be better to live harmoniously and just invent the cuckoo-clock, says Eco, but creativity seems linked to improvisation and adaptation to difficult circumstances, a theory shared by Hans Magnus Enzensberger, a critical admirer of 'Italian genius'.[28] Utopia might be desirable but social conflict and difference is a condition of human society. Conflict is not something to be suppressed. The problem is to make it productive of new ideas that confront rather than ignore realities. In this respect Eco is part of a fine tradition going back as far as Machiavelli and embracing liberal thought. If Italy has been described as a 'difficult democracy', it is also a country which has developed a remarkable openness of debate and enquiry.

However, this level of generalization is perilously close to banal stereotype. It gets away from the false cosmopolitanism that Gramsci saw as a peculiarly Italian vice and according to which everything foreign is automatically better. Instead there is the danger of forgetting that there is often no such thing as 'Italy'. Geographers, sociologists and students of language have for some time pointed to the plurality of cultures and economies hidden by the adjective 'Italian'. Historians of art, for instance, have called the peninsula an ideal laboratory for the study of the relationship between centre and periphery: 'A relative ease of exchanges with faraway countries has been accompanied by limited and difficult communications with inland areas close by. Even today it is easier to go by train from Turin to Dijon than from Grosseto to Urbino.'[29] Tullio De Mauro even suggests that acknowledging that 'the country is an interlacement of countries' is the basis for overcoming the barriers between the official unitary 'Italy' of the rulers and the 'Italies' of the ruled.[30]

In this perspective, Eco is Piedmontese not Italian, and in debates on cultural phenomena within a national forum he frequently refers to himself in this way. A good example is found in the discussion of comic actors: 'For my part I personally prefer Totò, and the reason Placido misunderstood me was that he, being a Southerner, instinctively distrusted the likes of me, a Piedmontese' ('The Phantom of Neo-TV'). Being from this region actually means being identified with a kingdom that annexed southern Italy (or, euphemistically, 'unified Italy'), and significantly the allusion is humorous and about humour, that greater defuser of cultural tensions. Certainly Eco is a 'northerner' and his political-cultural formation is closely bound up with the cities of Turin (where he studied), Milan (where he lives) and Bologna (where he teaches). Arguably he is an advocate of a 'modern industrial culture' that, historically, belongs to the North.

However, Eco's writings question any simplistic model of 'modernization' and explore areas unimagined by the official culture: 'We should start by dispelling the illusion of those convinced that emigration, social mobility, motorways and the car would blow away the dark clouds of obscurantism. . . .

technological development provokes rather than reduces the need for the sacred' ('For Grace Received'). Italy is also the land of thaumaturges and unrecognized poets, uncharted and ignored. The average parish priest may deny the existence of a thaumaturgic press, 'like a vice-chancellor asked about photo-novels for housewives'; but, writes Eco, its circulation makes that of the weekly *L'Espresso* look insignificant. It is not a regional phenomenon (though more widespread in the South). Likewise the 'vanity press' analysed in 'The Italian Genius Industry'. Both have a national diffusion but they appear locally in the form of publications directed by a particular mission, sanctuary or publisher and are too readily dismissed by intellectuals as signs of 'provincialism' and 'backwardness'. Again Eco insists on taking seriously what others have no time for. If the humour is sometimes uncomfortably at the expense of those who are duped or dupe themselves into believing in miraculous powders or the equally wondrous powers of the religion of Art, he nevertheless reveals in microcosm cultural realities of significant proportions.

As a piece of cultural analysis 'The Italian Genius Industry' ranks as an Eco *tour de force*, and one to which he is evidently still attached since it is reproduced wholesale in the description of the publisher Manuzio, in *Foucault's Pendulum* (except that the 'Fourth Dimension Author' or FDA has now become the 'Self-Financing Author'). The seemingly harmless but possibly suspect (the Italian title of the piece, '*genio italico*', has a Fascist ring) poets, writers and philosophers inhabit the fourth dimension of literature because (self)excluded from the third dimension, constituted by recognized literature. Ignored by the official culture (none of their work is reviewed in the press), they form a parallel universe complete with journals and their own 'Who's Who'. Overwhelmingly kitsch in the titles and characters not only of the books but of the authors, the Fourth Dimension also harbours talents like Blotto, whose 'unbridled linguistic invention' rivals that of the *neo-avanguardia*. In his pursuit of the marginal, the peripheral and the 'provincial' Eco invents a kind of fisheye lens whose distortions give unsuspected insights into the core culture itself.

This ability of Eco's to reverse cultural optics, to find an unexpected angle or to create an unlikely juxtaposition, makes his writing both immensely readable and illuminating. To what extent this is to do with being Italian is difficult to judge. It is certainly difficult to imagine Eco as an Englishman or an American. More important than his debt to national tradition is probably his ability to mediate between different cultures (whether defined by geography, social class or professional activity) in an age in which established cultural frontiers have been dramatically contested and redrawn and in which the challenge of 'globalization' has made interdisciplinarity an imperative.

Choice of essays and presentation

The first outline of this collection was drafted in 1984, since when (after being rescued from the bottom drawer by Geoffrey Nowell-Smith) it has undergone major revisions. David Robey suggested including the essays and preface from *Apocalittici e integrati*. Then Umberto Eco sent a number of things subsequently included mainly in Parts I and III ('Yesterday evening, getting back to Milan, I set about looking through my archives until 3 a.m., and here's the result').

The objectives in making the collection are:

1. To convey some sense of the development of Eco's writings on cultural issues from the early 1960s to the late 1980s, documenting as well as re-presenting past works.
2. To focus on journalism and occasional essays.
3. To include historically significant pieces not previously translated (notably from *Apocalittici e integrati*).
4. To include material written about Italy and for Italians and which have tended not to be translated for that reason.
5. To communicate the wit and brio of Eco's writing.

The subdivision into four parts is designed to group essays around certain themes – the debate on mass culture, mass media (especially television), counter-culture, and what Eco referred to as 'Italian follies'. The essay 'Apocalyptic and Integrated Intellectuals' is put at the beginning because it precedes the others chronologically and provides the framework for the analyses of mass culture that constitute the bulk of the collection. Otherwise the reader should not feel obliged to read the parts sequentially.

Many of the pieces first appeared as part of continuing debates and are full of allusions to contemporary events as well as to a stock of knowledge the average Italian reader might be expected to possess. The introduction aims to give a general context, but notes are used for more specific references. A good example occurs in 'A Dollar for a Deputy', in which Eco's jokes about politicians are incomprehensible to anyone not knowing that Mr X has a moustache and Mr Y has a hunchback. Eco didn't footnote any of the essays except 'Political Language', so information on the books, authors etc. mentioned in the text have been added.

Much of the work of interpretation has, of course, gone into the translations themselves, which are the product of close collaboration between the editor (himself a translator) and the other translators, Jenny Condie, Liz Heron and Geoffrey Nowell-Smith (except where versions existed in English as with 'The Future of Literacy' or 'Independent Radios'). We have tried to be faithful to Eco's style of writing, for this is intrinsic to what he has to say. While there is inevitably a loss involved because of the transposition into another language and cultural context, making these texts available to readers of English offers the possibility of new (and undreamt of) readings and interpretations.

PART ONE

Mass Culture:
Apocalypse Postponed

CHAPTER 1

Apocalyptic and Integrated Intellectuals: Mass Communications and Theories of Mass Culture

IT IS QUITE WRONG to subsume human attitudes, in all their variety and subtlety, under two such generic and polemical concepts as 'apocalyptic' and 'integrated' ['*apocalittico*' and '*integrato*']. There are, however, certain requirements to be met in choosing the title for a book (a matter for the culture industry, as we shall see, though in this context the term should not be understood in its overused sense). Furthermore, in writing an introduction to the essays that follow, there is no avoiding the necessity of providing a general methodological outline. It is also convenient to define what one does *not* want to do by typifying a series of cultural choices in their extreme forms, when of course they should instead be analysed concretely and with calm detachment. Yet I reproach those critics I call apocalyptic or integrated intellectuals because it is they who are responsible for the spread of equally vague 'fetish concepts' – and for using them as targets for fruitless polemic or for commercial operations which we ourselves consume on a daily basis.

Indeed, in order to define the nature of these essays, in order to take the first steps towards making myself understood by the reader, I too am forced to resort to a concept as vague and ambiguous as 'mass culture'. And it is precisely to this vague, ambiguous and inappropriate term that we owe the development of the two types of attitude which I shall be aiming (with sharp but necessary polemic) to challenge.

If culture is an aristocratic phenomenon – the assiduous, solitary and jealous cultivation of an inner life that tempers and opposes the vulgarity of the crowd – then even to conceive of a culture that is shared by everyone, produced to suit everyone and tailored accordingly is a monstrous contradiction. (In Heraclitus's words: 'Why drag me up and down, you boors? I toiled for those who understand me – not for you! To me, one man is full thirty thousand, countless worth none.'[1]) Mass culture is anti-culture. But since its birth comes at a time when the presence of the masses in the life of society is the most striking phenomenon of the age, then 'mass culture' does not signal a transitory and limited aberration; rather, it is the mark of an irretrievable loss, in the face of which the man of culture (last survivor of a prehistory destined to extinction) cannot do otherwise than give an extreme, apocalytpic testimony.

Set against this is the optimistic response of the integrated intellectual. The combined efforts of TV, newspapers, radio, cinema, comicstrips, popular novels and the *Reader's Digest* have now brought culture within everybody's reach. They have made the absorption of ideas and the reception of information a pleasurable and easy task, with the result that we live in an age in which the cultural arena is at last expanding to include the widespread circulation of a 'popular' art and culture in which the best compete against each other. Whether this culture emerges from below or is processed and packaged from above to be offered to defenceless consumers is not a problem that concerns the integrated intellectual. Not least because, if apocalyptics survive by packaging theories on decadence, the integrated intellectuals rarely theorize. They are more likely to be busy producing and transmitting their own messages in every sphere, on a daily basis. The apocalypse is a preoccupation of the dissenter, integration is the concrete reality of non-dissenters. The image of the Apocalypse is evoked in texts *on* mass culture, while the image of integration emerges in texts which *belong to* mass culture. But do these two views not perhaps represent two aspects of the same problem and, if so, to what extent? And is it not the case that apocalyptic texts constitute the most sophisticated product on offer for mass consumption? Such a hypothesis would mean, then, that the formula '*Apocalittici e integrati*' does not refer to the clash between two opposing attitudes but is rather an expression made up of two complementary adjectives – adjectives which could both be equally applied to the creators of a 'popular critique of popular culture'.

After all, the apocalyptic intellectual offers the reader *consolation*, for he allows him to glimpse, against a background of catastrophe, a community of 'supermen' capable, if only by rejection, of rising above banal mediocrity. At the very least, the elected few who write and read: 'Us two, you and I – the only ones to understand, and be saved: the only ones not part of the mass.' When I say 'superman', I'm thinking of the Nietzschean (or pseudo-Nietzschean) origin of many of these attitudes. However, I use the term in the cunning sense suggested by Gramsci, for whom the model of the Nietzschean superman could be found in the heroes of nineteenth-century serial novels, such as the Count of Monte Cristo, Athos, Rodolphe de Gerolstein or (a generous concession) Vautrin.[2]

If this seems a strange connection to make, then consider for a moment the fact that one of the typical features of mass culture has always been the way it implants in the minds of its readers, from whom a controlled equilibrium is expected, the expectation that – in view of the existing conditions, and precisely on account of these – they may some day hatch out from their chrysalis to become an *Übermensch*. The price to pay is that this *Übermensch* busies himself with an infinity of minor problems while conserving the fundamental order of things; an example of this is the petty reformer Rodolphe in *Les Mystères de Paris*, and Marx and Engels were not the only ones to notice it: Belinsky and Poe both drew attention to it in two separate reviews which seem curiously to reiterate the polemic in Marx's *The Holy Family*.[3]

In one of the essays I examine a Superman that is typical of contemporary mass culture: the comic-strip Superman. I am able to conclude that this ultra-powerful hero uses his extra-ordinary gifts to bring about an ideal of absolute passivity, turning down any project without a prior seal of approval for its good sense, thereby becoming a paragon of high moral standards untouched by political concerns. Superman will never park his car in a no parking zone and he'll never be a revolutionary. If I remember correctly, the only one of Gramsci's *Übermenschen* who has a political conscience and is resolved to change the order of things is Dumas's Giuseppe Balsamo. But significantly, because Balsamo (alias Cagliostro) is so taken up with using his many lives to accelerate the pace of the French Revolution – organizing conspiracies among the enlightened, setting up mystical meetings of Freemasons and hatching gallant plots to embarrass Marie Antoinette – he quite forgets to work on the Encyclopédie or to foment the seizing of the Bastille (neglecting thereby to contribute either to mass culture or to the organization of the masses).

On the other side of the barricades we have the apocalyptic critics' superman: his method of countering the reigning banality is by rejection and silence and he is sustained in this by a total lack of faith in the possibility of any action transforming the state of things. Having established that superhumanity is a nostalgic myth (without a precise historical setting), this too becomes an invitation to passivity. Integration, thrown out of the door, comes back through the window.

But this world, which one side ostentantiously rejects and the other accepts and builds on, is not just a world for Superman. It is ours as well. This world begins with the subordinate classes gaining access to cultural goods and with the possibility of producing these goods industrially. The culture industry, as we shall see, begins with Gutenberg's invention of movable type, or even earlier. And so the world of Superman is also the world of man today. Is present-day man mercilessly condemned to becoming a 'superman' – i.e. to being an inadequate – or will he manage to find, somewhere in this world, some way of instituting a fresh, civilized exchange of views? Is this a world for the *Übermensch* only, or might it also be a world for man?

I believe that, if we are to work *in* and *for* a world built on a human scale, then this human scale should be defined not by adapting man to the *de facto* conditions but by *using these conditions as the point of departure*. The universe of mass communication is – whether we recognize it or not – our universe; and if it is of values that we wish to speak, the objective conditions of communication are those provided by the existence of newspapers, radio, television, recorded and recordable music, the new forms of visual and audiovisual communication. Nobody is free of these conditions, not even the virtuous man who, angered by the inhuman nature of this universe of information, transmits his own protest through the channels of mass communication, in the columns of a great newspaper or in the pages of a paperback printed in linotype and sold in railway station kiosks.

Some fetish concepts come from the virtuous apocalyptic. And the fetish concept has a particular ability to obstruct argument, straitjacketing discussion in emotional reaction. Take the fetish concept of 'culture industry'. What could be more reprehensible than coupling the idea of culture – which implies a private and subtle contact of souls – with that of industry – which evokes assembly lines, serial reproduction, public distribution and the concrete buying and selling of objects made into merchandise. A medieval manuscript illuminator painting images in a Book of Hours for his patron was obviously anchored to an artisan-patron relationship. While on the one hand each image referred to a code of beliefs and conventions, on the other it was addressed to the individual patron, establishing a precise relationship with him. But as soon as somebody invents a method of printing with wooden blocks so that the pages of a bible are endlessly reproducible, something new happens. A bible that can be printed in quantity costs less and can be distributed to more people. But isn't a bible sold to many people a lesser bible as a result? Hence the name *biblia pauperum*. On the other hand, external factors (ease of diffusion and price) influence the nature of the product as well: the pictures will be adapted for understanding by a wider, less cultured audience. So wouldn't it be better to link the illustrations to the text with a play of fluttering scrolls, strongly reminiscent of the comic-strip? The *biblia pauperum* begins to submit to a requirement which will be attributed, centuries later, to modern mass media: the adaptation of taste and language to the average person's receptivity.

Then Gutenberg invented movable type and the book was born. Being a serially produced object, the book had to adjust its language to the receptivity of a literate audience which had by now grown (and, thanks to the book, was continuing to grow) much vaster than the readership of the manuscript. And this wasn't all: by creating a public, the book creates readers who will in their turn condition the book itself.

The first popular printed books of the sixteenth century repeat the formula of the *biblia pauperum*, but this time on a secular level and using more refined typographical methods. They were produced by small printing presses for itinerant booksellers and mountebanks who sold them to the common people at fairs and in public squares. These chivalrous epics, laments upon political events or real-life stories, pranks, jokes or nonsense rhymes were badly printed and often omitted to mention the place and date of publication, for they already possessed the principal characteristic of mass culture: namely ephemerality. They also shared the chief connotation of the mass-produced object: they offered sentiments and passions, love and death in a format appropriate to the reaction they aimed to elicit in the reader. The titles of these stories already contain advertising blurb, along with an explicit judgment on the outcome of the story, as if to give advice on how best to enjoy it: 'Danese Ugieri, a pleasing and beautiful work concerning arms and love, newly reprinted and now including the death of the giant Mariotto, which is not to be found in the other versions'; or, 'A new tale of the cruel and pitiful case in Alicante, with a mother who kills her own child and feeds its insides to the dog and its limbs to her husband.'

Meanwhile, the images conformed to charming but basically modest standards and aimed, as befits a serial novel or a comic-strip, to make a violent impact. It is obviously not possible to speak of mass culture in the sense in which the term is understood today; the historical circumstances were different, as was the relationship between the producers of these printed books and the populace. The division between popular culture – for culture it was in the ethnological sense of the term – and learned culture was of a different type. But it is already possible to see how serial reproducibility and the fact that the readership was growing and broadening its social base combined to create a series of conditions that profoundly influenced the character of these little books. They became a genre in themselves with their own sense of tragedy, heroism, morality, sacredness and the ridiculous, adapted to the tastes and ethos of the 'average consumer' – the lowest common denominator. By propagating among the common people the terms of an official morality, these books acted as instruments of pacification and control, while their professional subject-matter – outbursts of bizarre behaviour – provided material for escapism. They nonetheless gave rise to a popular breed of 'literary men', and helped make their public literate.

Then along came the first gazettes. And with the birth of
the newspaper, the relationship between external conditioning
and the cultural object became even clearer: what is a newspaper if not a product consisting of a fixed number of pages
that is obliged to appear once a day and in which the things
it prints are no longer determined solely by the things that
should be printed (according to a wholly internal necessity),
but by the fact that, once a day, a newspaper has to find enough
things to print to fill a set number of pages? At this point we
enter fully into the realms of the culture industry. This industry
would appear then to constitute a system of conditioning
which every cultural operator, if he wishes to communicate
with his peers, has to take account of. If he wishes, that is, to
communicate with other men, for now all men are on their
way to becoming his peers, and the cultural operator has ceased
to be the functionary of a patron, and instead has become the
'functionary of humanity'. The only way the cultural operator
can carry out his function is by entering into an active and
conscious dialectical relationship with the conditionings of the
cultural industry.

It is, after all, no accident that newspaper civilization develops in conjunction with democracy, the political awakenings
of the subordinate classes, the birth of political and social egalitarianism, and at the time of bourgeois revolutions. But on
the other hand, nor is it accidental that those who are whole-
hearted and coherent in their polemic against the culture industry trace the root of all evil not to the first television broadcast
but to the invention of printing together with the ideologies
of egalitarianism and popular sovereignty. In fact, the indis-
criminate use of a fetish concept such as 'the culture industry'
basically implies an inability to accept these historical events,
and – with them – the prospect of a humanity that is capable
of changing the course of history.

Once the culture industry is correctly understood to be a
system of conditioning linked to the phenomena listed above,

the discourse becomes less generalized and is articulated on two, complementary planes: firstly the analytical description of the various phenomena; and secondly their interpretation in the light of the historical context in which they appear. But such a discourse entails a further realization: that the system of conditioning called the culture industry does not conveniently present us with the possibility of distinguishing two independent spheres, with mass communication over here and aristocratic creation over there, the latter coming first and remaining untouched by the other. The system of the culture industry imposes a mechanism of reciprocal conditioning so that the very notion of culture *tout court* is affected. If the term 'mass culture' represents an imprecise hybrid in which both the meaning of culture and the meaning of mass are unknown, it is nonetheless clear that it is now no longer possible to think of culture as something which is articulated according to the inexorable and incorruptible necessity of a Spirit that is not historically conditioned by the existence of mass culture. From this point onwards, the notion of 'culture' itself has to be re-elaborated and reformulated; just as it was also necessary to rearticulate the role of the man of culture following the assertion that history is created in material circumstances by men seeking to resolve their own economic and social problems (in the process bringing about a dialectical conflict between the classes).

'Mass culture' thus becomes a definition of an anthropological order (like 'Alorese culture' or 'Bantu culture'), and is useful for indicating a precise historical context (the one in which we are living) in which all communicative phenomena – from offers of escapist enjoyment to the appeals to our inner soul – appear dialectically connected, each carrying the imprint of their context, making it impossible to reduce them to analogous phenomena belonging to other historical periods.

Clearly, then, the attitude of the man of culture towards this situation must be the same as that of somebody who, confronted with the system of conditioning of the 'era of industrial mechanization', did not ask how to return to nature, i.e. to a time before the advent of industry, but instead asked in what circumstances man's relationship with the production cycle made him a slave to the system, and what was required in order to elaborate a new image of man in relation to the objective conditions; a man not free *from* the machine, but *free in relation to the machine*.

Now there is nothing that obstructs a concrete analysis of these phenomena so much as the diffusion of fetish categories. And among the most dangerous of these, we have yet to discuss that of 'mass' and 'mass man'.

More will be said about the lack of validity of these concepts in the essays that follow (attempting to set limits for the discourses in which they may be employed); meantime it is worth recalling the historical lineage of this Manichean opposition between the lucidity of the intellectual in his solitude and the stupidity of mass man. Its roots are not to be found in *The Revolt of the Masses* but rather in the polemic of those we now remember as 'Mr Bruno Bauer and company', that circle of young Hegelians[5] grouped around the *Allgemeine Literatur-zeitung*:

> The worst evidence in favour of a work is the enthusiasm with which it is greeted by the masses . . . All the great feats of history have until now been fundamentally wrong and devoid of real success because the mass took an interest and were enthusiastic about them . . . The spirit now knows where to look for his sole adversary – in the phrases, self-deceit, spinelessness of the masses.

These words were written in 1843, but they could, in the right context, be used again today, providing the material for an excellent *feuilleton* on mass culture. Of course, it is not my intention to contest anybody's right to theorize on the opposition between the Spirit and the Mass, to believe that cultural activity must be defined in these terms, and to bear witness to this cleavage in ways that may well inspire great respect. But it is worth clarifying the ancestry of such a stance and throwing some light on the historical context of a polemic that was destined to be renewed with the apparent advent of mass society.

A good proportion of the pseudo-Marxist theories of the Frankfurt school,[6] for example, show links with the 'Holy Family' ideology of Bauer and his following, including the idea that the thinker (the 'critic') cannot and should not suggest remedies, but at most give notice of his dissent: 'Criticism does not constitute a party, it does not want to claim a party as its own, but to remain alone, alone while it engrosses itself with its object, alone when it takes a stand against it. It detaches itself from all things . . . It feels any link to be a chain.' This passage, from issue IV of the *Allgemeine Literaturzeitung*, was the inspirational basis for an article by Koeppen in the *Norddeutsche Blätterne* of 11 August 1844, on the problem of censorship: 'Criticism is above affections and sentiments, it knows neither love nor hatred for anything. Thus it does not set itself against censorship and fight it . . . Criticism does not lose itself in events and cannot lose itself in events; it is therefore a nonsense to expect it to destroy censorship with events and to procure for the press the liberty to which it is anyway entitled.' These excerpts may be legitimately compared with the statements made a century later by Horkheimer in his polemic with a pragmatist culture accused of deflecting and consuming energies meant for reflection in plans for action, to which he opposed his 'method of negation'.[7] And it was no coincidence that one scholar closely associated with Adorno, as friend and collaborator, Renato Solmi,[8] identified in the writer's works a speculative tendency, a 'critique of praxis', by means of which the philosophical discourse avoids a consideration of the conditions and the forms of that 'passage' which thought should identify in a situation while simultaneously subjecting it to radical critique. For his own part, Adorno ended his *Minima Moralia* by presenting philosophy as the attempt to contemplate all things from the standpoint of redemption, revealing the world with all its deep divides as it will appear one day in the messianic light. However, thought thereby involves itself in a series of contradictions such that they have all to be endured with lucidity; 'Beside the demand thus placed on thought, the question of the reality or unreality of redemption itself hardly matters.'[9]

Now it is easy to reply that Marx's answer to Bruno Bauer was as follows: 'When the masses acquire class consciousness, they will be able to put themselves at the head of history and present themselves as the only real alternative to your "Spirit"' ('in order to appreciate the *human* nobility of this movement, one must have witnessed the application, the thirst for knowledge, the moral energy, and the desire for unhalting progress of the French and English workers'). Meanwhile the implicit response of the mass culture industry to its accusers is: 'Once the masses overcome class differences, they become the protagonists of history, so that their culture, which is a culture produced for them and consumed by them, is something positive.' In these terms the function of the apocalyptic intellectual has a special validity – that of denouncing the optimistic ideology of the integrated intellectuals as profoundly false and in bad faith. However, the reason for this is that the integrated intellectual, like the apocalyptic, adopts the fetish concept of 'mass', and with maximum ease, using it in a positive or negative sense at will. The integrated intellectual produces for the masses, plans mass education, and in this way collaborates in the process of 'massification'.

Whether the so-called masses go along with this, whether they have stronger stomachs than their manipulators think, whether they know how to use their powers of discrimination on the products on offer, and how to turn messages to unforeseen and positive uses – all this is another question. The existence of a category of cultural operators who produce for the masses, using them in effect as a means of making a profit rather than offering them real opportunities for critical experience, is an established fact. Moreover, the cultural operation is to be judged for the intentions it manifests as well as for the way in which it structures its messages. Yet, in judging these phenomena with the aid of the apocalyptic intellectual, we must nonetheless oppose him on the same grounds as Marx opposed the 'mass' theorists, namely that 'If man is formed by circumstance, then the circumstances must be made human.'[10]

The apocalyptic intellectual must on the other hand be reproached for never really attempting a concrete study of products and how they are actually consumed. Not only does the apocalyptic reduce the consumer to that undifferentiated fetish that is mass man, but while accusing mass man of reducing even the worthiest artistic product to pure fetish, he himself reduces the mass-produced object to a fetish. Rather than analyse these products individually in order to render their structural characteristics visible, the apocalyptic negates them *en bloc*. When he does analyse them, he betrays the presence of a strange emotional tendency in himself and reveals an unresolved love-hate complex, giving rise to the suspicion that the first and most illustrious victim of the mass product is the virtuous critic himself.

This is one of the strangest and most fascinating features of that culture industry phenomenon we have identified as apocalyptic criticism of the culture industry. It resembles the barely disguised manifestation of a frustrated passion, a love betrayed, or rather, the neurotic display of a repressed sensuality, similar to that of the moralist who, in the very act of denouncing the obscenity of an image, pauses at such length and with such voluptuousness to contemplate the loathsome object of his contempt that his true nature – that of a carnal, lustful animal – is betrayed.

The phenomenon has been remarked upon with regard to numerous polemics against kitsch, particularly in the German cultural context. Thus Karl Markus Michel[11] could observe many years ago that, since even the person who feels himself to be immune to any form of sentimentality is sometimes powerless to prevent tears from pouring down his cheeks despite being fully aware of the low quality of the stimulus causing this reaction, the desire for kitsch is often so intense in its critics that it has to be fulfilled by condemning it. Such condemnation is strengthened with reference to art, which is then praised in terms thoroughly compliant with all the established rules of kitsch emotiveness. So the response of the intellectual undermined by a passion for kitsch resembles that of the rich man who, importuned by a beggar, orders his servant: 'Drive this man away. He's breaking my heart!'

Drive this man away. He's breaking my heart! It's impossible not to think of this phrase when we read the following passage by Günther Anders[12] from his study of television, entitled *The world as phantom and as matrix?*:

> In an exhibition of television, I had the dubious fortune of seeing and hearing an actor doing a sketch in the next room while seven of his TV performances were being screened contemporaneously. There were several things worthy of note in this: 1) the actor was divided into seven identical brothers as far as the eyes were concerned, yet he had only one, undivided voice which echoed in both rooms; 2) the images appeared more natural than the original because to confer naturalness on his reproduced image, the actor had had to put on make-up; 3) (which was more ghastly than remarkable) the multiple incarnations of the actor no longer shocked anybody: so accustomed have we become to expecting little else but serial products.

What emerges above all from this passage is a sort of morbid attraction for the enigma of mirrors and the multiplication of the human image. At root, there is a sort of metaphysical terror, the same as assails the primitive man when he realizes that somebody is copying his likeness and believes that his soul is being taken away from him along with his image. Now it is wholly legitimate to carry out a poetic reflection on the enigma of mirrors; and to accomplish this in the name of lyrical digression or imaginative paradox may well produce excellent results as in Rilke's poetry or when Borges writes: 'From the remote depths of the corridor, the mirror spied upon us. We discovered (such a discovery is inevitable in the late hours of the night) that mirrors have something monstrous about them. Then Bioy Casares recalled that one of the heresiarchs of Uqbar had declared that mirrors and copulation are abominable, because they increase the number of men.'[13] However, in this case, Anders is not creating art. He is reflecting upon a communication phenomenon typical of our time. We know – and in many respects his intuitions are valid – that his definition of the phenomenon went something like: TV reduces the world to a phantom and thus blocks all critical reaction and any effective response from its viewers. But at the end of the day, what Anders is describing to us is TV's effect *on him*. Nobody is able to satisfy our curiosity about what that actor on the screen was saying. Was he saying, 'Yes, the right answer!' or, 'We go over now to Dallas prison, bringing you pictures of Oswald's transfer'? Because if the latter, we want to know for whom and for how many the live footage of Ruby shooting Oswald makes the world appear as a series of phantom forms, suspending it in a zone of unreality. This was certainly not the case with those jurors repeatedly rejected by Ruby's defence on the grounds that, having seen the murder on television, they would have formed an idea of the facts that all the procedural sham and juridical pretence involved in a courtroom trial would have been powerless to challenge.

Yet it is clear that in this case our critic is not interested in the message's content, its structural patterns, nor in the process of reception. What emerges most strikingly is a form of morbid attraction for the *mysterium televisionis*. So that, far from helping us to free ourselves from the spell, the most the critic does is to hold us there for even longer. Perhaps he hopes to induce his own peers to switch off the television. But the fact that it remains switched on for everybody else is evidently one of those things which criticism is powerless to prevent (remember: 'Criticism does not lose itself in events and cannot lose itself in events.' The fact that in other cases Anders did indeed bravely lose himself in events – we may recall his polemic against the atom bomb, a stand aimed at influencing reality – testifies in his favour. However, it was no accident that he was reproached for this recently in Italy by another apocalyptic critic, who accused him of squalid demagogy).

The Anders passage is reminiscent of another commentary, written in an altogether different historical situation and for different reasons, but which has – as we shall see – subtle psychological and ideological (in the pejorative sense of the term 'ideology') links with his. The words are from the *Apologia ad Guillelum, Sancti Theodorici Remensis Abbati* by St Bernard. St Bernard had been irritated by someone who was a typical producer of 'mass culture', at least within the limits in which it was possible in the twelfth century to produce mass culture: namely Abbot Suger. In a historical context in which the instruments of culture were in the hands of the ruling class while the subordinate classes were for the most part excluded from the exercise of writing, the only way to educate the masses was by translating the official contents of culture into images. Suger had adopted the programme of the Synod of Arras, summed up by Honorius of Autun in the formula: *'pictura est laicorum literatura'*.

Suger's programme is well known: the cathedral was to become a sort of immense book of stone in which the rich use of gold and gemstones would induce a sense of devotion in the faithful, and the beams of light falling from the great windows would suggest the participative warmth of divine power. Moreover, the sculptures over the portals, the reliefs on the capitals and the images on the stained glass windows were designed to communicate to the faithful the mystery of the faith, the order of natural phenomena, the hierarchies of the arts and of the trades, and the events in the nation's history.

St Bernard, a believer in an unadorned, severe architecture in which mysticism is suggested by the limpid nakedness of the house of God, reacted to this programme with an outburst of graphic accusations, ridiculing the monstrous iconographic efflorescences of the capitals:

> What excuse can there be for these ridiculous mon-strosities in the cloisters where the monks do their reading, extraordinary things at once beautiful and ugly? Here we find filthy monkeys and fierce lions, fearful centaurs, harpies, and striped tigers, soldiers at war, and hunters blowing their horns. Here is one head with many bodies, there is one body with many heads. Over there is a beast with a serpent for its tail, a fish with an animal's head, and a creature that is horse in front and goat behind, and a second beast with horns and the rear of a horse. All round there is such an amazing variety of shapes that one could easily prefer to take one's reading from the walls instead of from a book. One could spend the whole day gazing fascinated at these things, one by one, instead of medi-tating on the law of God. Good Lord, even if the foolishness of it all occasion no shame, at least one might balk at the expense?[14]

No matter that in this particular passage, the argument is against the images sculpted on capitals in monastic cloisters, images designed therefore for literate monks, not for the illiterate masses. It nonetheless summarizes a discussion which was concerned above all with the decoration of ordinary churches. An observation that comes naturally to mind is that St Bernard is betraying himself here, at what his accusation shows more than anything else is the perturbation of a man among the first to be won over and seduced by those images. In the absence of other documents, no passage could communicate to us more effectively the fascination and power of romanesque-gothic bestiary. St Bernard's tone betrays that same lacerated mixture of love and hatred apparent, in the same text, in his attitude towards the landed property he ascetically rejects:

> But we no longer belong to such people. For the sake of Christ we have abandoned all the world holds valuable and attractive. All that is beautiful in sight and sound and scent we have left behind, all that is pleasant to taste and touch. To win Christ we have reckoned bodily enjoyments as dung.[15]

Well yes, it's dung, but what a lot of frustrated passion over some lost dung . . .

But we shouldn't be ungenerous: such force of feeling rebounds positively in the ascertic's favour, his renunciation having obviously not come easily. However, if we were to judge Bernard by a contemporary yardstick, we would have to object to the fact that, while dwelling with unequivocal sensuality upon the diabolical nature of the images ('Drive this man away, he's breaking my heart!'), he does not touch upon the fundamental problem. After all, medieval society is organized in such a way that one class produces a culture made to its own measure and communicates it (whether through images or through sermons in a bare, unadorned church) to the subordinate classes, who are neither involved in the elaboration of that culture nor share responsibility for public affairs. Consequently, Bernard's discourse concentrates on only two modes of communication within the context of a single cultural model.

The medieval cultural model was of such an organic and integral nature that Bernard obviously could not have reacted otherwise, and for us seriously to make the above objections would denote a lack of historical knowledge. But what we cannot reproach St Bernard for, it is our duty to challenge in our contemporaries who behave like him.

The phenomenon known as mass culture comes about at a historical moment when the masses enter the public life of society as protagonists, sharing in responsibility for the commonweal. Often, these masses have imposed an ethos of their own, in various historical periods they have asserted particular needs, they have disseminated a language of their own; they have, that is, elaborated cultural proposals from below. But paradoxically, their way of enjoying themselves, of thinking and imagining, does not originate from below; it is suggested to them instead through the mass media in the form of messages formulated according to the codes of the ruling class. With mass culture a unique situation has arisen whereby members of the working class consume bourgeois cultural models believing them to be the independent expression of their own class. For its own part, bourgeois culture – in the sense in which 'high' culture remains that culture expressed by bourgeois society over the last three centuries – identifies mass culture as a 'subculture' which does not belong to it, without realizing that this mass culture still shares the same roots as 'high' culture.

Suger was well aware that the monsters over the entrances to cathedrals constituted visual translations of theological truths elaborated in the realms of university culture. What he tried to do was to bring together both ruling and subordinate classes in a single cultural model, if for no other reason than because he recognized, in good faith, that the two classes represented the two extremes of one and the same people: God's people, the people of France. St Bernard attacks the monsters, but only because he does not judge them to be instrumentally useful for establishing this same spiritual unity, believing it attainable by other means. On the other hand, in his elaboration of an iconographical repertory for the use of his own artists, Suger also makes sensitive use of the imaginary repertory of the common people.

However, with modern mass culture, the situation is much harder to define.

Yet, on reflection, there is something monstrous about a society in which the working class reacts to the screening on TV of a nineteenth-century *pochade* presenting *fin de siècle*, upper-middle class mores, as an opportunity for identifying, projecting itself and having a vehicle for escapism. This is an extreme example, but it reflects a common situation. From the godlike models of the cinema and the protagonists of romantic novels to women's television programmes, mass culture for the most part depicts human situations that have absolutely no connection with the situations actually experienced by its consumers but which, despite this, come to represent for them model situations. At the same time, however, it is possible in this sphere to encounter phenomena that defy any attempt to place them within a theoretical framework. Let's say that in a TV advertisement you want to use the model of a refined young woman who *has to* use a vacuum cleaner. She has to use it in order not to ruin her hands and to keep them beautiful and well-manicured. You show these images to inhabitants of an underdeveloped region for whom not the vacuum cleaner but the house in which you use a vacuum cleaner still constitutes an unattainable dream. It would be easy to assume that for these people such an image seems a phantom from another world that has nothing to do with them. Yet some surveys of the reactions of southern Italians to TV stimuli suggest that, in many cases, the viewer's reaction is of a critical and active nature; the revelation of a world that is still a possibility rather than an actuality for them can provoke rebellion, realism, or anyway some kind of judgment.

Here then is an example of a message being interpreted according to a different code from that used by its originator. It is enough to cast doubt on the whole notion of 'de-individualizing messages', 'mass man' and 'escapist culture'.

Consequently we cannot define the problem once and for all in terms of the worrying paradox of a culture produced for the masses which originates from on high rather than emerging from below: the situation is characterized by unpredictable outcomes that often contradict our premises and intentions. Any definition of the phenomenon in general terms runs the risk of contributing further to the generic nature of the mass message. The critic of culture finds himself duty-bound to embark on a study in which both fits of temper and neurotic indulgence are forbidden. The first thing he must learn to doubt are his own reactions as these *do not constitute a set of standards*. The critic (who no longer belongs to France and to God, but to a multitude of peoples and races with whom he is still not fully acquainted, for he is living in a civilization of mutants) must begin anew with every object and every consumer, as if he were preparing to discover something for the first time.

However, let us read the Günther Anders passage again. It begins on a chilly note: 'In an exhibition of television I had the dubious fortune of seeing and hearing . . .' So, just as he is about to invite us to read several hundred pages of his thoughts on the television phenomenon, Anders warns us that on the only occasion in which he undertook a concrete examination of the phenomenon of image transmission, he did so with boredom and a sense of disgust. But let's not accuse Anders of superficiality just yet. He remains one of the most illustrious representatives of a certain misunderstood humanist tradition. What he is displaying here is not an act of personal dishonesty, but a mental vice which has claims to nobility –

and which is often justified on account of its desperate good faith. It will come as no surprise, then, when the apocalyptic critic derides the suggestion that the mass media (like machines) are instruments, and as such may be instrumentalized. For in reality, the apocalyptic critic refused from the outset to examine the instrument and to test its possibilities. The only inspection he made was from the other side of the barricade, using himself as the guinea-pig: 'Apples make me come out in a rash, so they are bad. I am not interested in what an apple is and what substances it contains. If other people eat apples and are none the worse for it, it means that they are degenerates.' If by chance there existed some racket in the fruit and vegetable market which resulted in the population being forced to eat only unripe apples, or forced to eat only apples, it would escape the apocalyptic critic's attention, nor would he make any apology for this. From here, it's a short step to saying that rackets, like the Mafia, are a biological phenomenon and that no force in the world can eradicate them. By now, it is no longer of interest to know whether the apocalyptic critic was motivated by honest intentions, and whether he was urging us to eat meat as well as apples. As far as the consumers of apples are concerned, he's on the side of the racketeers.

So let us attempt to articulate the point of view in some other way. The progress of the working classes towards an active (formally speaking, at least) participation in public life and the broadening of the social base of information consumption have created a new area of anthropological study: 'mass civilization'. In this civilization, all members of the community become, to some degree, consumers of an intensively produced and non-stop stream of messages which are generated industrially and transmitted through the appropriate commercial channels governed by the laws of supply and demand. Once these products have been defined as *messages* (and the definition 'mass culture' has been carefully substituted with 'mass communication' or 'mass media'), one can proceed to an analysis of their structure. This structural analysis must not concentrate solely on the message's form, but define the extent to which the form is determined by the objective conditions of the transmission (which thus also determine the message's meaning and its informative power, i.e. whether it actively propounds something new or is purely a reiteration of something already said). Secondly, having established that these messages are addressed to a totality of consumers whose reduction to a unitary model is only accomplished with difficulty, their modes of reception – which differ according to historical or sociological circumstance and individual differentiation – must be established by empirical means. Thirdly (and this will be necessary in historical research and in the formulation of political hypotheses), having established the extent to which the saturation of the various messages may truly contribute to the creation of a model of mass-man, an examination must be carried out to identify what kinds of operation are possible in the current context, and what kinds require different conditions of existence.

The essays which follow will throw light on only some aspects of these questions.[16] The first is a summary of the critical stances taken up towards the argument. The second ('The Structure of Bad Taste'[17]) will attempt to elaborate a set of critical tools with which to assess in structural terms the aesthetic value of messages produced for an *average* public. The third ('A Reading of Steve Canyon'[18]) will attempt to provide an example of how direct experience is drawn on: a page of comic-strip will be subjected to the most analytical and meticulous reading, leading to the elaboration of a list of problems involving the whole range of the mass media, and entailing a methodological definition of the various types of possible research. The second section of the book will be about 'characters' as behavioural models, from myths with a purely projective function to constructions of a more conscious art which, by allowing us to enter into a critical relationship with the character, satisfy certain expectations of characterization and permit aesthetic enjoyment in the true sense.[19]

A third section will contain discussion of problems concerning the visual and aural elements of this civilization which is not simply one *of vision* but also *of noise*. These will mainly consist of survey notes, proposals for team research, clarifications and hypotheses in pedagogic and political terms. The final section brings together occasional essays and articles published in newspapers and magazines, in which the conflict between apocalyptic and integrated intellectuals is discussed on an intuitive and polemical level. I thought it useful to include these occasional 'notes' for the very reason that a discussion on mass media is continually 'occasioned', being linked to the observation of social mores, and stimulated also by marginal factors. A critic recently complained that my essay on the popular song contained as many as five pages written in the conditional tense. From a stylistic point of view, there is little to be proud of in having set such a record. But from a methodological point of view, all the essays in this volume have been conceived in the conditional tense. In bringing together the published ones and linking them to the unpublished ones, I made no attempt whatsoever to eliminate the odd contradiction. With the alteration of point of view, these problems are continually taking on new aspects – and casting doubt on what has already been said. A discussion of phenomena that are so closely linked to everyday experience, having defined a process and its effects, inevitably encounters new phenomena that apparently contradict earlier diagnoses. Such a discussion cannot amount to more than a chain of hypothetical syllogisms with the premises in the subjunctive tense and the conclusion in the conditional. If there is one idea governing these writings, it is that today it is impossible, despite some attempts, to elaborate '*Theorien der Massenmedien*': such a thing would be akin to a 'theory of next Thursday'.

Precisely because these phenomena cannot be subsumed under a unitary theoretical formula, they must be submitted to a process of examination that does not shrink from putting them through every conceivable test. An examination which is above all not afraid of using approaches that are too noble for the modest objects under study. One of the objections levelled as research of this type (which has also been levelled at some of these essays) is that the cultural apparatus used is inappropriate for the study of trivia such as Superman comics or Rita Pavone pop songs. The sum of these minimal messages that accompany our daily life constitutes the most manifest cultural phenomenon of the civilization in which we are living. As soon as it is decided to turn these messages into objects for criticism no approach can be unsuitable and they must be treated as worthy of the greatest attention.

And anyway, the objection is rather old hat. It recalls the objection of those who regarded a science as worthy only if it was concerned with examining incorruptible realities (like the celestial spheres or the *quidditatis*) while judging as inferior studies of things liable to corruption. This meant that knowledge was not judged on the basis of the dignity of the method, but on the basis of the object's dignity.

Consequently, in introducing a discussion on things that are 'minimal' and without history, it is impossible to resist the temptation to shield ourselves with a recourse to history, borrowing the words of one who believed that the discussion of 'humble and low matters' was a dignified activity. Leonardo wrote:

> The lie is so vile, that even if it were speaking well of Godly things it would take off something from God's grace; and truth is so excellent that if it praises but small things, they become noble . . . And truth is so excellent in itself, that, even if it dwells on humble and lowly matter, it rises infinitely above the uncertainties

and lies about high and lofty matters . . . But you who live on dreams are better pleased by the sophistical reasons and frauds of wits in great and uncertain things than by those reasons which are certain and natural and not so exalted.[20]

A final note, which reconfirms the 'conditional' nature of these studies, and the suspicion that they must continually be begun afresh. I would like to dedicate the book to those critics whom I have so summarily defined as apocalyptics. Without whose unjust, biased, neurotic, desperate censure I could never have elaborated three-quarters of the ideas that I want to share here; without them, perhaps none of us would have realized that the question of mass culture is one in which we are all deeply involved. It is a sign of contradiction in our civilization.

1964

CHAPTER 2

The World of Charlie Brown

HE DOESN'T DRINK, he doesn't smoke, he doesn't swear. He was born in Minnesota in 1922. He's married and has five children, I believe. He works alone, has no neuroses of any kind. This man whose life is so disastrously normal is named Charles M. Schulz. He is a Poet.

When I say 'poet', I say it because I am sure it will make some people mad: the professional humanists, who don't read comic strips; and those who accuse intellectuals who do of being snobs when they claim to like them. But this much should be clear: if 'poetry' means the capacity of carrying tenderness, pity, wickedness to moments of extreme transparence, as if things passed through a light and there were no telling any more what substance they are made of, then Schulz is a poet. If poetry means fixing typical characters in typical circumstances, Schulz is a poet. If poetry means producing from everyday events, which we are accustomed to identify with the surface of things, a revelation that causes us to touch the depth of things, then, every so often, Schulz is a poet. And if poetry were merely finding a particular rhythm and improvising on it in a ceaseless adventure of infinitesimal variations, making a constantly new universe from the otherwise mechanical encounter of two or three elements, well, in this case, too, Schulz is a poet. More so than many others.

But poetry is all these things and others as well, and we do not mean to become involved here with aesthetic definitions of Schulz. When we say Schulz is a Poet, we say it chiefly as a challenge, to take a stand. The declaration 'Schulz is a poet' amounts to saying 'We love Charlie M. Schulz unconditionally, intensely, fiercely, intolerantly; and we will allow no debate, and anyone who disagrees is either a villain or an illiterate.'

There. These things had to be said, otherwise the reader would not understand the nights spent by a committee of Italian translators, who have devoted to these strips the meticulous passion that Max Brod devoted to the manuscripts of Kafka, Valéry Larbaud to the French version of *Ulysses*, and Father Van Breda to the shorthand notes of Edmund Husserl; the reader would not understand the philological debates on the closest Italian equivalent of the famous 'Good Grief' (which finally became 'misericordia!') and on how to render most fully all the charge of despair and passivity understood in 'I can't stand it' (which could not be translated in a single way, but differently according to context), and the complex hermeneutics that, barely touched, burst in the air like soap-bubbles – and then the long, exhausted breaks during which the experts argued the *vexata quaestio* as to whether Gordon was Flash's surname or given name, some suggesting that he should really be called Gordon Flash; and if, for instance, the loftiest moments of the Disneyan epoch, the days of Steamboat Willie, surpassed, in their barbarian and primitive form, those of the more relaxed epic of the sophisticated saga of the Plumbers – and, further, on the suitability of adding, in a first Italian edition of *Peanuts*®, a critical appendix with variants, an apparatus of explanatory notes, a trilingual bibliography raisonnée and, bluffing but determined to give the unprepared reader a sense of the greatness of the undertaking, a collation of alternative interpretations offered both by the School of Tübingen and by that of Bratislava, well known for its *Beiträge*, essential to a correct reading of Schulz – and so on and on. Fantasies gradually assumed weight and consistency, and in the end were believed in, and why not? Isn't Charlie Brown a moment of the Universal Consciousness, a Hero of Our Times, a 16mm Leopold Bloom, a Positive Type, our pocket, portable Everyman, the suburban Philoctetes of the paperbacks, a Jeremiah of the strip-Bible which mercenary apocrypha have occasionally presented to us in receptive and malevolent translations, undermining our faith, and thus demanding a legion of Erasmuses to re-establish the texts and the glosses?

Enough. Those who were to be offended have duly taken offence and gone away. Let us sit down for a moment and talk. I will tell you briefly why *Peanuts* by Charlie M. Schulz is something important, true, tender and gentle.

It is not true that comic strips are a harmless amusement, which, though created for children, can also appeal to adults, seated in their easy-chairs after dinner, a bit of escapism to be enjoyed without harm and without gain. The mass culture industry produces comics on an international scale and distributes them on every level: as they (and as the pop song, the thriller, the TV broadcast) prevail, true popular art, the art that rises from below, dies, autocthonous traditions die, no more legends are born to be told around the hearth, and balladsingers no longer arrive, to display their narrative panels, during festivals in the farmyard or the village square. The comic strip is commissioned from above, it operates according to all the mechanisms of hidden persuasion, it presupposes in the consumer an attitude of escape that immediately stimulates the paternalistic aspirations of the producers. And, as a rule, authors conform: thus the comic strip, in most cases, reflects the implicit pedagogy of a system and acts as hidden reinforcement of the dominant myths and values. *Dennis the Menace* confirms the basically happy and irresponsible image of a good middle-class family that has turned Deweyan naturalism into an educative myth ready to be misunderstood, mass-producing a long line of neurotics; and *Little Orphan Annie* (as highly respectable sociological investigations have demonstrated: cf.

the study by Lyle W. Shannon) becomes for millions of readers the supporter of a nationalistic McCarthyism, a paleocapitalist classism, a petty bourgeois philistinism ready to celebrate the pomps of the John Birch Society; *Maggie and Jiggs* reduces the sociological problem of American matriarchy to a simple, individual situation; *Terry and the Pirates* lent itself faithfully to a nationalist-militarist education of the young American generations; *Dick Tracy* brought the sadism of the action-thriller within everyone's reach not only through its plots but also through the very sign of an extremely neurotic and sanguinary pencil (and it is of no matter that it considerably refreshed the palate of its audience); and *Joe Palooka* continues singing his hymn to the prototype of the innocent and upright Yankee, the same to whom all electoral persuasions of conservative stamp make their appeal. Thus even protest and social criticism, when they did exist, were politely confined within the system and reduced to storybook dimensions. We all know that the figure of Donald Duck's Uncle Scrooge sums up all the defects of a generic capitalism founded on the worship of money and the exploitation of one's fellow-man solely for profit: the Dickensian name of this character serves to direct this implied criticism towards a notion of nineteenth-century capitalism (akin to the use of child labour in coal mines and corporal punishment in schools) which modern society obviously no longer fears and which anyone can feel free to criticize. And if the famous strips of Al Capp, through the adventures of Li'l Abner, present a criticism of American tics and myths, at times with irrepressible nastiness – for instance, the satire of an opulent society based on consumption, which the story of Shmoo related for some time – all the same this criticism, too, is always seen against an indestructible background of optimism and good humour, while the scene of the events, the village of Dogpatch, in its pastoral dimension, regularly dulls the bite of the various attacks on situations originally concrete and troubling.

Should we then say that the comic strip, bound by the iron rule of the industrial-commercial circuit of production and consumption, is destined to give only the standard products of a sometimes unconscious, sometimes programmed paternalism? And that, while it has developed the stylistic formulas, narrative lines and unquestionable original suggestions of taste, stimulating for its mass audience, the comics will nevertheless always and in every way exploit these achievements in a constant function of escape and masking of reality?

Now, in theory, we could answer that, ever since the world began, major arts and minor arts have almost always been able to flourish only within a system that allowed the artist a certain margin of autonomy in exchange for a certain percentage of observance of the established values; and that, all the same, within these various circuits of production and consumption, there have been artists who, using the same opportunities afforded the others, managed to alter profoundly their consumers' way of feeling; and these artists, working within the system, performed a critical and liberating function. As usual, it is a matter of individual genius: to be able to develop a language so incisive, clear and effective as to dominate all the conditions within which that language must operate.

I believe that, in this sense, the comic strip has offered us two paths. The first is the one whose most recent and perhaps finest representative is Jules Feiffer. The satire of this author, so accurate, catching with such precision the ills of a modern industrial society, translates them into exemplary types, and displays in the revelation of these types so much humanity (nastiness and pity at the same time) that, in whatever newspaper these stories appear, however successful they may be (even if everyone smiles and accepts them, including those readers who should be insulted and terrified), their success in no way lessens their power. A Feiffer story, once published, cannot then be exorcized; once read, it sticks in the mind and silently works there.

There is also a second path, and to exemplify it I would choose a now-classic strip, George Herriman's *Krazy Kat*, which came into existence around 1910–11 and ended in 1944 with the death of the author. The dramatis personae were three: a cat of unspecified sex, probably female; a mouse, Ignatz; a dog acting as policeman, Offissa Pupp. The drawing was remarkable, with certain surrealistic inventions, especially in the improbable lunar landscapes, deliberately intended to divorce the events from any verisimilitude. The plot? The cat madly loves the mouse, and the wicked mouse hates and tyrannizes the cat, preferably by hitting him on the head with a brick. The dog constantly tries to protect the cat, but the cat despises this unrestrained love of his: the cat adores the mouse and is always ready to excuse him. From this absurd situation without particularly comic ingredients, the author drew an infinite series of variations, based on a structural fact that is of fundamental importance in the understanding of comics in general: the brief daily or weekly story, the traditional strip, even if it narrates an episode that concludes in the space of four panels, will not work if considered separately; rather it acquires flavour only in the continuous and obstinate series, which unfolds, strip after strip, day by day. In *Krazy Kat* the poetry originated from a certain lyrical stubbornness in the author, who repeated his tale ad infinitum, varying it always but sticking to its theme. It was thanks only to this that the mouse's arrogance, the dog's unrewarded compassion, and the cat's desperate love could arrive at what many critics felt was a genuine state of poetry, an uninterrupted elegy based on sorrowing innocence. In a comic of this sort, the spectator, not seduced by a flood of gags, by any realistic or caricatural reference, by any appeal to sex and violence, freed then from the routine of a taste that led him to seek in the comic strip the satisfaction of certain requirements, could thus discover the possibility of a purely allusive world, a pleasure of a 'musical' nature, an interplay of feelings that were not banal. To some extent the myth of Scheherazade was reproduced: the concubine, taken by the Sultan to be used for one night and then discarded, begins telling a story, and because of the story the Sultan forgets the woman; he discovers, that is, another world of values.

The best proof that the comic strip is an industrial product purely for consumption is that, even if a character is invented by an author of genius, after a while the author is replaced by a team, his genius becomes fungible, his invention a factory product. The best proof that *Krazy Kat*, thanks to its raw poetry, managed to overcome the system is that at the death of Herriman nobody chose to be his heir, and the comic-strip industrialists were unable to force the situation.

And now we come to Schulz and *Peanuts*, which we would assign to the 'lyric' vein of *Krazy Kat*.

Here, too, the situation is elementary: a group of children, Charlie Brown, Lucy, Violet, Patty, Frieda, Linus, Schroeder, Pig Pen, and the dog Snoopy, involved in their games and their talk. Over this basic scheme there is a steady flow of variations, following a rhythm found in certain primitive epics (primitive, too, is the habit of referring to the protagonist always by his full name – even his mother addresses him in that fashion – like an epic hero); thus you could never grasp the power of his *poésie interrompue* by reading only one, or two, or ten episodes: you must thoroughly understand the characters and the situations, for the grace, tenderness and laughter are born only from the infinitely shifting repetition of the patterns, and the same results are born also from fidelity to the fundamental inspiration; they demand from the reader a continuous act of empathy, a participation in the warmth that, from within, pervades the lines of events.

And further: the poetry of these children is born from the fact that we find in them all the problems, all the sufferings of the adults, who remain offstage. In this sense Schulz is a Herriman already approaching the critical and social tendency of a

Feiffer. These children affect us because in a certain sense they are monsters; they are the monstrous infantile reductions of all the neuroses of a modern citizen of the industrial civilization.

They affect us because we realize that if they are monsters it is because we, the adults, have made them so. In them we find everything: Freud, mass-cult, digest culture, frustrated struggle for success, craving for affection, loneliness, passive acquiescence, and neurotic protest. But all these elements do not blossom directly, as we know them, from the mouths of a group of children: they are conceived and spoken after passing through the filter of innocence.

Schulz's children are not a sly instrument to handle our adult problems: these problems they experience according to a childish psychology, and for this very reason they seem to us touching and hopeless, as if we were suddenly aware that our ills have polluted everything, at the root.

But still more: the reduction of adult myths to childhood myths (a childhood that no longer comes 'before' our maturity, but 'after' – and shows us its fissures) allows Schulz a recovery; and these monster-children are capable suddenly of an innocence and a sincerity which call everything into question, sift out the detritus, and give us back a world that is still and always very sweet and soft, tasting of milk and cleanliness. Thus in a constant seesaw of reactions, within a sole story, or between one story and another, we never know whether to despair or to heave a sigh of optimism. But, in any case, we realize that we have emerged from a banal circuit of consumption and escapism, and we have almost reached the threshold of meditation. The most amazing proof of this and other things is that, while distinctly 'cultivated' comics, like *Pogo*, appeal only to intellectuals (and are consumed by the mass-audience only through distraction), *Peanuts* charms both sophisticated adults and children with equal intensity, as if each reader found there something for himself, and it is always the same thing, to be enjoyed in two different keys.

The world of *Peanuts* is a microcosm, a little human comedy for the innocent reader and for the sophisticated.

In its centre is Charlie Brown: ingenuous, stubborn, always awkward and doomed to failure. Requiring, to a critical degree, communication and popularity, and repaid by the matriarchal, know-it-all girls of his group with scorn, references to his round head, accusations of stupidity, all the little digs that strike home, Charlie Brown, undaunted, seeks tenderness and fulfilment on every side: in baseball, in building kites, in his relationship with his dog, Snoopy, in play with the girls. He always fails. His solitude becomes an abyss, his inferiority complex is pervasive – tinged by the constant suspicion (which the reader also comes to share) that Charlie Brown does not have an inferiority complex, but really is inferior. The tragedy is that Charlie Brown is not inferior. Worse: he is absolutely normal. He is like everybody else. This is why he proceeds always on the brink of suicide or at least of nervous breakdown; because he seeks salvation through the routine formulas suggested to him by the society in which he lives (the art of making friends, culture in four easy lessons, the pursuit of happiness, how to make out with girls . . . he has been ruined, obviously, by Dr Kinsey, Dale Carnegie, Erich Fromm and Lin Yutang).

But since he acts in all purity and without any guile, society is prompt to reject him, through its representative, Lucy, treacherous, self-confident, entrepreneur with assured profits, ready to peddle a security that is completely bogus but of unquestioned effect (her lessons in natural science to her brother Linus are a jumble of nonsense that turns Charlie Brown's stomach. 'I can't stand it,' the unfortunate boy groans, but what weapons can arrest impeccable bad faith when one has the misfortune to be pure of heart? . . .)

Charlie Brown has been called the most sensitive child ever to appear in a comic strip, a figure capable of great shifts of

mood of a Shakespearean tone; and Schulz's pencil succeeds
in rendering these variations with an economy of means that
has something miraculous about it: the text, always almost
courtly, in a language worthy of Harvard (these children rarely
lapse into slang or commit anacoluthon), is enhanced by a
drawing able to portray, in each character, the subtlest psychological nuance. Thus the daily tragedy of Charlie Brown is
drawn, in our eyes, with exemplary incisiveness.

For eluding this tragedy of non-integration, the table of
psychological types offers some alternatives. The girls elude it
thanks to an obstinate self-sufficiency and haughtiness: Lucy
(a 'géante', to be admired with awe), Patty and Violet are all
of a piece; perfectly integrated (or should we say 'alienated'?),
they move from hypnotic sessions at the TV to rope-skipping
and to everyday talk, interwoven with sarcasm, achieving peace
through insensitivity.

Linus, the smallest, is, on the other hand, already burdened
with every neurosis; emotional instability would be his per-
petual condition if the society in which he lives had not already
offered him the remedies: Linus already has behind him Freud,
Adler, and perhaps also Binswanger (via Rollo May), he has
identified his baby-blanket as the symbol of a uterine peace or
a purely oral happiness . . . sucking his finger, blanket against
his cheek (if possible, with TV turned on, in front of which
he can huddle like an Indian; but also without anything, in an
oriental-type isolation, attached to his symbols of protection),
he then finds his 'sense of security'. Take away his blanket and
he will be plunged once more into all the emotional troubles
lying in wait for him day and night. Because – we must add
– along with the instability of a neurotic society he has
absorbed all its wisdom. Linus represents its most technologically up-to-date product. While Charlie Brown is unable to
make a kite that will not get caught in the branches of a tree,
Linus reveals suddenly, in bursts, fantastic abilities and dazzling skills: he performs feats of amazing equilibrium, he can

strike a quarter flung in the air with the edge of his blanket, snapping it like a whip ('the fastest blanket in the West!').

Schroeder, on the other hand, finds peace in aesthetic religion. Seated at his little toy piano from which he draws tunes and chords of transcendental complexity, slumped in his total worship of Beethoven, he saves himself from everyday neuroses by sublimating them in a lofty form of artistic madness. Not even Lucy's constant, loving admiration can budge him (Lucy cannot love music, an unprofitable activity, whose reason she doesn't comprehend; but in Schroeder she admires an unattainable summit. Perhaps she is stimulated by the adamantine shyness of her pocket Parsifal, and she stubbornly pursues her work of seduction without making a dent in the artist's defences). Schroeder has chosen the peace of the senses in the delirium of the imagination. 'Do not speak ill of this love, Lisabeta: it is good and fertile. It contains nostalgia and melancholy, envy and a bit of contempt, and a complete, chaste happiness' – this is not Schroeder speaking, of course: it is Tonio Kröger; but this is the point; and it is no accident that Schulz's children represent a microcosm where our tragedy and our comedy is all performed.

Pig Pen, too, has an inferiority to complain about: he is irreparably, horrifyingly dirty. He leaves home neat and spruce, and a second later his shoelaces come untied, his trousers sag over his hips, his hair is flaked with dandruff, his skin and clothes are covered with a layer of mud ... Aware of this vocation to the abyss, Pig Pen turns his plight into a boast; he speaks of history. This is not a Beckett character speaking; these are, more or less, the words of Pig Pen; Schulz's microcosm reaches the last outcrops of existential choice.

Constant antistrophe to the humans' sufferings, the dog Snoopy carries to the last metaphysical frontier the neurotic failure to adjust. Snoopy knows he is a dog: he was a dog yesterday, he is a dog today, tomorrow he will perhaps be a dog still; for him, in the optimist dialectic of the opulent society that allows upward moves from status to status, there is no hope of promotion. Sometimes he essays the extreme resource of humility (we dogs are so humble, he sighs, unctuous and consoled); he becomes tenderly attached to those who promise him respect and consideration. But as a rule he doesn't accept himself and he tries to be what he is not: a split personality if ever there was one, he would like to be an alligator, a kangaroo, a vulture, a penguin, a snake ... He tries every avenue of mystification, then he surrenders to reality, out of laziness, hunger, sleepiness, timidity, claustrophobia (which assails him when he crawls through high grass), ignorance. He may be soothed, but never happy. He lives in a constant apartheid, and he has the psychology of the segregated; like an Uncle Tom, he has finally, *faute de mieux*, a devotion, an ancestral respect for the stronger.

Suddenly, in this encyclopaedia of contemporary weaknesses, there are, as we have said, luminous patches of light, free variations, allegros and rondos, where all is pacified in a few bars. The monsters turn into children again, Schulz becomes only a poet of childhood.

We know it isn't true, and we pretend to believe him. In the next strip he will continue to show us, in the face of Charlie Brown, with two strokes of his pencil, his version of the human condition.

Note: This essay was originally published in Italian in 1963 as the introduction to the first translated volume of *Peanuts* entitled *Arriva Charlie Brown!*

1963

CHAPTER 3

Reactions of Apocalyptic and Integrated Intellectuals: Then (1964)

A DISCUSSION of *Apocalittici e integrati* and of its critical reception in 1964 is interesting because, despite the provocative tone and the original analyses it contained, the book was not thought by its author to be saying anything new but rather to be taking stock of what, by this date, was a seasoned debate. A debate to which many writers around the world had contributed (a glance through the footnotes, which refer also to some excellent studies that had already appeared in Italy, is sufficient confirmation of this) and which, in the more progressive university circles in Italy, as in other countries, was giving rise to a number of research and teaching initiatives.

And yet the reason for this book's success, for the huge controversy it aroused (together with the adoption of the expression 'apocalittici e integrati' as a slogan which has since entered current usage) lay precisely in the fact that the book seems to have taken a section of Italian culture by surprise.

The most typical reaction is perhaps to be found in a review by Pietro Citati in *Il giorno* (14 October 1964), entitled 'Pavone and Superman arm-in-arm with Kant'. If the title is tongue-in-cheek, the article itself has a troubled tone: the book is said to be lively and intelligent but the reviewer complains that while 'in all good scientific research the material under study selects its own instruments, and these are in perfect accordance with it . . . Eco cites Husserl, Kant and Baltrusaitis for no good reason, almost as if he wished to be forgiven for the humbleness of his own theme.' Leaving aside the idea that the instruments used in the analysis of a subject must identify with it, as if a study of criminology had to be undertaken by inflicting stab wounds, and Kant could be cited only in discussions about philosophy (which would be to do him a somewhat humiliating disservice), the fact is that Citati is highly suspicious about using the instruments of High Culture in order to explain and analyse Low Culture. 'This widening of the field of study reveals an obvious assumption: all things are equally worthy of consideration, Plato and Elvis Presley both belong to history in the same way.' In fact, such an assumption was obvious, but Citati objected for it seemed to him to represent the crowning of the secret ideals of mass culture: 'I don't know if these ideals run the risk of being realized. But if this were to come about, in a few years' time the majority of Italian intellectuals will be producing films, songs and comic strips; the cleverest of them will be slipping a few lines of Celentano into their own poetry . . . while in all the university chairs, young dons will be analysing the phenomena of mass culture . . . and perhaps all of us are already living in order to stimulate increasingly accurate statistics, ever more exhaustive analyses, or furious denunciations.'

Citati's text was remarkably prophetic: today, thirteen years later, a good number of Italian intellectuals are producing films and songs, poets are composing collage works using lines from Celentano, while in the universities theses on the comic strip abound and the Citati piece is interesting simply because it allows us to analyse the situation facing the Italian intellectual in 1964. This analysis will be all the more thorough if we consider that, although the piece was meant to be prophetic, it was in fact an unwittingly up-to-date account of what was actually taking place: in fact, by 1964, Calvino and Fortini had already been writing songs for some time, Pasolini and Robbe-Grillet were making films, the Novissimi poets were composing verse using fragments of popular language, while at the University of Rome's Education Department the late Romano Calisi was engaged in setting up, with the encouragement of pedagogist Luigi Volpicelli, a national archive of the comic strip.

What Eco's book did was to take this new situation fully on board, but in doing so, as has been pointed out, it took the less informed by surprise and gave rise to a series of newspaper and magazine articles in which writers expressed their delighted or dismayed astonishment under titles such as: 'Mandrake goes to University' (*ABC*), 'From Aesthetics to Rita Pavone' (*Paese sera*), 'From Joyce to Rita Pavone' (*Il punto*), 'Comic strips have blue blood too' (*Oggi*), 'Cultural Passports for Mandrake and Mickey Mouse' (*Lo specchio*), 'Now hully gully too is a "message"' (*Il giorno*), 'Thank goodness for Superman' (*Il Resto del Carlino*), 'The comic strip is added to the university syllabus' (*La Gazzetta del Popolo*), and so on. It's worth noting that, in almost all of these articles, the term 'comic strip' appears in quotation marks (not yet having been accepted into the Italian language as a *bona fide* term), and most of all, that what most struck reviewers' imaginations was the fact that the comic strip had become an item of study, when in fact less than a quarter of the book was actually dedicated to the comic strip form, the rest being a discussion of the problems of television, petit-bourgeois literature, recorded music, and the popular novel of previous centuries.

Even the *Times Literary Supplement*, reviewing the book with exemplary promptness, made its shock announcement with a front-page illustration which, for that journal in those days, represented quite a break with tradition: it showed a comic-strip dog, albeit derived from Lichtenstein, remarking 'sniff sniff, arrrff!'

Of course, not all of these articles were as provincial in outlook as their titles suggest; some appeared with titles which were more 'critical' and thoughtful. All of them discussed the conflict between apocalyptic moralists and integrated optimists, but in some the subject of mass communications was examined in a decidedly more political key.

Thus, leaving aside those reactions which were merely sensationalist, reviewers may be divided into two camps: embittered conservatives, and progressives under stress. There is little to say about the embittered conservatives: the book itself had foreseen their reaction. An intelligent conservative instead had to adopt as his own the argument against ingenuous apocalyptics, putting forward a more mellow apocalyptic stance while in the same breath praising the book. This was the approach of A. G. Solari (widely held to be the pseudonym of Giose Rimanelli) in his article 'Cultural passport for Mandrake and Mickey Mouse' published in *Lo specchio* (6 September 1964). In a sympathetic reading of the book, couched in terms of shrewd concordance, he places Eco among the upholders of Reason: a sly backhander this, since for the Left in those days the accusation of holding Enlightenment views was a hard one to swallow. Historically speaking, it was equal to an accusation of being right-wing, but the Rusconi editions, in which the classics of the anti-Enlightenment tradition would be reinstated, had not yet appeared, and to launch an attack from the pages of *Lo specchio*, outdoing the author on the left wing, was a brilliant move. By means of this polite condemnation, Eco was shown in his true colours as a champion of avant-garde tendencies (remember *Open Work!*[1]), the notorious other face of mass culture. Which, on reflection, was the Adornist position of the time, Adornism having reached Italy from Frankfurt via the conservative mediation of Elémire Zolla[2] (one of the polemical targets of *Apocalittici*) and having been adopted in this form by many on the Left.

Montale, however, reacted with his usual coherence: prepared to face the new developments with curiosity, ready to declare himself trouble, pessimistic, but not dogmatic. Entitling his short article in *Il Corriere della sera* (2 August 1964) 'From good to better', he agreed with the author that the mass media existed and that they had to be dominated and made to comply with human aims. But what are the aims of man? 'Here we are navigating in darkness.' Let's not exaggerate; people also said of the telephone that it would damage the intimacy of the home, but we absorbed that one too. We may as well say that life is a stream that flows where it will and it's easy to become part of that stream; while the apocalyptics keep watch, silent and unpopular, conscious that they are protesting 'against the means and yet still part of the means'. But, 'the cold war being waged for and against the mass media will probably seem senseless in a few decades. No social revolution will substantially change the technical-mechanical aspect of the world.'

Interesting for other reasons are the reactions of a section of the Marxist cultural current which was in that period opening itself up to a more careful consideration of these phenomena, replacing second-wave Adornism with a realistic and analytical outlook. Mario Spinella in *Rinascita* (3 October 1964: 'Apocalittici e integrati') linked the polemic against aristocratic culture to Gramscian thought, taking the book's point of departure, i.e. Marx and Engels's polemic with Bruno Bauer, as his own. He accused Eco of not having dedicated enough space to the problem of the socio-economic context within which the mass communication media operated, and attempted to explain the reasons why Eco preferred to carry out an analysis of the textual frameworks, inviting him to consider the historical setting of the products under analysis. He did, however, credit this particular brand of 'structuralism' with being more critically aware of its own limits than that of French origin, and his article ended with an evaluation of Eco's book as 'the best that has so far been written on the subject', one reason being 'the engaged tone of his more recent statements about Marxism'. In *Mondo Nuovo*, Francesco Indovina stated that 'only by means of contributions of this type . . . will it be possible to evolve a coherent strategy for transforming the phenomenon into a positive critical experience for the "masses". Eco's approach seems to me to be significant because of the attempt to link the economical, political and social conditions of the phenomenon with the actual structure of the mass message itself: if, in fact, such a connection is not made, it seems to me that there is a risk of going round in circles without getting anywhere, leaving the field open to *manipulators*.' Vittorio Spinazzola's evaluation of the book appeared in *Vie Nuove* (10 December 1964) under the title 'An as yet uncharted territory for Italian scholars'. He reproached Eco for a certain randomness in his selection criteria, complained about the theoretical weaknesses, the wavering between pure description and the attempt to grasp the formidable ideological and economic implications of these problems, but judged it finally to be a pioneering work in which the author had 'boldly faced the risks involved'.

ARCI's *Le ore libere*[3] dedicated three successive editions to a debate which took various tones and whose participants included Rossana Rossanda, Luciano Paolicchi, Franco Fortini, Mario Spinella, Gianni Toti, Pietro A. Buttitta, Mino Argentieri, Walter Pedullà and Nanni Saba. Reactions varied from those who declared themselves to be 'neither apocalyptic nor integrated', to those who confessed that yes, they had read the odd Flash Gordon comic-book (but it was just 'one of those venial sins that don't even have to be confessed'), and others who took a more considered viewpoint. But taken all round, the debate was fairly representative of the whole range of theoretically divergent opinions which the Marxist Left typically expressed on the argument. Even more significant was the fact that the subject received such a thorough reading from so many representative figures. In an article in *L'Avanti* (3 October 1964) Walter Pedullà defined Eco's stance of a third force between apocalyptic and conformist as that of 'a realist who accepts the dialogue and makes concessions in order not to lose all. His book is a sort of splendid Yalta memorial to mass culture.'

Among the favourable reviews, it is interesting to record an article by Oreste del Buono ('Serious thoughts on frivolous problems', in *La Settimana Incom*, 30 August 1964) in which one of the few reproaches levelled at Eco is that he is 'perhaps somewhat too benevolent' towards Charlie Brown – a compromising severity for the man who was later to be Editor in Chief of *Linus*,[4] but then that's the beauty of reading through these old reviews. Among the distinctly unfavourable reviews was an article by Michele Rago in *L'Unità* (29 November 1964: 'Mass culture and the culture of the masses') in which he criticizes the book for its superficiality, its haphazardness, and the clever sleight-of-hand polemics, although he admits to sharing a number of its basic preoccupations. There was also a very irritated article by Gianfranco Corsini (*Paese Sera*, 19 September 1964) who, previously an enthusiastic reviewer of *Open Work*, now reproached Eco for here having tried to fuse, in a haphazard way, the canons of that first book with the pastiches of *Diario minimo*,[5] with rather unhappy results. And finally, there was a piece by Enzo Siciliano in *La Fiera Letteraria* (27 September 1964) in which, under the title 'A good beginning isn't enough', he launches into a discussion with threefold implications. He begins with praise tempered by an indulgent 'All right, all right, all right', and follows this with a series of objections to the 'Enlightenment' tendency which seem to be of a traditionalist sort; he then reminds the author of the importance of historical analysis and, implicitly, of social practice, thus ending the article on a somewhat 'Leftist' note.

This takes us to the first months following publication. Gradually, the articles in specialist journals appear. But by now the book has taken off: there are new editions, a couple of unabridged translations and others of selected parts of the work (as the author tells us, he has never thought of this work as forming an organic whole and has preferred to allow only translations of selected essays), and the title has become a catch-phrase, still in use though often without a knowledge of its origin.

1964

CHAPTER 4

The Reactions of the Author: Now (1974 and 1977)

EVERY TIME there was talk of bringing out a new edition of this book, I tried to stop it, and for two reasons. For one, its writing was a chance affair, as in fact many critics realized; and also because this is one of those subjects where you wake up every morning and everything has changed, so it needs to be written all over again. This explains why a book like *Open Work* was practically rewritten, the form of *La struttura assente*[1] changed with every new translation, while in the case of *Apocalittici* I've always allowed new editions to be printed in the original version. And I've always given the go-ahead on new editions because booksellers told me that people were requesting it. You can't cancel your own past, like the dictator in *Nineteen Eighty-Four*: and so here we have it, this is what I was thinking in 1964. And if it were 1964 today, I'd probably publish the same book all over again. Every culture has the 'novelties' it deserves.

How did *Apocalittici* come to be written? Manners, popular culture, detective stories, comic strips were all things that had interested me greatly for a long time. Only I was writing about them in newspaper articles and pieces like those of *Diario minimo* which in those days were published in *Il Verri*. In 1959 I wrote a piece entitled 'Estetica dei parenti poveri' ('Aesthetics of the poor relation') in which I listed, in paradoxical tones, a number of possible research projects, including the evolution of the graphics of physical features from Flash Gordon to Dick Tracy; existentialism and Peanuts, gesture and onomatopeia in the comic strip; standard outlines of narrative situations; the influence of the magnetic echo in vocal evolution after the Platters; aesthetic use of the telephone; aesthetics of the football match. All these themes are now the subjects of books. One of them, the one on standard situations, had already been written many years beforehand by Propp, but I wasn't aware of that in 1959.

I'd already tackled the subject of television in a paper I gave to the international conference on aesthetics in 1956, and I published an essay on 'topical' characters of popular fiction in the *Rivista di Estetica* in 1958. But these were all marginal interests. What really stimulated me was a book that I totally rejected, but one that will remain the obvious or hidden target of *Apocalittici*: this was Elémire Zolla's *L'eclissi dell'intellettuale*. Basically, it was responsible for opening the discussion of mass culture in Italy, even though it did so in a negative way.

I believe, however, that the revelation came between 1961 and the beginning of 1962. I had been invited by Enrico Castelli to take part in a symposium at the Istituto di Studi Filosofici in Rome on the subject of demythicization and image and I was worried because taking part also were famous experts on mythology like Kerényi, scholars of hermeneutic philosophy such as Ricoeur, Protestant theologians, religious historians, Jesuits and Dominicans, philosophers of all sorts. What was I going to say to them? Then I think that the problem of myth and image isn't exclusive to the primitive and classical eras. Stored in a cupboard I have two or three hundred copies of the original comic books with full-colour stories of Superman and I think that basically he is a myth of our time, the expression not of a religion but of an ideology . . . So I arrive in Rome and begin my paper with a pile of Superman comics on the table in front of me. What will they do, throw me out?

No sirree, half the comic books disappeared; would you believe it, with all the air of wishing to examine them, those monks with their wide sleeves spirited them away before I could say Jack Robinson. Aside from this omen, a discussion gets under way and I decide that this is a question that deserves more attention.

That very same year I read *L'Esprit du temps* by Edgar Morin,[2] where he writes that in order to analyse mass culture you have to secretly enjoy it, you can't talk about the juke box if you resent putting money into it . . . So why should I not use my comic strips and detective books as items of study?

There was also the fact that in 1961 Aldo Visalberghi was preparing a series of issues of the *Rivista Pirelli*[3] dedicated to TV (entitled 'Towards a civilization of vision?', which was, I might say, the most exhaustive study of the subject at the time) and he asked me to contribute, so I worked like crazy reading everything that American sociologists had produced on the subject. I churned out scores of pages, only a few of which Visalberghi actually used because one of the other contributors had already written about the same things. But just by way of example, my essay did include mention of the 'Phenomenology of Mike Buongiorno' and this later became a subject in its own right.[4] Then in 1963, the magazine *De Homine* published a bumper special issue on mass culture and this stimulated me into compiling a long register which later turned into the first chapter of *Apocalittici*. Moreover, in 1961 Gilbert Cohen-Séat had organized a conference on visual culture in Milan and in 1962 I'd dragged him into the offices of Bompiani to work with Sergio Morando on what was to become the *1963 Almanac*, 'The image civilization'. Then that same year, while I was on my honeymoon, I'd gone to Grosseto for a symposium on television in which the challenger from the Left was Armando Plebe, while the Absolute Elsewhere was represented by Achille Campanile, who during the discussion came out with one of his memorable statements: that to read the newspaper in the morning and then look for confirmation in the evening news on TV was like posting a letter which you ended by saying 'Telegram to follow'.

So you see, a whole series of interests prompted me to write various things. At the same time, the first analyses of mass communication were beginning to be made in the universities: between the end of 1963 and 1964 I was running an open workshop in Turin on 'mass aesthetics and communication' in which I examined the questions that were later to become those of *Apocalittici*; but something was wrong, maybe too many people were coming to the lecture which was, after all, only an open workshop (I do know that I've never since set foot in the University of Turin) and it ended up with me meeting the students in the evening in a sociology centre that wasn't attached to the university. Looking over my notes taken at that time, I realize that Guido Viale[5] was among the students, and that we were analysing the narrative structures of women's weekly magazines. The ways of the Lord . . .

But the subject was obviously in the air in those days, because then an advertisement appeared for an absurdly named university chair: Pedagogy and Psychology of Mass Communications (because to call it just Theory of Mass Communications didn't seem academic enough in those days); and of course, the post remained vacant because naturally none of the candidates was a psychologist, mass mediologist and pedagogist all in one, so I thought, why not try for it? Since you had to have a list of publications, I gathered together all the essays and articles I'd written on the subject (that's why it's not surprising that so many reviewers criticized the book for being a hotchpotch) and I showed them to Bompiani.[6] Fine, says he, what's the title? Well, I reply, something along the lines of Psychology and Pedagogy of Mass Communications. You're mad, Mr Eco, he says, and he was right, poor devil. Well then, let's say: The Problem of Mass Culture. Don't make me laugh. (It was hopeless, I was testing the laws of the culture industry.) Right, says Bompiani, let me look at the essays again. And he happens to open the final part of the manuscript, where all the newspaper articles were collected together and which I'd entitled 'Apocalittici e integrati'. There we are, says Bompiani, there's our title (as when one of the Three Kings trips up, falls over and curses and St Joseph says, Ah, that's a nice name for the child!). But it doesn't have anything to do with the rest of the book, I object. Yes it does, he replies. And that's why I wrote the introduction, which is in fact an essay in the true sense and discusses the contrast between the apocalyptic and the integrated. The apocalyptics are absolutely right, this is exactly the way that books get 'packaged'.

How would I write this book today? In the 1964 preface, I said that to theorize on mass communication is like theorizing about next Thursday. Just think how the sociological studies on the future of young people published in those years predicted a generation uninterested in politics, whose aims would be a good job, a stable marriage, a house and a car.

In 1974 the book was reissued in the paperback series 'I satelliti' (among other things excluding for reasons of economy a series of writings that in the present edition have been reincorporated) and I added the following observations by way of an update. I cite them here because, as will be obvious, they too are now partly out of date.

What has changed in the meantime? In the first place, these questions no longer seem so offensive and eccentric as they did then: the increasingly in-depth study of mass communications phenomena is widespread in Italy today, on the scientific level as well as on those of education and political action; I think I can claim that this book has been one of the factors which contributed to this growing interest. As a consequence, much of the research which had simply been outlined in this work has since become reality.

In the general refining of methods, semiotic tools have come to the fore (in the present text, they are given brief mention in the essay on bad taste); tools which I later put to use in my studies of television messages, narrative structures in the novels of Ian Fleming,[7] relationships between rhetoric and ideology in Eugène Sue's *Les Mystères de Paris*,[8] newspapers, and in the analyses of advertising in *La struttura assente* (1968) and *Le forme del contenuto* (1971).[9]

As for the central themes of *Apocalittici e integrati*, some confirmation has meanwhile appeared in the shape of a large body of research on the phenomenon of reception, which has now defined the limits of content analysis and theoretical analyses of messages, introducing the vast semiotic dimension constituted by the variability of addressee codes, which deform and inflict in various ways the original meanings of the messages themselves. So that, whereas this book still contained the 'Enlightenment' belief that desirable cultural action would bring about an improvement in the messages, we would now be more in favour either of political action that attacked the messages – in their original form – at the very moment in which they are 'read' (transforming what used to be a reformist strategy of communications into a continuous guerrilla warfare of reception), or of the spread of alternative information, similar to the type we have seen from 1968 onwards.[10] This is why I feel that certain observations contained in the essay 'High, middle, low' on the active role of those involved in the cultural sphere as 'official representatives of humanity' are rather outdated and perhaps naive; not because that path doesn't also exist, but because it's not the only path. And other, less corporate forms of agency have emerged. 'To have one's say' has not just been a slogan. All this, however, seems to me to lend further validity to the argument against the differentiated notion of 'mass' or 'mass man'. Although on this score the book should today consider the two contrasting yet close positions assumed by Marcuse[11] and McLuhan[12] – positions which may only on the surface be categorized according to the now traditional dichotomy between 'the apocalyptic and the integrated'.

However, with some people viewing the communications industry in advanced technological society as a massive one-dimensional levelling operation carried out on its users, and some seeing in it the birth of a new global village, where a renewed sensitivity feeds optimistically not from the contents but from its form and the dazzling multiplicity of the messages, it seems to me that one of the hypotheses running through the whole of this book remains valid (and confirmed by events): namely that a quantitative growth of information, no matter how muddled and oppressive it appears, can produce unforeseen results, according to the law that there is no reformist neutralization in the circulation of ideas. Rather, every cultural development – no matter what ideological project is behind it – produces results which, in dialectical relation to given circumstances, outstrip the forecasts made by strategists or scholars of communication.

Events from May 1968 to the present day show that the communications civilization does not necessarily produce either one-dimensional man or the blissfully dazed savage of the new global village; in different places and times, depending on the different recipients, the same type of communication bombardment may produce either habituation or revolt. Which shouldn't lead us to abandon ourselves to the free market in communications and its liberal wisdom, but rather to explore the mechanisms further, in order to make their contradictions explode by using alternative approaches, both from within and without.

As I have come to these conclusions today after only writing the book yesterday, one might think a reading of these pages, including the parts that should have been edited, rewritten or rejected, could provide new readers with concepts and material for use in their own personal *iter*.

*   *   *

Well, today, in 1977, I have to correct the impression I had in 1974: at the time I was almost ashamed of the fact that in 1964 I had hoped for some sort of intervention from the inside, for a cleaning up of the cultural industry on the part of its own operators. But in the last four years other things have happened. For example, the rebellion of journalists, who managed to impose democratic control over the decisions of management and owners. Not much, but a great step compared to the situation in 1964. The changes in television. It's easy for today's young people to see it as the expression of the dominant ideology. But they should have seen it in the 60s. The existence of two ideologically competing television news programmes was unthinkable when I was writing this book. And finally, the birth of alternative radio stations, a novel way of using the mass media.[13]

It would seem that the '68 generation attacked the mass media civilization with a 'Marcusian' vision pretty close to that of the apocalyptics in my book. The apocalyptics had therefore attracted a 'popular' rather than an aristocratic following; but having taken the apocalyptic approach to extremes, this same generation pushed the old-style apocalyptics to the Right, or rather, it revealed what I had already shown to be their aristocratic roots: just look at Horkheimer's career.[14] This generation, armed with video-recorders and producing slogans, posters and murals, uses the same instruments as the mass media to make its statements, discovering that the same technical means may be used to make *different* statements. And the comic strip? Can anyone now maintain that comic strips cannot be used for critical purposes? If anything, we are witnessing the growth of 'revolutionary' comic strips . . . [15]

What is happening is that the ground is shifting, both from the inside and the outside. And if you write books on mass communication you have to accept that they are provisional. And that they may be up-to-date and then outdated in the space of a single morning.

But basically, if this book still interests me it is for other reasons: it is because it has definitely opened the way to semiotic studies for me. With *Open Work*, I studied the language of the avant-garde movements; with Apocalittici, I studied the language of their opposite (or, as some will say, of their fatal complement). But in the face of two apparently different phenomena, in which language was used in such different ways, I needed a unifying theoretical framework. And this framework became clear to me precisely while I was writing the essay on kitsch, where I began to make use of Jakobsonian linguistics. And in this perspective, the essays I'd be prepared to salvage with minor adjustments are those on Steve Canyon (with the addition of technical analysis), kitsch, the practical use of the fictional character, and Superman.[16]

As far as the general sense of the book goes, it will perhaps remain readable because of the way in which it made so many reviewers wonder whether I am an apocalyptic or an integrated intellectual, coming up with the most diverse answers. I am still not sure whether this is because I was ambiguous, problematic or dialectical. Or whether it was because they were none of these things and needed a black and white, yes or no, right or wrong answer. As if they'd been contaminated by mass culture.

1974 & 1977

CHAPTER 5

Orwell, or Concerning Visionary Power

WHEN ERIC ARTHUR BLAIR finally settled on George Orwell as a pen-name, having previously rejected H. Lewis Allways, Kenneth Miles and P. S. Burton, it was more or less by chance. The decision to entitle his novel *Nineteen Eighty-Four* was also made more or less by chance: apparently he also considered 1980 and 1982 and it's said that the date he finally chose was obtained by reversing the last two digits of 1948, the year in which the final version of his novel was completed. Orwell was looking for a date sometime in the fairly distant future in which to set his story (today we might term it science fiction), or to his negative utopia, but a date still near enough in the future to enable him to express the fears that were actually troubling him in those years: that sooner or later, something of the sort he envisaged in his novel might actually come about.

Yet however fortuitous the choice of a date, chance too, once it has determined an event, has a way of creating its own requisites: now that the fatal date of 1984 is upon us, there is no getting away from the spectres it evokes. They have come to be part of our collective imagination.

In November 1983, the weekly magazine *Time* ran a cover story on Orwell, listing in alarmed tones the myriads of conferences, seminars, articles, essays, and TV documentaries that were accumulating in preparation for the fatal date of 1 January. The article announced a new critical edition of Orwell's works, the placing of a wax model of the author in Madame Tussaud's, a dozen or so conferences varying from science-fiction fan gatherings to events at the Smithsonian Institute and the Library of Congress, the publication of a 1984 Calendar documenting the 'erosion of civil liberties in America', and ending with speculation about doublethink T-shirts and a barbecue in honour of Big Brother.

Now we all know what celebrative excitement is about, and passing fads are extremely susceptible to the glamour of centenaries, golden weddings and anniversaries. But if so much folly is unleashed around a date that cannot even be defined in codifiable terms (it's neither a birthday, a birth, an expiry date, nor an appointment), the reason cannot be a frivolous one. Orwell's terrible tale has made its mark upon our era, has given it an obsessive image: the threat of a millennium just around the corner, and the words, 'there will come a day . . . ', have relegated us all to waiting for that day, without giving us the psychological distance necessary to ask ourselves whether, in fact, 1984 has not been with us for quite some time already.

It's not as if a great many people haven't read this book as the description of a present time. Indeed as a satire – which is in fact Orwell's own definition of it, albeit a satire devoid of humour – of the Soviet regime. And in fact, ever since the book was published, reactions to it have been conflicting, passionate and discordant, and on the whole rather short-sighted. Some have seen it as a timely lampoon in support of the Cold War; some, forgetting that Orwell remained a declared socialist until his death, as a conservative pamphlet; some – for the same reasons, but from the opposite political camp – considered Orwell to be a slave of imperialism; others insisted that the author was an honest anarchist wounded by his terrible experiences as a volunteer in the Spanish Civil War, during which the group with which he was serving had been killed in cold blood by Communist fighters. Such a turmoil of passions meant that for a long time the book was prevented from being read *sine ira et studio* in order to see what it was really talking about.

What we can say is that there is very little about the book – although this very little is quite important – that is prophetic. At least three-quarters of what Orwell narrates is not negative utopia, but history.

The book appeared in 1949 and at that time you didn't need much of a prophetic bent (the most a convinced socialist needed was courage and intellectual honesty) to talk about Big Brother and his arch-enemy Goldstein, the heresiarch Jew. The Stalin–Trotsky power struggle, the great purges, the Soviet encyclopedia which claimed for Russian scientists the great scientific discoveries of the century, the attribution to the dictator of all the feats of history that had led the regime to triumph, even the continual rewriting of history (one of the most appealing and terrifying inventions of the novel) – all this was already the order of the day, even if it was dismissed from consciousness. Nor can we forget that Koestler's *Darkness at Noon* had already been published in 1940.

But Orwell was not simply a disappointed revolutionary and betrayed fighter, he was also an Englishman emerging from the Second World War and the victory over Nazism; many of the atrocities carried out in Oceania recall Nazi practices and rituals: the pedagogy of hatred, the racism that divides Party members from the proles, the herding of children into a sort of *Hitlerjugend* where they are taught to spy and to report on their parents, the puritanism of the chosen people for whom sex may serve only as a eugenic instrument . . .

What Orwell does is not so much invent a possible yet incredible future as build up a collage of a past which is all too credible because it has already been possible. And, just as he implies that the regimes of the three warring superstates are basically the same, he also insinuates suspicion into the reader's mind that the monster of our century was totalitarian dictatorship and that, as far as the fatal mechanism of totalitarianism was concerned, ideological differences actually counted for very little. This, for example, was Bertrand Russell's reading of *Nineteen Eighty-Four*.

This has doubtless been one of the reasons the book has become an alarm call, a rebuke and a denunciation, and also why it has fascinated tens of millions of readers all over the world. Yet I believe that there is also another, more profound reason. In the course of the four decades that now stand between us and the publication of *Nineteen Eighty-Four* the impression has daily been growing that if, on the one hand, the book was talking about something that had already happened, on the other hand it was talking about what was actually happening rather than about what could happen.

Let's take the most shiningly obvious of all indicators: television. Baird designed his first set in 1926, the first experimental broadcasts were carried out around 1935, and in Britain and America the first talk of non-experimental broadcasting was immediately after the war. So Orwell presents us with something that had not yet become a mass medium but which did already exist: he was not writing science fiction. The possibility of indoctrinating people through the new media was not a negative utopia: Goebbels's philosophy of the radio as a propaganda instrument and a means of exerting ideological control had already received wide discussion; Adorno and Horkheimer began their *The Philosophy of the Enlightenment* in 1942; and another great book, Huxley's *Brave New World*, had as far back as 1932 explored technological invention as an instrument of oppression.

However, what is new and prophetic in Orwell is not the idea that television allows us to see people who are far away, but that people who are far away can see us. It is the idea of closed-circuit control, later to be employed in factories, prisons, in public places, supermarkets and the fortified apartment blocks of the affluent middle classes – an idea to which we have already become accustomed – that Orwell discusses with visionary power. And it is because of ideas such as this, ideas which history was verifying daily, that readers have continued to read *Nineteen Eighty-Four* as a book of present-day relevance rather than as a book about the future. Orwell rendered visible through narrative something that only later Foucault would identify as Bentham's idea of the Panopticon, a prison in which detainees could be observed without themselves being able to observe.[1] Except that Orwell, ahead of his time, suggests something more: the threat that the whole world will be transformed into an enormous Panopticon.

It is at this point that we discover the significance of Orwell's negative utopia and also why he is at pains to remind us, with what to many will have appeared simple non-commitment, that there is no difference between the regimes of Oceania, Eurasia and Eastasia. Orwell's satire hits out not only at Nazism and Soviet Communism but at bourgeois mass culture itself.

Where, indeed, should we look to find a situation in which the ruling class is summoned to a rigid control of its morality on the basis of a criterion of efficiency, while the underclass, the proles, are accorded a wide margin of liberty for unruly behaviour, including not only the free expression of sexuality but even its programmed titillation through industrialized pornography? Who are the consumers of pornographic films? Not the poor (as opposed to the Nomenklatura) of the Soviet regime; it's the underdogs of the capitalist countries, with the difference, certainly not insignificant, that the latter eat, drink and clothe themselves better than the proles of Oceania.

And where should we look for the development of Newspeak, the new language that reduces vocabulary in order to diminish the range of thought and sentiment? The socialist countries have developed a standard language of ideology and propaganda composed of slogans and prefabricated phrases, but if the aims of this language are the same as those of Orwell's Newspeak, its grammatical structure is not. Newspeak would appear to share more of the characteristics of the language of television quiz shows, Anglo-Saxon tabloids, and advertise-ments. Many of the words listed by Orwell in the brief linguis-tic treatise contained in the novel's appendix seem to have been plucked out of some TV advertisement; they're like the words you hear housewives and children saying every day, in the version according to the purveyors of gift-wrapped happiness. Just what is the difference, I ask myself, between words like *uncold, doublepluscold, oldthinkers, bellyfeel* (Newspeak) and *supercleanplus, easyfix, grannybakes* or *fruitogel* . . .

And lastly (Goldstein's brilliant idea), Orwell not only antici-pated the division of the world into zones of influence with alliances that shifted according to circumstance (whose side is China on today?) – a conclusion that could already be drawn from events at Yalta – but he foresaw a situation that has actually come about, namely that war is not something that will at some point break out, but something that breaks out every day in certain areas, without anybody trying to conceive of a definitive solution, with the result that the three big oppos-ing alliances are free to issue warnings, blackmail each other, and make pleas for moderation. It's not that nobody dies, indeed the death of a few people is part of the deal; thus war, from being an epidemic phenomenon, becomes an endemic one. But then after all, Big Brother is right, 'war is peace'. For once, Oceanic propaganda isn't lying: it's stating such a shocking truth that nobody is able to comprehend it.

Orwell's is much more than a straightforward satire on Stalinism; in fact, for him it is not at all necessary that Big Brother should really exist. It was still necessary for Stalin to exist, but not Andropov who, as I write, some newspapers are insinuating is already dead or confined to a wheelchair, yet it's totally irrelevant whether he gets his health back or his funeral is celebrated in Red Square. The trouble is that, likewise, it's irrelevant at the end of the day who the President of the United States is or who's really in charge in China (quite independent of the different techniques elaborated by each power for the purpose of winning international consensus). Orwell guessed that, in the future-present which is his theme, the power of the great supernational systems would proliferate and that the logic of power is no longer, as in Napoleon's time, the logic of one man. Big Brother is useful because you still need to have a love-object, but a television image will do.

All this explains the fascination of this novel, even if – and at this point I think I can say as much without being suspected of anti-Orwell malice – it is not a masterpiece of writing. His moralism is voiced out loud rather than underwritten by the action; stylistically, it isn't much better than a good adventure novel and, from the point of view of narrative technique, Le Carré would certainly do a better job today. Everything, even the most appealing pages, reminds us of something we've already read: think of Kafka, for example. The pages on torture, on the subtle bond of love which binds victim to torturer, we've already read elsewhere, if not in Sade. The idea that the victim of an ideological trial must not only confess but repent, convince himself of his mistakes and feel sincere love for his persecutors, identify himself with them (and only then is it worthwhile killing him), is presented by Orwell as new, but this is not the case: it is normal practice for all self-respecting inquisitions.

And yet at a certain point, indignation and visionary power take the author by the hand and lead him beyond 'literature', so that Orwell doesn't just write a work of narrative, but a cult book, a mythical book.

The pages on the torture of Winston Smith are shocking, indeed they have a cult greatness, and the portrayal of his persecutor seizes our imagination because we have met him somewhere before, even if he was distinguished; somehow we have already taken part in this litany and we fear that all of a sudden the persecutor will take off his disguise and appear by our side, behind or facing us, and smile at us with an expression of infinite tenderness.

And at the end when Winston, stinking of gin, weeps as he gazes into the face of Big Brother, and truly loves him, we ask ourselves whether we too are not already loving (under who knows what image) our own Necessity.

At stake here is not (only) what we usually recognize as 'literature' and identify with good writing. What is at stake is, I repeat, visionary power.

And not all visions have to do with the future, or the hereafter.

1984

CHAPTER 6

The Future of Literacy

ACCORDING TO Plato (in the *Phaedrus*) Thoth, or Hermes, the alleged inventor of writing, presents his invention to the Pharaoh Thamus, praising this new technique which will allow human beings to remember what they would otherwise forget. But the Pharaoh is not satisfied. My skilful Thoth, he says, memory is such a great gift that it ought to be kept alive by training it continuously. With your invention people will no longer be obliged to train memory. They will remember things not because of an internal effort, but by virtue merely of an external device.

We can understand the Pharaoh's concern. Writing, like any other new technological device, would have made sluggish the human power which it replaced and reinforced – just as cars have made us less able to walk. Writing was dangerous because it decreased the powers of the mind, by offering human beings a petrified soul, a caricature of mind, a machine memory.

Plato's text is, of course, ironic. Plato was writing his argument about writing. But he is putting it into the mouth of Socrates, who did not write. Therefore Plato was expressing a fear that still survived in his day. Thinking is an internal matter; the real thinker would not allow books to think in his place.

Nowadays nobody shares these concerns, for two very simple reasons. First of all, we know that books are not ways of making somebody else think in our place; on the contrary they are machines which provoke further thoughts. Secondly, if once upon a time people needed to train their memory in order to remember things, after the invention of writing they had also to train their memory in order to remember books. Books challenge and improve memory. They do not narcotize it. This old debate is worth reflecting on every time one meets a new communicational tool which pretends or appears to replace books.

During the last year some worried and worrying reports have been published in the United States on the decline of literacy. One of the reasons for the recent Wall Street crash, according to some observers, has been not only an exaggerated confidence in computers but also the fact that none of the yuppies who were controlling the stock market knew enough about the 1929 crisis. They were unable to face a crisis because of their lack of historical information. If they had read some books about Black Thursday they might have been able to make better decisions and avoid many well-known pitfalls.

I agree. But I wonder if books would have been the only reliable vehicle for acquiring information. Time was when the only way to acquire a foreign language (apart from travelling abroad) was to study the language from a book. Now kids frequently learn other languages by listening to records, watching movies or TV programmes in original versions, or deciphering the instructions on a drinks can.

The same happens with geographical information. In my childhood I got the best of my information about exotic countries not from textbooks but from adventure novels (Jules Verne, for example, or Emilio Salgari, or Karl May). My children at a very early age knew more than me on the same subject by watching movies and TV.

The illiteracy of the Wall Street yuppies was due not only to an insufficient exposure to books but also to a form of visual illiteracy. Books about the 1929 Black Thursday exist, and are still regularly published (the yuppies can be blamed for not being bookstore and library-goers), while television and

cinema are largely unconcerned with any rigorous reconstruc-
tion of historical events. One could learn the history of the
Roman Empire very well from the movies, if only those movies
were historically accurate. The fault of Hollywood is not to
have set up its films as an alternative to the books of Tacitus or
Gibbon, but rather to have imposed a romantic, pulp version of
both Tacitus and Gibbon. The yuppies' problem is not only
that they watch TV instead of reading books; it is that in New
York only on Channel 13 is there anyone who knows who
Gibbon was.

I am not stressing these points in order to assert the possibility of a new literacy which would make books obsolete. God
knows, every penny I ever made in my life – as publisher, as
scholar, or as author – has come from books. My points are
rather the following:

1. Today the concept of literacy comprises many media. An
    enlightened policy on literacy must take into account the
    possibilities of all these media. Educational concerns must
    be extended to the whole of the media. Responsibilities
    and tasks must be carefully balanced. If tapes are better
    than books for learning languages, look after cassettes. If
    a commentated presentation of Chopin on compact disc
    helps people to understand Chopin, don't worry if people
    don't buy a five-volume history of romantic music.

2. Do not fight against false enemies. Even if it were true
    that today visual communication has overwhelmed writ-
    ten communication, the problem is not one of opposing
    written to visual communication. The problem is rather
    how to improve both. In the Middle Ages visual com-
    munication was, for the masses, more important than
    writing. But Chartres Cathedral was not culturally
    inferior to the *Imago mundi* by Honorius of Autun.[1]
    Cathedrals were the TV of their times, and the difference
    with our TV was that the directors of the medieval TV

read good books, had a lot of imagination and worked for the public good.

We are regularly misled by a 'mass media criticism of the mass media' which is superficial and almost always belated. The mass media are still repeating that our historical period is and will be more and more dominated by images. Mass media people have read McLuhan too late. The present and the forthcoming young generation is and will be a computer-oriented generation. The main feature of a computer screen is that it hosts and displays more alphabetic letters than images. The new generations will be alphabet and not image-oriented.

Moreover, the new generation is trained to read at an incredible speed. An old-fashioned university professor today cannot read a computer screen at the same speed as a teenager. These same teenagers, if they should happen to want to program their own home computer, must know, or learn, logical procedures and algorithms, and must type on a keyboard, at great speed, words and numbers.

I have said that we should not fight against false enemies. In the same vein let me say that we should not endorse false friends. To read a computer screen is not the same as to read a book. I do not know if you are familiar with the process of learning a new computer program. Usually the program is able to display on the screen all the instructions you need. But generally users who want to learn the program and to save their eyesight either print out the instructions and read them as if they were in book form, or buy a printed manual. It is possible to conceive of a visual program which explains very well how to print and bind a book, but in order to get instructions on how to write a computer program we need a book.

After spending a few hours at a computer console I feel the need to sit down comfortably in an armchair and read a newspaper, or maybe a good poem.

I think that computers are diffusing a new form of literacy

but are unable to satisfy all the intellectual needs that they stimulate. I am an optimist twelve hours a day and a pessimist the remaining twelve. In my optimistic mood I dream of a computer generation which, obliged compulsively to read a computer screen, gets acquainted with reading but at a certain moment comes to feel dissatisfied and looks for a different form of reading, more relaxed and generating a different form of involvement. In Hugo's *Notre Dame de Paris*, Frollo, comparing a book with his old cathedral, says: 'Ceci tuera cela.' I think that today, speaking of computers and books, one could say: 'Ceci aidera cela.'

Do not fight against false enemies. One of the most common objections to the pseudo-literacy of computers is that young people get more and more accustomed to speaking through cryptic short formulas: dir, help, diskopy, error 67, and so on. Is that still literacy?

I am a collector of old books and I feel delighted when I read the seventeenth-century titles which take up a whole page and sometimes more. Introductions were several pages long, started with elaborate courtesy formulae praising the ideal addressee, usually an Emperor or a Pope, and went on for pages and pages explaining in a very baroque style the purposes and virtues of the text to follow.

If baroque writers were to read our modern scholarly books they would be horrified. Introductions are one page long, briefly outline the subject matter of the book, thank some National or International Endowment for a generous grant, briefly explain that the book has been made possible by the love and understanding of a wife or husband or children, credit a secretary for having patiently typed the manuscript. We understand perfectly all the human and academic ordeals suggested by those few lines, the hundreds of nights spent highlighting photocopies, the innumerable frozen hamburgers eaten on the go (no caviar for the scholar) . . . I guess that in the near future three lines saying

TWO

SMITH

ROCKEFELLER

(to be read as: I thank my wife and my children, the book is due to the generous assistance of Professor Smith and was made possible by the Rockefeller Foundation)

would be as eloquent as a baroque introduction. It is a problem of rhetoric and of acquaintance with a given form of rhetoric. In years to come, I think, passionate love letters will be sent in the form of a short instruction.

There is a curious notion according to which in verbal language the more you say the more profound and perceptive you are. Mallarmé, however, told us that it is sufficient to spell out 'une fleur' to evoke a universe of perfumes, shapes and thoughts. Frequently, for poetry, the fewer the words the more things they imply. Three lines of Pascal say more than three hundred pages of a long and boring treatise on morals and metaphysics. The quest for a new and surviving literacy ought not to be the quest for a pre-computer verbal bulimia.

The enemies of literacy are hiding elsewhere.

Let us now reconsider the debate between Thoth and Thamus. Thamus assumed that the invention of writing would diminish the power of human memory. I objected that human memory has been improved by the continual exercise of remembering what books say. But to remember written words is not the same as to remember things. Probably the memory of the librarians of Alexandria was quantitatively greater than that of the illiterate savage, but the illiterate savage has a more specialized memory for things, shapes, smells, colours. In response to the invention of writing, Greek and Latin civilization invented the *artes memoriae* so that orators and teachers could survive as thinkers in times when books were in short supply.

The memory of Cicero or Aquinas was more flexible and powerful than ours. Though Thoth's invention may not have, Gutenberg's has certainly weakened the mnemonic capacity of our species. To counteract the negative effects of printing, the old school insisted on training young people to learn poems, dates and lists of historical figures by heart.

Our permissive society, relying on the abundance of tapes and other forms of recording, has further rendered memory as a mental ability somewhat obsolete. The use of computers will work in the same direction. You may recall a short story by Isaac Asimov where, in a future world dominated by intelligent machines, the last human being who still knows the multiplication tables by heart is wanted by the Pentagon and by various secret services because he represents the only calculator able to function in the event of power shortages. The way our present society tends to encourage well-trained memories is through TV quiz programmes and so-called trivia games.

Menaced by the growth of an image-oriented culture, our technological society has already spontaneously reacted in terms of free-market dynamics. After all, since the invention of TV the quantity of printed matter in the world has not decreased. On the contrary it has grown to an extent unprecedented in previous centuries – even though this increase has to be set against a corresponding increase in world population.

In simple terms, it seems that previously illiterate people, once exposed to television, at a certain moment start to read newspapers. I appreciate that such a merely quantitative evaluation is not very illuminating in terms of highbrow culture, since there are newspapers that are worse than TV programmes. But when speaking of literacy it is better to forget the shibboleths of highbrow culture. Speaking of literacy in the world today we are not only concerned with the happy few of Bloomsbury, but with the masses of the Third World.

The real question rather is how to confront a series of phenomena which are menacing the universe of books and the cultural heritage that books represent. I shall list some problems, without pretending to propose solutions. It is pretty late in the day and I have started my twelve hours of pessimism.

1. Books are menaced by books. Any excess of information produces silence. When I am in the USA I read the *New York Times* every day except on Sunday. Sunday's *Times* contains too much information and I do not have time enough to consume it. Bookstores are so crowded with books they can only afford to keep the most recent ones.

2. Books are still an expensive commodity, at least in comparison with other forms of communication such as TV. An international committee to oppose the taxation of books in the European Community has just been created and since I am its president I cannot but agree with its demands. But good ideas have unfortunate side effects. Lowering the price of books will encourage their publication and circulation but will at the same time increase their number – with all the dangers referred to under 1, above.

3. New technologies are competing with each other. Books are now more widely available than in any other period of human history, but all publishers know the extent to which photocopying technology is jeopardizing their interests.

   A photocopy of a paperback is still more expensive than the original, but publication in paperback is dependent on the success of the hardcover edition and for many important scientific books only hardcover publication is possible. I am a writer. I live on my royalties, and once my American publisher told me he was thinking of suing a professor who had told his thirty students to make photocopies of one of my books, too expensive for them to buy. I asked the publisher to refrain from any legal action, since in the professor's place I would have done the same.

The main international scientific publishers have found a way to escape this predicament. They publish a very limited number of copies, they price the book at $300, and they take it for granted that copies will be bought only for major libraries and the rest will be piracy. So prices increase and the physical act of reading scientific material becomes more and more unpleasant, since everyone knows the difference between reading a crisp original page and a xerox. Moreover, the very act of photocopying a book tends to make me feel virtuous and up-to-date in my scholarship: I have the text, and afterwards I no longer feel the need to read it. Today scholars are accumulating enormous stocks of xeroxed material that they will never read. Ironically, the technology of photocopying makes it easier to have books, not easier to read them. Thus billions of trees are killed for the sake of unread photocopies.

4. Trees, alas. Every new book reduces the quantity of oxygen. We should start thinking of ecological books. When, in the last century, the book industry stopped making books from rags and started to make them from trees, it not only menaced our survival, it jeopardized the civilization of the book. A modern book cannot survive more than seventy years. I have books from the 50s that I can no longer open. In the next fifty years the modern section of my personal library will be a handful of dust. We know that acid-free paper is expensive, and that chemical procedures for preserving already existing books can be reasonably applied only to a limited number of them. To microfilm all the books contained in a huge library will certainly save their content, but will limit the opportunity to consult them to a small number of professional

students. A way to escape this danger is to republish books every few years. But decisions of this type are regulated by the market and by public demand. According to this criterion, a thousand years from now *Gone with the Wind* will survive, and *Ulysses* will not.

The only solution would be to appoint special committees to decide which books to save (by chemical rescue, by reprint, or by microfilm). The power of such committees would be enormous. Not even Torquemada, or Big Brother in *1984*, had such an authority to select.

I am an author. I want not to be saved by a special committee. I want not to be saved by mass demand. I want not to be saved in the form of a cryptic microfilm. I want to survive for centuries and centuries, unknown to everybody, in the secret of an old forgotten library, as happened to the classical authors during the Middle Ages. I cannot. I know for sure that I cannot. Should I sell myself to Gorbachev, to Reagan, to the Pope, to Khomeini, in order to have as a reward an acid-free edition?

5. Finally, who will decide which books to give to the Third World? I recently attended a meeting at the Frankfurt Book Fair, organized by German publishers, about the need to send books to the young people of Nicaragua. I was sympathetic to the initiative, and I trust the group that invited me. But the problem is bigger than that. The whole of the Third World is escaping from illiteracy in the sense that the kids there will probably learn to read and write. But they will not have the economic possibility of having books. Who will choose the books for them? The American fundamentalist churches which are engaged in an economic push to spread their doctrines through Latin America? The Soviet Union? The Roman Church?

I suppose that three-quarters of the world population

today cannot afford books. They can only accept some of them graciously. Who will decide for them? The immediate future offers the opportunity to make millions and millions of people think in one way or another, depending on the economic and organizational effort of those who decide to send them books. I feel worried by the power that somebody – I don't know who, but certainly not my university – will have in the next few decades.

1987

PART TWO

Mass Media and the Limits of Communication

CHAPTER 1

Political Language: The use and abuse of rhetoric

ARISTOTLE DIVIDED DISCOURSES into judicial, deliberative, and epidictic. The judicial doesn't need to be explained; epidictic discourse is discourse in praise or blame of someone or something (a typical example being the *Encomium of Helen* by Gorgias). Today we'd include under the heading of epidictic discourse the advertising message, which effectively consists of a eulogy of a given product.[1] Deliberative discourse consists of political, and, one might now add, trade union discourse. In short, it is a matter of convincing the audience of the necessity or risk entailed by doing or not doing something that concerns the economic and political future of the community.

There are three types of discourse examined by Aristotle in the book devoted to Rhetoric. Among moderns the term 'rhetoric' has undoubtedly fallen into disuse and has assumed connotations of pompous vacuousness. However, one should go back to the original meaning.[2] Rhetorical discourse, for the Greeks, was discourse that treated with that which is probable and aimed to persuade listeners of the acceptability of an assertion. Just to illustrate the point, saying two and two make four, or that two parallel lines never meet, or that a proposition cannot be both true and false, has not (and does not) belong to rhetoric. One is dealing instead with statements which (even if not considered 'true' in any absolute sense) are based on a system of precise and convention-governed axioms. Given the axioms, and given the rules for deriving demonstrations therefrom, one enters a certain logic and cannot dispute certain conclusions. They are apodictic.

Let us suppose, however, that we have to discuss whether it is right or not to take something from someone who has robbed you. As will become apparent, there doesn't exist a mathematical law that lays down the precise conditions under which a conclusion can be said to be true. It is necessary, if one wants to construct a syllogism, to start from a premise that is only *probable*. For example, I can argue as follows: 'What others possess having taken it away from me is not their property; it is wrong to take from others what is their property, but it is not wrong to restore the original order of property, putting back into my hands what was originally in my hands.' But I could also argue: 'Rights of property are sanctioned by the actual possession of a thing; if I take from someone what is actually in their possession, I commit an act against the rights of property and therefore theft.' Of course a third argument is possible, namely: 'All property is *per se* theft; taking property from property-owners means restoring the equilibrium violated by the original theft, and therefore taking from the propertied the fruits of their thefts is not just right but a duty.'

As one can see, these three arguments (in a crude and elliptical form that condenses the chain of rhetorical syllogisms or *enthymemes*) are all acceptable enough, so long as one accepts the premises (that are not axioms but opinions). The task of confronting deliberative (or political) discourse is that of demonstrating, through other arguments, the acceptability of these opinions, taking them as accepted by the audience in order to draw conclusions accordingly.

Two approaches shape two instances of political discourse – the theoretical, for which discussing the rights of property is a matter for political economy, and the propagandistic, which is not to be conflated with the 'demogogic' in the worst sense of the word. No public speaker at a meeting, no journalist in an article, can start laying down fundamental premises every time he expresses an opinion and calls for decisions to be made: he simply takes generally accepted opinion in order to persuade the audience/readers of a given set of consequences; or else he asserts an opinion that is not generally accepted so convincingly that it becomes indisputable. And the three arguments put forward as examples are neither fictitious nor paradoxical but make up the kernel of many of today's debates and could be aired on an edition of *Tribuna politica*.[3]

All these observations point to the fact that political discourse (just like philosophical, critical or any other discourse dealing with abstract values in the context of a highly formalized body of axioms) must persuade. In other words, it must get the listener to agree to the speaker's point of view, even if other options remain available. It is, therefore, a form of rhetorical discourse.

However, rhetoric in this sense is an honest and productive exercise. Instead of imposing my will on another I seek to get his agreement, his active support, and so I argue in order to persuade him accordingly. While doing so I am obliged to re-examine my premises and arguments. Consequently the discourse I am addressing to another person is also being addressed to myself in order to clarify what I want. In an extreme case, and in circumstances of maximum intellectual honesty, a rhetorical discourse designed to convince others of something could bring me to reject what I had intended to say. Rhetoric (in this respect) as technique of persuasion is a means of creating awareness.

However, we cannot deny that there exists another sense of 'rhetoric' understood as discourse that masks under empty and grandiloquent forms a basic lack of substantial argument. If I say 'Forward, forward, let us follow the immortal destiny of those men bound to us in singleness of purpose', I'm simply saying, 'Let's do what everyone who thinks in the same way as me wants', except that on the strength of the emotions I have evoked I might then sweep along some imbecile who doesn't share my views. This second idea of rhetoric is genetically dependent on the first and constitutes its natural stage of degeneration. In fact, technicians of persuasion have since classical times identified those premises and arguments that seem best designed to persuade. Acceptable premises are called *endoxa* and consist of opinions held by the majority and difficult to challenge. For example, a typical *endoxon* is: 'You must never make a mother weep.' Everyone, initially, would maintain that this is an incontrovertible truth. Obviously it isn't, because if I have to condemn a man guilty of rape and murder to life-imprisonment, I must do so even if his mother will be broken-hearted. Yet an appeal of this kind coming from the lips of an unscrupulous lawyer for the defence would still be liable to conjure up unchecked emotions in a jury, if only for a moment or two. Here then is a first instance of degeneration of rhetoric: namely, using opinions that are widely held and difficult to criticize without there being time to consider other and equally established opinions. As for the arguments available, rhetoric has for over 2,000 years classified batteries and repertories of argumentation which, used opportunely, cannot fail to achieve consensus, even though one knows perfectly well that other arguments work equally effectively. Perelman, for example, cites two typical arguments (also called *loci*) which, although mutually contradictory, can each in turn evoke consensus. The first is the locus of quantity: 'You must do this because most people do.' The exact opposite is the locus of quality: 'Nobody does this; if you do, you'll set yourself above all the others.' It's not hard to see that the knowing use of premises and loci consolidated over time enables one to obtain favourable emotional responses, almost as a conditioned reflex, and this constitutes an obvious example of degenerated rhetoric.

All of Mussolini's speeches belong to this second type of

political argumentation. Take an expression like 'Only God can bend our will; men and things never can', and compare it with a generally accepted opinion of a different kind sufficient to undermine it: 'God acts only through men and things as his instruments.' Often humour is achieved thanks to a paradoxical collision of opposing and equally acceptable premises; think of Bergson's quip: 'Stop! Only God has the right to kill those of his kind.' Or an advertisement that simultaneously exploits the loci of quantity and quality: 'A tiny number of people will buy this rare product. Join this select band now!'

Lastly, there's a third layer of rhetorical usage that is found both in 'creative' and 'degenerated' rhetoric: namely that of the rhetorical figures such as metaphor, metonymy, oxymoron, hypallage, or paronomasia (pun). The list of these figures includes over one hundred types and it isn't possible to enumerate them here.[4] Let's simply recall that we're dealing with the capacity to say something, perhaps something fairly familiar, in a new and surprising way so as to attract attention and, so to speak, appeal to the aesthetic sense of the audience. A rhetorical figure used well and at the right moment is charged with numerous connotations. If I make a speech to consumers asking them to limit their spending in the face of the devaluation of the dollar, and instead of saying 'we the consumers at this critical juncture' were to say 'Oh, my fellow voyagers on the tempestuous seas of international finance', not only would I be saying the expected in an unexpected manner but I would be calling upon feelings of solidarity, communicating the drama of the occasion, making my listeners share in a common adventure and asking for their trust on that basis. When these figures are being used for the first time we certainly witness a creative act that makes us see reality with new eyes; poets have this important role.[5] However, the recurrent figure is already overlain with certain emotional values and ideological connotations by convention. Using it, then, is not merely laziness on the part of the speaker. Such use also constitutes a safe if dishonest investment in the emotional disposition and laziness of the audience.

There is one final way of making full use of rhetorical figures, which consists in real verbal abuse of power and not just degenerated rhetoric. In brief, this is the discourse of the swindler: an overuse of figures, an interweaving of premises and arguments of which one loses the thread, dressing up a discourse in all the trappings of scientificity and its accompanying authority merely to confound an audience. This type of discourse can be used either by those who know what they want to say but only want a few others to know, or by those who don't know what they are saying and hide their own confusion in an accumulation of rhetoric.

All these forms of rhetorical discourse can be found in the linguistic activity of this country (and others) in the area of political debate. Unmasking these usages of persuasive discourse should not be seen as simple *qualunquismo* or apparent rejection of all politics and politicians. Rather it means hunting out all abuses of power and acknowledging clarity when it is found. In short the purpose is to restore clarity of thought and, subsequently, the freedom of information that is every citizen's right.

Political language is always addressed to specific audiences. The politician who speaks in parliament or in the piazza knows the set of opinions and openness to argument of his listeners. Calibrating his speech in such a way as to get across to a given audience, and hence calibrating the argumentation by modulating the sharpness of an assertion here or underlining one point while dropping another there, all these are perfectly legitimate techniques of persuasion, not abuses of power. We too, when we try to convince a friend of something, resort to arguments that touch the heart.

However, the means of mass communication have now put the politician in a position, whether writing or speaking, to address simultaneously a whole spectrum of people that are remote from him and differentiated by background, region, culture and personal inclination. The limit case is provided by political debates on television. Research carried out a few years ago on the style of argumentation of Italian politicians appearing on *Tribuna politica* showed that very often the arguments of a Liberal or a Christian Democrat, a Communist or a Socialist were very different from one another at the public meeting in the piazza.[6] Yet once presented to a television audience they appeared, in the final analysis, remarkably similar. Knowing they were talking to a far more differentiated audience, each speaker tended to soften the edges, select arguments acceptable to the majority, possibly use generally known terms. The upshot was that everyone converged towards a kind of middle-of-the-road argument in which, for all the differences, there visibly emerged a uniformity of opinion. What is found on television is also found in the press, though to a lesser extent since newspapers have specific readerships (and extremely specific ones in the case of party organs). But even here we cannot overlook the levelling role of the means of mass communications.

Yet this is not the main danger facing political discourse in Italy. What is striking isn't so much the uniformity (with some dramatic exceptions) as the apparent incomprehensibility, sometimes to the point of pernicious vacuousness. As for vacuousness, one can point to instances of degenerated rhetoric in the use of tried and tested formulae that promise acceptability and reassurance. For example, a few years ago we find papers reporting two parliamentary speeches in this vein: 'Minister Such-and-such stated: We will give the regions concrete powers. The Right Honourable Something-or-other reiterated: One must oppose whoever pushes the country in the wrong direction.' If we avoid accusing the speakers of talking in generalities it is nonetheless significant that the paper in question instantly selected them as the most significant. Obviously there is little more abstract than the expression 'concrete powers', and saying that one must oppose whoever pushes the country in the wrong direction is not saying anything without analysis of the direction and the related error. But what is worrying is that in the course of the article there appear expressions in inverted commas such as, 'The government must press on, selecting the proposals and studies so far undertaken, and identifying the substantial points of a new law so as to go beyond the stage of pure and simple proposals and move promptly to that of decision-making.' The sentence just says that the government should, in order to resolve the problem, elaborate precise laws and then apply them. Which is, as everyone knows, what a government does or should do every day, without the announcement of the fact constituting a news story.

These are typical examples of formulae not difficult to comprehend and not unappealing, but vague and evasive. However, a second type of degenerated rhetoric consists in the use of rhetorically complex formulae designed to hide (or filter for the benefit of those in the know) a decision or political opinion that is either too risky or unsafe.

The series of quotations that will now be presented is culled from a debate involving politicians of various parties that took place in parliament, at public meetings and in leading newspaper articles in June 1968 during a ministerial crisis which threatened to bring down the centre-left coalition. Since situations of this kind have occurred several times in Italy in living memory, the example might well serve as a general model applicable to analogous situations. The first intervention, made by the press agency Nuova Stampa, specifies that the planned Leone government 'should not be considered a monochrome Christian Democrat one but a government of Christian Democrats in monochrome.' The experts in political matters read between the lines the importance of the distinction: it consists in a government of Christian Democrat politicians but one in which the Christian Democrats as a party do not assume full responsibility. However, in order to express the substantial concept without divulging it, a rhetorical procedure is employed, namely *antimetathesis*; that is, the repetition of the same words in transposed order in two successive phrases. The Right Honourable Malagodi, on the other hand, expresses 'the wish that the new government can act to serve only the objective interests of Italy and not with the view to the manifestation of eventual and future political forms whose concrete content is today difficult to imagine and evaluate.' The sentence exemplifies another rhetorical figure, namely *periphrasis* or *circumlocution*, and aims to show that the party that enunciates it would not support the government in a vote of confidence. With the polemics hotting up, the Right Honourable Zannier defines the situation on 12 June as follows: 'There is an entirely open-ended problematic. For now it is a moment of stastis.'

Giving 'open-ended problematic' the obvious sense of 'unstable situation', we thereby arrive at the first formulation: 'static instability'. In rhetoric this is called an *oxymoron*. The oxymoron is, according to Horace, a *'rerum concordia discors'*, the clash of two opposites, such as 'cautious enthusiasm, clear ambiguity, luminous obscurity, strong weakness'. When well used it can poetically bring alive the meaning of an expression; wnen used badly it serves to diminish meaning, i.e. to say nothing. But wanting to say nothing can constitute a precise political message, otherwise it would be impossible to explain Nenni's phrase of 21 June: 'Now one must decide. [. . .] There remains nothing for us but to abstain'. So, starting with the oxymoron, we come upon another odd operation that is called *epanortos*. The operation consists in expanding on the initial phrase with another that alters its meaning. On 17 June, for instance, a definition emerges according to which: 'This will be a government of business [. . .] or better, government in waiting.' Anyone who is persuaded that a government that 'waits' does less than a government that gets on with business is being misled: the government in waiting should be a government 'in the fullness of its prerogatives', and therefore a government that, in order to wait in a dignified manner, should do an enormous number of things. The explanation is that 'the waiting' does not regard the government but the parties that, while the government governs, should wait and clarify their ideas. Hence the 'precipitous wait'.

The oxymoron is so daring that, at the time, nobody wanted to claim paternity for it. The *Popolo* of 17 June announces the definition but attributes it to the Socialist Cariglia. *Avanti*, the same day, states that it was the Christian Democrat Gava; the *Corriere della Sera*, also that day, decides to attribute it to the Christian Democrat Sullo. By this point the Socialist parliamentarians have to make a statement on the matter, taking up the polemic on 'disengagement' once again. On 13 June, Mariotti asserts that disengagement should have shown the Socialists' determination to return to government 'with the proviso that the Centre-Left guarantees to contest and democratically change the existing system at the level of society'. Yet on 18 June, the Social Democrat Preti states that one should engage because 'in the Italian and European society of today the Socialist Movement does not have the function of assuming a contestatory role.' From which can be derived two exemplary oxymorons: 'contestative disengagement' and 'engagement that does not contest'.

By this stage the taste for disengagement is spreading to the Christian Democrats as well, first to its left wing and then to the whole party. The government will be Christian Democrat but not the expression of Christian Democrats.

This important decision is announced through a sequel of semantic operations that in rhetoric go by the name *reticence*. For the *Popolo*, the Socialist Mancini said that the Christian Democrats were disengaging; for *Avanti*, the Christian Democrat Party said it. In either case it is evident that the Christian Democrats are disengaging with respect to a government of Christian Democrats that stands thanks to help from the Socialists. Mancini, with extreme semiological finesse, grasps the contradiction and discloses it in the form of an *antitheton* (which is, according to Isidore of Seville, a figure whereby opposites are opposed to opposites and generate the beauty of an enunciation); in effect the situation now requires the Christian Democrats to engage and form a government with respect to which it is busy disengaging, while the United Socialist Party is disengaging vis à vis a government with regard to which it should be engaging. We are simultaneously presented with another well-known figure, *paradox*, and an oxymoron, no two, because the *antitheton* opposes an 'engaged disengagement' to a 'disengaged engagement'. And by this point one might conclude that the Italian political elite had been scrutinizing the now very fashionable works of Marshall McLuhan, who, with a deft touch defines alphabetic communication (in which there are no images) as 'visual' and television as 'tactile'. And when we are surrounded by sounds, lights, noises, words etc., in front of the television, lo and behold, McLuhan declares we are being subjected to a 'very cold' medium, and yet when we are freezing at the end of a telephone we are having 'very hot' communication. By the same token, the notion of disengagement is now defined as 'supporting with every effort the business which others are washing their hands of'.

We've reached the climactic moment. With a concise play of reticence, after three days of press reports warning of the imminent appointment of Leone as head of government, Sullo announces to the country that, having only just learnt that the government in waiting is to be offered to his friend Leone, the Christian Democrats are guaranteeing him affectionate solidarity. By solidarity is meant 'Leone forms the government choosing the Christian Democrats he wants but the Christian Democrat Party knows nothing about the matter.' How could it possibly know nothing? Through an artifice which, according to Frege's semantics, consists in changing the sense of a phrase without changing its referent: it is not the same to say

'Dante' or 'the author of the *Divine Comedy*'. Or, to be more precise, the thing designated doesn't change but the sense of the designation does. Dante for instance had an aquiline nose, but as the author of the *Divine Comedy* this fact doesn't matter. Hence Gui, Andreotti or Leone can be seen under two different *suppositiones*: as politicians (happening to be members of the Christian Democrat Party) and as Christian Democrat politicians. It will be in their former capacity that they will participate in the government which is not, let it be noted, a monochrome Christian Democrat one but a monochrome government with Christian Democrats. The same thing happens as in a Dario Fo song sung by Janacci that speaks of 'The Twenty-One – meaning the tram'. The Twenty-One and the Christian Democrat politician can be said to rediscover their real nature after decades of being repressively identified with a party in which they didn't entirely fulfil themselves.

The cycle of our rhetorical drama set in many (political) acts is complete. The possibility of a contestative disengagement, a procrastinated engagement, a dissident consensus, a parallel divergence, a sharpest of blunt edges, a circle with hypotenuse, and a radical solution that leaves things as they are – this whole series of verbal artifices that only unreasonable people could define as senseless is justified as a justification of a moderately decisive decision taken by two parties of government. And the decision can be communicated, without rhetorical figures, in the following way: 'Give us time to think it over.' If the rhetorical overlay appears absurd, the blame lies not with the art of rhetoric, which expresses what one wants to say, but with the fact that, in politics, whoever wants to govern never has the right to think it over.

On the other hand one shouldn't think that all expressions put in rhetorical form necessarily hide emptiness. Sometimes they hide a potential, a conflict of alternatives, and, far from constituting verbal contrivances without content, they represent verbal contrivances that confusingly circumscribe a content; it's just that one doesn't yet know who will manage to fill them with content of their own.

In the history of parliamentary and ministerial rhetoric the expression 'parallel convergences' has become celebrated – another oxymoron but this time one that didn't attempt to disguise a state of indecision because it referred to a precise formula for governmental equilibrium. Let's not forget that expressions that are perhaps less baroque but equally hermetic are found in the lexicon of all the parties and political currents. Candidates might include: 'non-integration objectives', 'more advanced equilibria', 'new majority', and even, in its Italian usage, 'cultural revolution'. Each of these formulae referred or refer to precise enough political projects. Every political commentary could, in a bout of sincerity, translate each of them into a definition expanding on and clarifying exactly what the relevant formula was meant to express. Yet one would soon notice divergences of interpretation both over marginal (to the outsider) and crucial political issues. This is because, when occasions arise in which decisions have to be made about a course of action, a politician (either by chance or out of a feeling for words) invents and propounds a formula that alludes to a direction to be taken. The formula is not empty, and the course of action is specific. However, in that course of action there are many options still open. Which of these will the formula apply to? What happens in the world of politics is a sort of blind struggle to control the power definitely and unequivocally to fill the formula with a particular meaning. In the period of waiting, and at the height of the struggle, the formula is not without meaning but has many and interrelated meanings. Whoever manages to make his own interpretation prevail will take control of the formula, making it into the verbal emblem of his brand of politics. Except when, in the very moment of triumph of a particular definition, the formula is conclusively emptied of any power of suggestion and loses its magic properties, no longer the epicentre of moral struggle.

There is undoubtedly a fascinating side to this process whereby a language often anticipates the realities that it must designate, and from the point of view of a study of rhetorical forms and pragmatics (rather than semantics) of language the pheno-menon has much to offer. But unfortunately we are analysing political language, that is to say language which should be spoken by the whole national community in order to inform all citizens of their representatives' intentions so that these can then be judged. At present the socio-cultural situation of this particular national community is the one exposed a couple of years ago by an RAI Audience Survey on the comprehension of political jargon in radio and television news programmes.[7]

The findings, now widely known, provide food for reflec-tion. Out of every hundred interviewees, twenty believed that the Confindustria (employers' association) was the trade union of workers in industry, and 40% said they didn't know what it was. Only 28% of a group of farm-workers in Andria knew the meaning of 'alternative', and only 19% the meaning of 'cabinet reshuffle'. Only 8% of a group of Voghera housewives knew the meaning of the word 'notion'. Thirty-five per cent of a group of Milan workers thought 'dialogue' meant conflict of opinions and 40% considered 'minister without portfolio' to mean 'Finance Minister'. Almost 50% thought that 'lay parties' meant parties in favour of Church/State collaboration, with only 26% giving the correct answer.

This, then, is the objective situation in which the public speaker is operating when he addresses the electorate. It is easy enough to see that when the Right Honourable Colombo refers to unemployment on television with the *euphemism* 'available manpower', he is not merely designating an unpoetic reality in an inoffensive manner; he is, in effect, hiding information from the addressee. But is he actually addressing the citizen?

This is a good place to analyse the cultural factors that push the politician to express himself in the ways outlined above. There are reasons to do with educational background: the residues of a humanist culture of a legal hue or the legacy of the uphill battle to master the dustiest of classics. The traditional political elite is composed of literary intellectuals rather than technocrats and most have not renounced the ornate forms of speech that symbolize prestige and status, and act as a substitute for the technological and economic power beyond their reach. Industrialists express themselves in far more concrete terms, and when Pasolini accused Italian politicians of speaking a technological language he was wide of the mark.[8] Italian political language is still pre-technological, agrarian.

But this isn't the only explanation. A further explanation that digs down to the determining effects of economic development tells us that the politician, when speaking in obscure terms, is actually sending a message in code that emanates from one power group and is destined for another.[9] The two groups, sender and receiver, understand one another perfectly well, and the wittiest of rhetorical turns is not, for the right people, mere *flatus vocis* but so many promises, threats, refusals and agreements. It is clear, moreover, that in order for communication between power groups to carry on undisturbed it must go over the heads of the public, just like the coded message passing between two armed camps in a war situation, which might be intercepted by chance by a radio ham but never understood. The fact of its not being understood by others is the indispensable condition for the maintenance of private relationships between power groups. Accordingly, political discourse in this vein, whatever the aims of the government in question, is anti-democratic because it leapfrogs the citizen and denies him any room to agree or disagree. It is an authoritarian discourse. Unmasking it is the only political activity that is worthwhile and addressed to citizens as a whole. This is the only real way to exercise rhetoric so as to create convictions rather than to induce subjugation. It is a cognitive exercise in which one still persuades, but persuades others to want to see things clearly.

It is moralistic to assert that political discourse must be freed of rhetorical techniques in order to relate to the truth. Running a city is a question of opinions, and it is in relation to this plurality of opinion that the game of reciprocal persuasion must be played. When a group claims that discussion is useless and a waste of time, it is better in the name of consistency for it to engage directly in revolutionary action (whereby popular power is its own *raison d'être*) and to bypass the labyrinths of persuasion. Better still would be resorting to a vile demonstration of an armed forced that tells no lies and acts as a call to revolution. However, the political discourse that replaces persuasive speech with incantatory formulae (or, worse still, with magic formulae containing secret messages passed from witch to witch) represents a linguistic and civic reality that every democratic community must attack with the weapon of clear-sighted analyses and demystification.

1973

CHAPTER 2

Does the Audience have Bad Effects on Television?

1. Years ago someone tried to substitute the question 'Do comics have bad effects on children?' with 'Do children have bad effects on comics?' (they had in mind all those imitations of *Peanuts*).

The idea seems worth pursuing because the question that has dominated the study of mass communications since the early 1960s has been: 'What do mass communications do to audiences?' It was only in the late 1960s that people began, timidly, to ask: 'What do audiences do to (with) mass communications?'

A Martian analysing the effects of television on the generation brought up on it (and relating them to major social transformations) would not have many doubts. Let's take the case of Italy, where television was born in the early 1950s and where a generation has now come into existence that has grown up with television.

Our typical Italian probably began to speak just before the time his parents bought a television set, which found its way into the home in about 1953. Between the ages of three and four he is accompanied day and night by the image of Marisa Borroni.[1] At five he delights in the jugglers who populate the shows of the day, and his sense of humour develops with the help of Nuto Navarrini's *operette*. Meanwhile his ideology owes much to the Verdi-style melodramas broadcast with relentless regularity. The boy starts to go to school and bases his notion of culture on *Lascia o raddoppia*[2] or, more worryingly, on the cultural programmes of the epoch.

Once able to read and write he enters the era of *Carosello*,[3] his initiation rituals go by the name of Festival of San Remo and *Canzonissima*,[4] and he doesn't even hear of Marx *à la* Groucho and Harpo because the films he sees on the small screen are second-rate 1940s productions. At eleven he learns geography from *Campanile Sera*.[5] Otherwise he is told about the world by the News. Along with Greek and Latin he learns meteorology from Col. Bernacca,[6] confronts his first political and social issues through *TV7*, and learns of the existence of violent forms of ideological conflict with the help of *Tribuna Politica*.[7]

By 1968 he is already at university. He has passed through Children's Television, State News and Father Mariano.[8] He represents someone with a totally televisual education in a country run by a majority party standing for fundamental Catholic values and slotted into the ideological ranks of the Atlantic Alliance.

If the apocalyptic theorists of mass communications, with their pretensions to an aristocratic Marxism of Nietzschean origins, their diffidence towards praxis and distaste for the masses, had been right, this boy would in 1968 have automatically applied for a post in a savings bank, having graduated on completion of a dissertation entitled 'Benedetto Croce and the Spiritual Value of Art', getting his hair cut every week and hanging the olive branch blessed by the priest on Palm Sunday over the picture of the Sacred Heart from the *Famiglia Cristiana* calendar. We know what actually happened. The television generation has been the generation of May '68, revolutionary organizations, anti-conformism, 'parricide', crisis of the family, rejection of the 'Latin lover syndrome' and acceptance of homosexual minorities, women's rights and class culture as opposed to the culture of the Enlightenment. If this is a trend, the next ten years of television should bring this generation, and the next, to take their horses to drink Holy Water at St Peter's.[9] So we might ask: why call for the banning of *Last Tango in Paris* when all the evidence suggests that they should be banning 'The News', *Cronache italiane, Tv degli Agricoltori* and *Ciocagiò*?[10]

2. Everything said so far has the appearance of mere paradox, and by way of reassuring the timid we can confirm that this is so. As for the less timid, those wanting to understand social phenomena rather than pigeonhole them, we'd say that it is paradox but that is not all.

The historical scene that I have set shows at least two things:

i) Television alone (or with other media) is not responsible for shaping a generation's way of thinking, even though this generation 'makes the revolution' using slogans drawn from television.

ii) If the generation goes against what television invited it to do (while showing signs of having fully absorbed its expressive forms and mental operations), it has read television differently from most of those who produce it, those who consume it and the sum total of the theoreticians analysing it.

In 1965 in Perugia (an occasion that's gone down in people's memories), Paolo Fabbri, Gilberto Tinacci Mannelli, Pier Paolo Giglioli, Franco Lumachi and myself presented a paper to a conference on audiences and television entitled 'Group Research: Towards a Model of Interdisciplinary Research on the Relationship between Television and Audiences'[11] in which the following thesis was put forward, taking issue with the official RAI audience research designed to measure audience ratings and appreciation.

We said: unlike toothpaste which fulfils its function when

bought and materially consumed, it is a matter of little consequence for television how many people watch a particular programme. At least, knowing the figures might help orient
programmes but it tells us nothing about their effects. Knowing such things might be useful in countries with several channels that depend entirely on advertising and must provide their
sponsors with statistics on audience size, but it hardly matters
in a country like Italy with two channels when knowing that
ten million saw the film on one channel only means that they
didn't have the courage to follow the organ music recital on
the other.

We said: measurement of appreciation does not (except for
commercial or political purposes) produce interesting data
from a civic, educational or sociological point of view. Anyone
who writes for the papers frequently gets letters that make one
feel like a cook who has prepared a cream and peach *gateau*
using eggs, dried figs, honey and *marrons glacés* only to be told:
'Dear Friend, you cannot imagine the pleasure your culinary
offering gave me. I love the strong hot flavours, especially the
anchovies, and your dish fulfilled my every desire.' The fact
that a programme was *liked* does not tell us what people *saw*.

We said: content analysis undoubtedly represents a step forward for the sociology of mass communications, a step away
from the measurement of the number of times the gum was
chewed (recorded in the auditorium with infra-red rays) during
the scene when the cavalry arrived, and away from experiments
seemingly demonstrating that after a John Wayne movie full
of fist-fights and shooting the spectator goes home at peace,
whereas after an Antonioni film he feels an irresistible urge to
chop up his wife. However, looking for ideological patterns,
models of behaviour and value systems in mass communications messages, one finds exactly what the authors had put
there because the programme producer and content analyst
both come from the same university, read the same books,
have the same background and education. Content analysis has

played and must continue to play a useful educational role when, rather than just providing a description of the ideology of the message, it brings the results of its research to the knowledge of the public, revealing what the message wanted to say, even if that's not what it said to everyone. However, as a record of mass communications' effects on people's minds it is totally irrelevant. It tells us what effects were intended, not the ones actually produced.

At the Perugia event we therefore drew the classic diagram of communications coming from mathematicians of information:

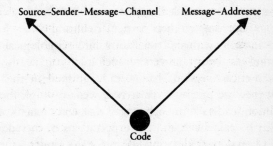

Source–Sender–Message–Channel   Message–Addressee

Code

and we tried to translate it into this second diagram:

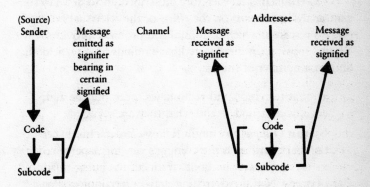

(Source) Sender — Message emitted as signifier bearing in certain signified — Channel — Message received as signifier — Addressee — Message received as signified

Code — Subcode — Code — Subcode

There exist, we said, depending on socio-cultural circumstances, a variety of codes, or rather of rules of competence and interpretation. The message has a signifying form that can be filled with different meanings. While there are basic codes accepted by everyone, there are differences in subcodes; hence the same word understood by everyone in its most diffused denotative meaning may connote something for some and something else for others.

A herd of cows is perceived in the same way by an Italian and an Indian but for the former it signifies abundance of food, for the latter abundance of ritual occasions. So the suspicion grew that the sender organized the televisual message on the basis of his own codes, which coincided with those of the dominant ideology, while the addressees filled it with 'aberrant' meanings according to their particular cultural codes.

In doing this we were translating into semiological terms something American university sociology (unlike the Germano-American version) had already grasped in the 1950s, namely that the message, on arrival, went through the filter of 'opinion leaders'[12] in such a way that comprehension was modified by exigencies and the expectations of the addressee group, often with devastating effects for the sender – the infamous 'boomerang effect'.

The Perugia project therefore prescribed, in addition to content analysis, research on the *effects* of the televisual message.

This research, which continues and probably provides some of the most scientifically credible findings in the field, has shown a number of things:

a) that television and radio news speak but the audience doesn't understand what they are saying;

b) that *Oedipus Rex* might follow *Carosello* but in certain backward areas the evening's viewing is perceived as a *continuum* without distinctions being made between News, Advertising and Entertainment Programmes;

c) that the very presence of television has, independently of the content of broadcasts, changed the relationship between the Italian people and their language, with some positive political consequences; that oral and local traditions have had to retreat before the forces of linguistic-cultural standardization, but have then been restored through centralized national broadcasting to their roots in the form of 'folk music' and dialect theatre.

Moreover, so-called 'aberrations' in the reception of messages have ceased to be seen as obstacles to comprehension (as might be the case with the advertiser trying to sell Orietta Berti[13] only to discover that he's persuaded young people to buy Cuban revolutionary music, and with good reason). Instead these aberrations are seen as the last hope of freedom available to the defenceless masses. As a result, encouraging rather than repressing this form of 'deviancy' took on a political and pedagogic colouring, with investigations being called 'counter-information' or 'semiological guerrilla-warfare'.

Furthermore broadcasters, acknowledging that some messages must, for the good of the community, be received as unequivocally as possible, have used their awareness of aberrant decodings to take the cultural circumstances of the audience more into account. This involved reducing the semantic gaps by adopting simpler language, respecting audiences' needs rather than talking over their heads in a slang made up of in-jokes comprehensible only to those in public bodies and their political patrons.

It could be concluded at this stage that the Perugia conference had made an impression and nothing else remained to be done. In that case the researcher wouldn't bother about questioning the methods and findings any further or asking whether the original hypotheses might have suffered from ideological distortions through *naiveté* or manipulation. The following section examines to what extent this initial presentation contains the embryo of future research. It should really have been presented by Paolo Fabbri, who recently published a weighty article on the question.[14] This provides the basis for what I am going to say, although, as will be made clear, there are places where I disagree with him.

3. What was equivocal about the Perugia model? I would say it was the term 'aberrant decoding' used to refer to the fact that addressees saw in the message things not put there by the sender. We've already established that 'aberrant' did not mean 'absolutely erroneous' but 'aberrant with respect to the intentions of the sender'. However, the connotative force of the term prevailed on all sides, not least because latent class complicity drew researchers closer to the senders than to the addressees.

It is the right of the Indian to see in the cow an object of veneration but aren't we always prey to the missionary feeling that it is our duty to convince him of the joys of the beefsteak – if only to help resolve the problem of endemic food shortages? So here we have fallacy number one: the addressee reads the message differently because he operates with flawed or abnormal codes.

Fallacy number two consists in checking comprehension through verbal tests. People were shown a programme and then asked what they had seen. Often answers hovered between hesitation, aphasia and borborygmus. It was plain enough – they hadn't just understood little, they hadn't understood at all. Consequently the option of filtering the message through mediators hadn't produced greater understanding but greater confusion. So much for the teaching of greater understanding, humanity, civility and progress.

Fabbri points out that an enormous gap separates *comprehension* and *verbalization* and that the conflation of the two derives from the myth of the word (which also dominates semiology), whereby something has meaning only when it can be verbalized, translated into words and *thought*. In his recent study,[15] Emilio Garroni addressed, at least from a methodoligical point of view, the question of a non-verbal universe that is still meaningful and yet not translatable into verbal interpretation. He has identified a universe of verbal or linguistic systems (L) with which a universe of non-linguistic systems (NL) intersects, producing a shared zone in which NL can be translated into L (as when we translate a traffic-signal into the injunction 'No Left Turn'), and leaving an exclusively NL zone in which we know that there's meaning and interpretation but this interpretation cannot be verbalized:

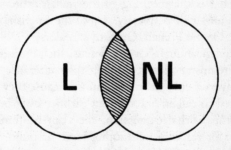

It's not a return to the age-old aesthetic question of visual configurations, like the masterpiece in which some things are comprehensible and explicable and others are comprehensible but not explicable while being, nonetheless, subject to rules of competence and interpretation. Just consider the semiotic nature of *sign-functions* such as architectonic objects: there are objects whose function one understands, by learning, and uses accordingly. However, one isn't able to recognize and verbalize the functional meaning of the object that one translates into an injunction or into behaviour. Let's concede, however, that a) these functions may be verbalized, and b) that if others exist which aren't verbalized the semiology of the future will manage to develop the metalinguistic means with which to unify group

NL and group L. What interests us here is that there exist signs whose meaning is *in theory* verbalizable, while there exist addressees whose verbal competence is too weak to let them carry out this complex act of decoding. Yet, even if they don't verbalize, it doesn't follow that they haven't grasped the meaning. It is not necessary that the meaning of a sign be made clear through an affirmative enunciation. What is the meaning of the expression 'Go to the devil!'? That I have to imitate Dante? Certainly not. That I have to go away? Undoubtedly. That the speaker is irritated with me? That as well. That the speaker doesn't acknowledge the logical basis of my assertions and demands? That too.

And what is the meaning of the Italian expression 'Mah!' said with an air of perplexity? Or of the English 'Oh, let me see . . . '? Or the French 'Ouff, tu sais alors . . . '? They don't have a fixed meaning, above all because their meaning depends on the circumstances surrounding their utterance and reception. However, they have a meaning because they have what Peirce used to call an 'interpretant': if they can't be translated into another verbal expression, they can be translated into behaviour or response of another kind (a sound, a touch of the hand, a gesture) that clarifies their meaning. For Peirce, then, the final interpretant of a series of signs that clarify one another is a habit – the way in which these signs, when put to a pragmatic test, show that they have produced or are producing a modifying action on the world.[16] Which explains why at the start of this paper I outlined, on the one hand, the history of televisual forms and, on the other, some generational responses: albeit in a fable-like way, the second served to interpret the first, or to show that they could be interpreted in another way.

If comprehension is not verbalization, research on effects of comprehension might well give results that are too limited. The subject might know how to verbalize in the terms of the interviewer but refuse (perhaps instinctively) this type of complicity with the dominant code. Equally, the opposite can occur; one sees people interviewed on television who (under the influence of the 'educated' TV cameras) express themselves in a language that is not theirs, reproducing that of television and, in the process, saying things which they wouldn't otherwise have wanted to. So the test of comprehension through verbalization can make one think either that *little* has been understood when sufficient has been understood or that everything has been understood when nothing has been.

Now we must ask ourselves:

a) whether under this seeming 'code deficit' there lie concealed autonomous subaltern cultures with their own differently organized codes, capable of providing rules of competence to their users concerning both expression and understanding the expression of others;

b) what it means to speak of different codes, how they are organized and whether they are 'codes' at all.

By now it has become apparent that the categories 'code' and 'message' are too blunt as tools of analysis, and a good deal of the incomprehension and errors listed so far derive from this inadequacy.

Let us therefore try to reformulate our analytic apparatus with the help of Hjelmslev's semiotic model.[17] According to this, signification takes place when contents are conveyed through the articulation of a *material of expression* (sounds, images, gestures, etc.). We can avail ourselves of an infinite variety of materials: culture makes us prefer some to others (for example, it is rare for us to signify through smells but it is much more common for us to do so through vocal sounds and graphic images) and then *segments* a given material into certain pertinent *formal units*. Of all the sounds that a human is capable of producing, a language selects as pertinent some thirty phonemes in all and articulates them to form a lexical repertory consisting of some 2,000 to 5,000 words that can be used on a daily basis.

Now it's a matter of making these *units of expression* correspond to *units of content*. Content, in its substance, is everything that can be attempted and everything that can be thought: a culture transforms it into *form* and makes only certain culturally elaborated units pertinent. For instance, both modern zoology and everyday speech know two species of rodent – 'rats' and 'mice' – while zoology in Latin knows only 'mus'. It is not a case of having either one or two units of expression but of having either one or two units of content. The codes, strictly speaking, are what make given units of content correspond to given units of expression. Yet the term 'code' is used to include formal systems, those of the plane of expression (the code of the English language recognizes a certain number of phonemes and lexical units) and those of the plane of content. The system of the plane of content, which is the way in which a culture makes the world knowable, is a plane of competence, as distinct from linguistic codes, and yet it is also called 'code'.

We know that for us the word 'snow' corresponds to a unit of the plane of content definable as H_2O in a special state: it is not water, nor is it ice; it is a sort of damp and flaky powder composed of innumerable tiny water crystals that fall from the sky and cover the ground like a white permeable blanket. However, an Eskimo knows – in the place of 'snow' – four units of content. For him, there are four states of snow, the one as different from the other as ice is from water for us. He has four words (his code is complete) but if he were to learn Italian the word 'snow' for him would correspond to only one of the four units that he knows (so that when he hears the word 'snow' he would exclude certain meanings that we associate with this form of expression) or else it would amount to a generic term like 'damp stuff'.

There are peoples who do not segment colours as we do: it

seems the ancient Romans and Greeks didn't know the difference between blue and green, reducing it to the difference, for us, between light and dark green or between pea and pastel green (recognizing in each instance that a person is dressed in green, a house is green, or that grass, in general, is green). Let us now imagine sending signals with traffic-lights to a subject who (for cultural reasons) segments the chromatic spectrum in the following way: black/colour/white (i.e. absence of light/various portions of the spectrum/simultaneous presence of colours). Our subject, as long as the lights are on, whether they signal red, green or amber, would think that they are always telling him the same thing with varying degrees of intensity, and so would stop and start without apparent reason, at least in our eyes.

Anyway, here is an initial question to put to future researchers on television's effects on audiences. When a subject shows that he hasn't understood a given message shouldn't we ask ourselves whether:

a) he's understood it but doesn't know how to verbalize it;

b) he doesn't know the unit of the plane of expression that the sender has used (if someone has never heard the word 'metempsychosis' it's simply a gap in lexical knowledge);

c) he knows the unit of expression, he possesses a segmented content like that of the sender but assigns to the unit of expression a different unit of content (he thinks 'metempsychosis' signifies a particular type of psychic disorder; in this instance, there is an imperfect knowledge of the code);

d) he possesses a differently segmented content so that the unit of expression received is made to correspond to units of content not corresponding to those of the sender.

Problem a) has already been discussed and invariably leads on to the others. Problem b) is simple enough and merely requires educational intervention. Problem c) is also resolvable through more thoroughgoing education. But problem d) is the one that is never taken sufficiently into consideration. In order to resolve problem d), a *semiotics of culture* must elaborate even sharper instruments of analysis. In particular, research on audience responses to television messages will have to go in some of the following directions.

4. The study of different ways of segmenting content, until now an area studied by cultural anthropology, is currently giving rise to a new branch of semiotics, namely the *semiotics of culture*.

A different segmentation of content does not necessarily mean that a culture being studied organizes elementary units differently from that of the culture doing the studying, as shown by the example of the Eskimos and snow. The difference can, however, affect the connotations we assign to these units.

Let us assume, for example, that there exists a culture (as indeed there does) that subdivides animals and vegetables in the same way as standard European culture, distinguishing wolves from dogs, rats from mice, maize from buckwheat, and buckwheat from nettles and tares, and so on. This culture could then, at a higher level of signification, reorganize these units into 'edibles' and 'non-edibles' in a different way. For certain Asian peoples the dog is edible, while other peoples (and not even very primitive ones) view our habit of eating frogs with horror. There are people fond of eating worms who would regard as poisonous the fermented barley that fetches such a high price, especially in bottles with a black label.

This alternative culture would, therefore, have subcodes different from our own. Like ours, the primary code would assign given units of expression to given units of content, while the subcode would make these units of content correspond to further units of content not corresponding to our own. Here then is how a different culture can understand what is said in a standard language and yet assign to the message different connotations.

Another difference could consist in norms of style and rhetoric that make certain ways of combining units of both expression and content seem either usual or eccentric. 'Lascia che io vadi'[18] is ungrammatical to a university graduate and perfectly grammatical to a Northern Italian peasant; and both expressions would correspond to the same unit of content. Yet the graduate would use 'lascia che vadi' to connote linguistic abnormality, while the phrase would be received as absolutely normal by other addressees. Or, to give another example, the sender could see it as normal that the characters of *The Betrothed* and *The Three Musketeers* dress in capes and feathered hats, and they would see it as stylish in a Californian hippy commune. Meanwhile, the uneducated addressee would refer both types of iconography to a vague connotation of 'antiquity' or 'legend'.

At a higher level of rhetorical conventions are found *textual conventions* and *genre typologies*. Our high culture possesses precise distinctions that separate the tragic, the comic and the melodramatic. An episode that began with the language and movement of classical tragedy and ended with the protagonist triumphing over his enemies, getting married and living happily ever after would be inconceivable. If that were to happen, one would have to stress the melodramatic language in order to underline parody and prepare the way for the paradoxical finale. However, the same play received in a different context could be taken as comic when tragic or as tragic when heavily paradoxical. The difference in behaviour of Don Quixote and Sancho Panza when faced with certain events perfectly illustrates the gap between genre conventions at the level of two historically contemporaneous cultures.

Now the real problem is to investigate subcodes and systems

of content of subaltern cultures. An initial requisite, before reception tests are started, is a geographical man of these cultures and the various systems of conventions and subconventions that they obey.

The task is difficult because it isn't yet clear what is meant by 'subaltern culture'.

The opposition is not between hegemonic culture, on the one hand, and time-honoured subaltern culture on the other: a primitive culture is every bit as grammar-oriented (in its own way) as a Western civilized culture. However, when one starts to talk about subaltern cultures within an industrially developed country, we know that we are no longer faced with a high culture and a primitive culture. The culture of the Samnites no longer exists. Instead we have the culture of the poor and the excluded. These are the subaltern culture(s). Nor are they 'pure', as they result from an incomplete adaptation involving the culture imposed from above and the vestiges of vanishing primitive cultures. The official model for a culture of this kind today is 'mass culture'; that is, the sum (or product) of the ensemble of models coming from the hegemonic culture via the mass media and the ensemble of interpretations that the subaltern culture has given it, leading to forms of behaviour, feelings, systems of opinion.

Obviously a worker, for instance, undergoes the influence of different models: on the one hand, there is his class culture, shaped in the factory and bearing the organizational imprint of the hegemonic culture (with respect to which it presents itself as an alternative); on the other, the model handed down from above as mass culture. What system of values and conventions emerges from this marriage? We have only just started to find out.

One thing we do know is that there doesn't exist a Mass Culture in the sense imagined by the apocalyptic critics of mass communications because this model competes with others (constituted by historic vestiges, class culture, aspects of high culture transmitted through education etc.). The difficulty with a map of the systems of content of the addressees today derives from the fact that this mass culture has not been studied in all its facets and, moreover, is in a continual state of flux brought about by the impact of the mass media and socioeconomic developments.

In answer to a 'deficit theory', Fabbri proposes the following hypothesis: while high culture is highly grammar-oriented (that is to say, it openly defines its own conventions of production through a metalanguage recognized by all its users), mass culture is only text-oriented.[19] He writes: 'In fact, one can observe that, as with folklore, mass culture functions best when the producer is invisible and the text presents itself as naturalized, the manifestation of a code as self-evident as it is explicit.' In other words, mass culture does not know precise conventions for the production of texts but uses model-texts in order to think, to produce and to understand other texts. One thinks of the format of the Western or of the 'love story with a happy ending' that can be used (by both senders and receivers) to describe and understand events like Watergate.

All this suggests that mass culture also possesses conventions and units of articulation but that these function at a macroscopic level with respect to those of high culture. This might explain why the celebrated Orson Welles broadcast on the invasion from Mars, explicitly presented as a fictional construct, was understood as live news. The conventions of production through which the author made his fiction explicit were not understood by the audience, which had instead identified that higher unit of broadcasting constituted by the format 'live reporting' and acted on the basis of this unit of expression and content.

5. There is a need, therefore, to address a number of questions and areas of research, as Fabbri mentioned, and among these the most pressing include:

A. What we call the 'message' is actually a text on which converge messages based on different codes. Not just in the sense that television is made up of words, images, sounds etc., but in the sense that what the message says at the level of certain basic codes can be negated, misunderstood or subverted at the level of higher couplings between units of content. In order to know what part of a message has *got through*, one must first know how many different messages were encapsulated in that text.

B. There exist discursive conventions and textual typologies. One needs to know which ones are dominant in a given community of receivers. If the News is read as a Western or a Western as the News, that must be known, and who is to say that the aberration is so 'aberrant'. Fabbri speaks of 'discursive pidginization' with reference to the different modes of decoding the overall form of discourses. 'Pidgin' is constituted by colonial and colonized languages as the result of processes of simplification, adaptation, elimination and interference. A housewife could interpret *The Stars Look Down*[20] as a love story pure and simple, a worker could subject it to the interpretative conventions governing labour disputes. He or she could introduce the same conventions into reading a comedy with love interest like the movie *The Apartment*, while a civil servant could read it, on the basis of institutional conventions, as a manual on how to gain promotion.

C. However, these texts have *deep semantic structures*, probably universal in nature, that could function at all levels, even when the senders of the message are unaware of the fact. A variety of semiotic research projects have dealt with this, but the hypothesis has never been applied to research on programme comprehension.

D. At this point it is worth noting that mass culture is not uniform in the way imagined by apocalyptic sociologists of Mass Culture. Textual conventions can vary from group to group, place to place, period to period. The texts in circulation in mass culture compete to bring about change, as do the alternative ones.

E. This helps explain why so much research that reveals incomprehension of messages actually testifies to what Fabbri calls 'detached involvement'. The addressee is not just a passive consumer of the message. As Benjamin knew,[21] he or she sometimes consumes the message distractedly, sometimes freely, seeing it as *day-dreaming* and without a cognitive function, and sometimes responds (especially if asked) with the *reticence* of someone who doesn't feel involved. On occasions this reticence is *politically institutionalized*, defence-mechanisms that lead to *self-exclusion*: 'Play the dirty game on your own.' With a survey this is sometimes registered by a mere 'I didn't understand' or 'I didn't like it.' Which isn't a lot. All these defences can then give rise to that *institutionalization of refusal* and *factious interpretation of messages* that I have elsewhere referred to as a semiological guerrilla-warfare and which today produces forms of counter-information that (fortunately) focus increasingly on how television is understood.

6. This is a panorama of possible research projects on reception that take account of a hugely complex phenomenon. I don't know whether they are realizable but they can certainly be proposed. The difficulties involved could make people say that these observations have no further purchase on the development of research on audience reception of television. It could end up with a 'free market' theory according to which *the audience does what it wants with the message*. A fairly dangerous utopia that springs from the naive idea that whoever sends messages is bad and whoever distorts them on reception is good, whatever the circumstances. Apart from the fact that there are messages which it would be socially desirable for everyone to receive according to some standard of comprehen-

sion and consensus (not excluding criticism, but removing distortions), the principal aim of this research should nonetheless be to understand the enormous changes in collective consciousness that the development of mass communications has entailed, rather than to concentrate on improving the effectiveness of the sender.

A final observation, levelled at some of Fabbri's positions. One should be careful to avoid a populist demagogy for which, since the systems of content of subaltern cultures are in their way regarded as organized and sufficient, there is no need paternalistically to try to convert their users to the dominant linguistic and cultural norms, because this would constitute an act of repression.

Let us return for a moment to the example of the traffic signals directed at an individual who can only identify white, black and an undifferentiated colour. Observe that he can live perfectly adequately in an environment in which to survive he needs to recognize only white, black and colour; his system of content would then be culturally organic, self-sufficient and perfectly respectable. The only drawback is that on arrival in the city he would end up under a lorry.

When Fabbri says, for instance, that the fact that an interviewee doesn't know the name of the Minister of Transport isn't evidence of political inadequacy, he is right. Moreover, he doesn't even need to know that, at ministerial level, transport is different from home affairs. He can have a political culture and hence a highly organized system of content that separates the 'holders of political power' or state representatives on the one hand from the 'holders of economic power' on the other. He can, all the while, make fine distinctions between his local grocer and Gianni Agnelli of Fiat but consider policemen, judges and ministers of every sort as expressions of the same slice of undifferentiated content. This is how every highly elaborated expression with which the sender might hope to communicate the subtle play of political alliance and opposition at the level of the state apparatuses would, in his case, acquire the same undifferentiated signifying capacity: they are talking about 'the others'. His organization of content would be respectable and even efficient in the event of a revolutionary insurrection, when prefects, judges and police are swept aside simultaneously. It emerges as pernicious, however, when in order to obtain a pension a person must know whom to approach. If he's a farm-hand it certainly wouldn't be the Minister of Transport.

The problem of linguistic freedom is also the problem of the *freedom to know of the existence of other organizations of content that don't correspond to one's own*. Linguistic freedom isn't just the freedom to administer one's own code but the freedom to translate between different codes. Colonial peoples, as long as they remained colonized, suffered from a lack in knowledge with respect to a civilization that knew very well how to distinguish between the peoples of the Congo and Berbers. For the peoples of the Congo, however, the Belgians, Germans and British were uniformly 'the white man'. And in order to be dominated they had to go on being unaware of the other segmentations of content. In order to carry out an anti-colonial revolution one needs to go to Oxford. The risk is that one remains there.

However, a more articulated piece of research on the effects of television doesn't have to assume the political responsibility of converting anyone to the dominant culture. It should, rather, provide the pedagogic means towards an education in *freedom of decoding* for the future.

Understanding what the others understand can certainly be useful in forcing them to know only what you know. Yet, fortunately, the vitality of the audience belies some of the projects outlined in *1984*.

The means of communication are not the only feature of the social landscape and the superstructures do not act in isolation.

Instead, to understand what the others understand can help

one to understand with whom one is speaking, however one is speaking.

To understand what the others understand can serve to get them to understand what is understood by other groups whose grammar they are ignorant of.

Getting them to understand the language of those who would want them mute as well as the language of those considered mute in the same way as themselves.

At this stage the researcher should stop being a paternalistic pedagogue who interprets the language of primitive people in order to teach them to read and write. To switch metaphors, the problem of future research on the comprehension of television messages will be that of a community which has stopped regarding itself as an object of surveys and is, instead, a subject that discusses and brings into the open its own rules of competence and interpretations, discovering, in the meantime, those of the others.

1977

CHAPTER 3

Event as Mise en scène *and Life as Scene-setting*

WHEN WE FOLLOW a fictional event (movie or TV serial) on the big or small screen we now know that, even if the cameras did represent things as they were (and years of studying the techniques of cinematic and televisual manipulation have taught us that filming means representing things as they are but also interpreting, selecting and reconstructing them), things are as they are not by chance or nature but because someone has arranged them, created the *mise en scène*, for the purpose of the shot.

It's not even worth consulting the most recent and definitive studies of the question (e.g., Bettetini's *Produzione del senso e messa in scena*).[1] You just have to refer to people's common sense. The viewer of average intelligence (if we exclude the ingenuous, the pathological or the viewer, not yet extinct, who can't tell the difference between the news, advertising and a film and sees the evening's television as an unbroken continuum of messages that originate in the real world) knows very well that when the actress kisses the actor in the kitchen, on board a yacht, or in a meadow, the actors are not the characters, the characters are not real people, and the kitchen or yacht are studio sets. Moreoever the meadow, even when real (usually located in the countryside around Rome or in Yugoslavia), is a meadow picked out, prepared, selected and hence *falsified* to some degree for the benefit of the shot.

No wonder the viewer with a measure of critical awareness knows he has to watch out not only for how something is filmed but for how reality (manufactured or selected) has been *prepared* in advance of the filming: *mise en scène* is already language, discourse.

So far it's a matter of common sense. However, common sense (and that often applies to critical awareness too) is much less informed when faced with what is called live television. In this instance one knows (even when suspecting that the live broadcast is prerecorded) that the cameras bring the pictures direct from the place where something is happening, something that would, I maintain, have happened independently of the presence of the TV cameras.

Right from the very beginnings of television there was an awareness that even the live broadcast presupposed choices, acts of manipulation. The author, in his piece 'Il caso e l'inteccio' (now in *Opera aperta*[2]), tried to show how two or three cameras filming a football match (an event competitive by definition in which no striker would miss a goal or goalkeeper allow one through for the sake of good entertainment) select from events, focus on certain actions and overlook others, pick out the spectators at the expense of the game and vice versa, frame the field in a given perspective, in short, *interpret* the match as seen by the director rather than reproducing some 'complete' match.

However, these analyses didn't put in question the indisputable fact that the event would have taken place anyway, independently of the filming. The filming interpreted the event which happened independently, recuperating a part of it – a slice of the action, a point of view – but it was always dealing with a point of view on an extra-televisual 'reality'.

Yet this idea was overtaken by a series of developments that quickly became obvious:

a) The knowledge that the event will be filmed influences preparation for it; with football this meant: the replacement of the brown leather ball by the TV chequered ball; the authorities' careful positioning of advertising in order to exploit camera movements and fool the state channel's regulations; changes in shirt design for chromatic reasons relating to the TV image.

b) The presence of TV cameras influences the course of events. One recalls the case of Vermicino.[3] Perhaps help would have been more effective in rescuing the boy trapped down the well if there hadn't been eighteen hours of television coverage. But the public would have been less involved, the confusion and traffic jams reduced. President Pertini might still have gone there but he'd not have stayed so long. Not from calculation of theatrical effect but because his presence was symbolic, designed to convey to millions of Italians the President's involvement. The fact that the symbolic gesture was, as I'd maintain, good in itself does not mean that it wasn't inspired by the TV cameras.

We might try to imagine what would have happened without the TV coverage. There are two possible scenarios: either the helpers would have been less generous (leaving aside questions of effectivity, it's clear that without the TV the gangling lads who rushed to the spot wouldn't have known that anything had happened); or the reduced crowds would have enabled more effective and rational measures to be taken.

In both the above examples we can glimpse newly emerging *mise en scène*. In the case of the match it is intentional and unlikely to have radically affected the course of the event. In that of Vermicino it is instinctive, unintended (in the conscious sense at any rate) but can radically affect the outcome.

In the last ten years, however, live television has undergone dramatic changes in terms of *mise en scène*. From papal ceremonies to political and entertainment events, we know that they would not have been conceived in the same way in the absence of TV cameras. The event that most clearly demonstrates this hypothesis is the marriage of the Prince and Princess of Wales. This event not only wouldn't have taken place in the way it did, it probably wouldn't have taken place if it hadn't had to be conceived with television in mind.

In order to establish how novel the Royal Wedding actually was one needs to refer back to an analogous event of some twenty-five years ago, namely the marriage of Rainier of Monaco and Grace Kelly. Apart from the difference in size of the kingdoms, the event lent itself to similar interpretations. There was the political-cum-diplomatic part, the religious ritual, the military liturgy, the love story. However, the Monaco marriage took place in the early years of television and was organized independently of television. Even if the organizers were perhaps aware of the television cameras, they had little experience of such things. So the event followed its own course and the television director had but to *interpret* it. In doing so he gave the romantic-sentimental aspects priority over the political-diplomatic ones, the private over the public. The event happened, and the cameras focused on the theme chosen by television.

During a parade of military bands, in which the marine contingent had a particular representative role, the TV cameras lingered on the prince at the balcony, who was leaning over and shaking the dust out of his trousers, laughing and smiling at his fiancée. A selection, to be sure – inspired by Mills and Boon rather than operetta – but made despite the event, taking advantage of its informal moments. Likewise, during the marriage ceremony, the director followed the same strategy – just as the band of the marines had been left out before, now the prelate performing the rites was excluded. All the while the cameras remained on the face of the bride, the princess formerly an actress, or rather the actress and future princess. Grace Kelly acted out her last love scene. The director told the story but parasitically (hence creatively), using in collage form elements of what would have been there anyway.

With the Royal Wedding things went very differently. It

was evident that everything that happened, from Buckingham Palace to St Paul's Cathedral, had been studied for television. The ceremony did not include unacceptable colours – the designers and the magazines had proposed pastel shades as the norm so that, chromatically, everything exuded not just springtime but television springtime.

And the dress of the bride, to the annoyance of the groom who didn't know how to lift it so as to make his betrothed more comfortable, wasn't made to be seen from in front, or behind, or from the side, but from above, as is evident from the closing compositional shots in which the architectonic space was reduced to a circle, dominated at the centre by the cruciform structure of the transept and nave, something under-lined by the long train of the dress, while the four quarters at the head of this emblem were realized, in the manner of a simple mosaic, by the coloured counterpoint of the clothes of choir, prelates and public, male and female. If Mallarmé once said that 'le monde est fait pour aboutir à un livre', the filming of the Royal Wedding said that the British Empire was built in order to produce splendid television.

I have in the past seen various London pageants, including Trooping the Colour where the most unpleasant impression was the horses, which are trained to do everything except abstain from legitimate bodily functions. It must be the emo-tion, the laws of nature, and the Queen on these occasions always proceeds amid mountains of dung because the horses of the Guard don't know any better. On the other hand, riding horses is a very aristocratic pursuit, and horse droppings are a familiar part of the English aristocrat's world.

There was no escaping from this law even during the Royal Wedding. However, anyone watching the broadcast will have noted that the horse droppings were neither dark nor differentiated but were also a pastel shade, between yellow and beige, shiny and in harmony with the surrounding ladies' dresses. One read later (and it wasn't hard to imagine) that the royal horses were fed pills for a week so as to guarantee dung of telegenic colouring. Nothing could be left to chance, everything was ruled by the television coverage.

To such an extent that on this occasion the amount of freedom for the TV directors to compose and interpret was minimal. It was a matter of filming what happened according to prepared schedules of time and place. The whole symbolic construction had been set in place at an earlier stage in the prior *mise en scène*; the entire event, from prince to horse droppings, had been prearranged as a defining discourse on which the eye of the cameras, following the fixed route, would focus, minimizing risks of televisual interpretation. Or rather, the interpretation, the manipulation, the preparation for television, preceded the whirring of the cameras. The event was born as fundamentally 'fake' from the start, ready for filming. London was arranged as a studio, constructed for television.

Which doesn't mean to say that there wasn't manipulation and interpretation, but it was all pretelevising; television filmed a theatrical show rehearsed in every detail like a Strehler play, but the theatrical show functioned as television-to-be.

We are now a long way from the first televised football matches. Television has induced a preconstruction of reality just when it (television) gives the impression of being an objective eye that opens the window onto what is there.

As a consequence, critical analysis has to switch its attention ever more to the set, to the masking of reality directly realized using what we call reality (bodies, buildings, roads), and away from the interpretative stage which we once considered the moment when looking became ideological. Now ideology moves back a step in the process. The television critic must look less at the screen, not just at the screen, and always behind the screen – interpreting the images as signs of other signs.

1982

CHAPTER 4

The Phantom of Neo-TV: The debate on Fellini's Ginger and Fred

FELLINI'S IMAGINATION works on three levels: memory, the analysis of manners, and the grotesque. Sometimes he fuses them, at other times he singles out, emphasizes it and makes it the dominant note of a particular film.

It could be said that *Amarcord* is dominated by memory, *La Dolce Vita* by the analysis of manners, *Juliet of the Spirits* or *Orchestra Rehearsal* by the grotesque. By the same token, we might say that in *I Vitelloni* the grotesque is held in check by memory and the analysis of manners, that *The White Sheik* hovers somewhere between the analysis of manners and the grotesque, and that *Satyricon* is wholly grotesque . . . I wanted to distinguish these separate levels because in *Ginger and Fred* all three are present.

Above all, there is the memory of the years of Fellini's and of our own youth, and of the myths of that time: in the film, the head of the TV station himself is shown to be a victim of this, without any irony on the director's part, while the memory of the film's two protagonists could be said to represent Fellini's own nostalgia. More so than in other films, memory exonerates, and is itself exonerated from the vulgarity of the present. Encountering the tenderness of Ginger and Fred's recollections, the grotesque circles around, menacing and offensive, but ultimately leaves both them and their purity untouched.

As for analysis of manners, there would seem on the surface to be plenty of it in a film like this, setting out as it does to expose the intrusiveness, greed, inanity and cruelty of television culture and the consumerism it promotes. And yet – and this is the strange thing about *Ginger and Fred* – for all its greatness, it's hard to define it as a comedy of manners about television. Fellini the analyst of manners emerges in the portrayal of Rome's Stazione Termini, of the desolate hotel in the outskirts (a cathedral rising out of a landscape strewn with stinking piles of rubbish) and in the glimpses of a city seen from the windows of a bus.

But as soon as we enter the world of television, it's as if Fellini puts his foot on the grotesque pedal and presses down on it relentlessly, brimful of unconcealed hatred and loathing. It's obvious that he's talking about television, and about the intrusive form it has taken over the past few years: notably in the shape of the hold-all variety show with its line-up of writers, MPs, freaks, cripples, dwarfs, dancers and heroic admirals, all reduced to fodder for show business consumption, or rather to first-act *hors d'oeuvres*, since the real show begins with the advertisements – advertisements oozing fat and sauce, greasy spaghetti and artificial cooked meats. It's easy to see why French culture, already anxious about the threatened invasion by American TV, and now even more so about the actual invasion by Italian TV, greeted this film (according to the papers) not only as an artistic event but as a battle cry, a proud and unequivocal call to arms after the fashion of Cambronne's 'Merde!'[1]

And yet, and yet . . . Fellini's television is too much. It's too much of everything, too emphatic. We laugh, we recognize what is referred to, but this television isn't drawn by Daumier, or even by Grosz, it's painted by Hieronymus Bosch. So the television in *Ginger and Fred* is a fine slice of grotesque – nothing wrong in that, but it goes beyond satirizing contemporary mores, and to such an extent that all the targets of

Fellini's scorn would find it easy to say, 'Yes, but we're not really like that.'

The question I'm asking doesn't concern Fellini: indeed, as far as Fellini is concerned, I don't believe he could have done otherwise. The question is why he couldn't have done otherwise.

As I left the cinema I thought that the drama and the vulnerable tenderness of this pathetic duo might perhaps have emerged with greater clarity and feeling had they been planted in a real television show face to face with some male or female presenter, and surrounded by real dancers. Apart from anything else, the latter are infinitely better at imitating the style of Broadway musicals than the Felliniesque Folies Bergères.

I said to myself that, had Fellini been capable, as he obviously wasn't, of imitating a real TV show, with its line-up of MPs, writers, out-of-work actresses, black singers, its phoney rapport with the audience and its fundamental and masturbatory relationship with itself and its own image, as well as with the image of other TV shows – in short, had Fellini succeeded (as he did in using Irving Berlin's melodies) in putting Giulietta Masina and Marcello Mastroianni in the midst of real television – wouldn't his satire have been all the more cruel?

Then I tried to imagine the result (it's always difficult to imagine what one would have done in the artist's place), and I thought no, it would have lacked spice.

In fact, Fellini is not talking about what I have referred to elsewhere as Paleotelevision[2] (the prototype of which might be the programme *Lascia o Raddoppia?* [Double Your Money].[3] Rather, he's talking about what I've called Neo-television, a complex phenomenon consisting of lots and lots of TV channels, all shot through with ads, and programmes that copy one another, taking turns to compete for the attention of the viewer who zaps compulsively on his remote control. Each programme talks about itself and addresses an audience that is part of the programme: the message, obsessively repeated, is not, 'This is how the world is', but 'I am here, do you see me? This is the only reality that you will recognize from now on.'

This multiplication effect cannot be seen in one programme alone: watching them singly, are we to be moralistic about the fact that, up there on the stage, after the MP comes the abandoned teenage mother, and then the flavour-of-the-month writer, the drug addict and the tap-dancer? So what? The world of mass media has seen worse, and if you don't like it, switch it off.

The Neo-TV effect is the result of the cancerous proliferation of the same programme format endlessly repeated. What characterizes Neo-TV is its repetitiveness and the ultimate impossibility of making distinctions, discerning and choosing. In order to portray this never-ending round, this serpent devouring its own tail, a director needs to make a film that lasts as long as television, that goes on day after day without ever stopping. Since this is not possible, an aesthetic short cut has to be found: the one Fellini has chosen is grotesque accumulation and he shows us a TV quite unlike real television, or any one programme, because it attempts to resemble, though not by mimesis, their unbearable whole. The true image of the 'Neo-TV plexus' is given us in the scene in which ten housewives throw themselves greedily at ten plates of pasta, tasting every single sauce, as if it were still possible for them to tell the good one apart.

In the pages of *La Repubblica* recently, Beniamino Placido[4] took up a remark I'd made during the course of a debate with Eugenio Scalfari and Giorgio Ruffolo in the same newspaper. I had written that one of the signs of a transformation in Italian mores was the increasing number of Northern Italian comedians, as compared with the large numbers of Southern Italian comedians in the cinema of some years ago. Placido didn't mention me by name, I believe out of a kind of exquisite delicacy, but ridiculed the fact that today's intellectuals prefer *Drive in*[5] to Totò.[6] Placido has misunderstood me, perhaps because another intellectual, and by no means an unknown one, stated some months ago that he really did prefer, if I remember correctly, *Drive in* to Plautus – and exquisite delicacy forbids me from divulging his name.

For my part, I prefer Totò, and the reason Placido misunderstood me was that he, being a Southerner, instinctively distrusted the likes of me, a Piedmontese. Actually there's no point in making ethical judgments about Neo-TV, because it's beyond morality. It's something that exists, like termites, desert dust storms, grape phylloxera or potota blight.

You can reject it, you can destroy it, but first you have to understand, with cool detachment, its relentless inner workings, one of whose features is perhaps the mechanical reactions of its audience. Some day this audience will throw the audience ratings bodies into chaos by flicking nomadically from one image to another, destroying itself along with its own spiritual masters, as well as the sponsors who were hoping to make a killing out of the proliferation of sameness.

If one had to level a criticism at Fellini, it would be that his reaction is evidently still of a moralistic kind. He expresses indignation. If this is the case, the public will not understand his message, because Neo-TV has educated it to live outside ethical boundaries. But we may yet see a sort of boomerang effect being produced from all this, a kind of stratagem of reason, a design of Providence. What might happen is that the public – and the sponsors – start demanding that Neo-TV provides them with the thing that Fellini has promised them. And then, because no programme-maker or scriptwriter could ever match Fellini's imagination, they'd all be dissatisfied and switch off the TV.

1986

PART THREE

———

The Rise and Fall of Counter-cultures

CHAPTER 1

Does Counter-culture Exist?

'COUNTER-CULTURE' is an overused term which, like Resistance, is invariably mentioned so as to reflect well on the person using it. Nobody is against the Resistance, and nobody nowadays would dare suggest that there was anything negative about counter-culture. As always in such cases, the concept itself must be revised by subjecting it to lexical analysis: not just looking at what the dictionaries say, but at everyday usage as well. If 'counter-culture' is an overused term, arguably this is because its antonym, 'culture', is equally overused. Impossible though it might seem, for every three people who talk about 'culture' at least one is thinking of a meaning quite different from that of the others.

Thus in order to define counter-cultural phenomena, we must first define what we mean by culture. Otherwise our argument is obstructed from the outset.

THE CONCEPT OF CULTURE

If the word culture indicates the possession of a stock of knowledge, then clearly the term counter-culture can mean one of only two things: either the lack of any such stock of knowledge, or the possession of *another* knowledge. But the former would mean plain and simple ignorance, the latter a second form of culture. Compared to the notions of physics held by the later Scholastics, Galileo possessed *another* knowledge: is it possible to talk of counter-culture in Galileo's case without over-emphasizing the antagonistic aspect of his polemic? When one speaks of counter-culture today, one is obviously alluding to class cultures, to youth culture as opposed to 'academic' culture, to cultures with their own ethical code, to subordinate cultures, and to the practical manifestations of outsider groups which are opposed to the theoretical assertions of the dominant groups. A range of phenomena so great as to be impossible to group under a single definition without thereby calling into question our society's notion of culture (and this is precisely the point). Or, to put it another way, without being forced to question the ways in which we use the word 'culture'. Or again, without emphasizing the polyphonic nature of the term 'culture' which, on slightly closer inspection, turns out to be like one of those terms which for Wittgenstein set up a network of 'family resemblances'. A typical example is *game*.[1] This can have different characteristics: competitiveness (but little girls' games with dolls don't fit this definition); duality (but that excludes the card game solitaire); physical exercise (which leaves out chess); disinterestedness (which excludes roulette); dependence on rules (but the happy prancing of a child on a lawn doesn't fit). Naturally one could have recourse to classic works of philosophy or cultural anthropology. However, the embarrassment we feel when faced with the term 'culture' has deeper roots and more immediate manifestations, and before we approach the problem of what is meant by Bantu culture, we should first ask ourselves why an economist is a man of culture and yet in every newspaper the economics page is separated from the arts page.

At this point, I think everyday language usage (and a critique of it) provides more insights than scientific discussion. So let's look at the definitions given by various standard dictionaries.

Garzanti. **Culture**: 'A quality of the cultured person; the body of systematically learned notions that are possessed by a person [...] the body of tradition and of scientific, literary and artistic knowledge of a people or of the whole of humanity [. . .] (ethnol.) civilization; also the body of artefacts belonging to a given civilization.'

Zingarelli. **Culture**: 'The complex of notions, traditions, technical processes, modes of behaviour and the like, transmitted and systematically employed, characterizing a given social group, people, or group of peoples, or the whole of humanity [. . .] synonym: **Civilization** [. . .] a quality of the cultivated person [. . .] the complex of hand-made products and techniques belonging to a particular, even extinct civilization.'

Devoto-Oli. **Culture**: 'The harmonious synthesis of a person's knowledge, sensibility and experiences; doctrine, learning [. . .] a particularly lucid and profound series of notions and experiences in a given field [. . .] the complex of spiritual acquisitions of a given place and time (nineteenth-century Neapolitan culture) [. . .] the complex of manifestations of the material, social and spiritual life of a people, in relation to the various phases of an evolutionary process, to different historical periods, or to environmental conditions; **material culture**, civilization as revealed through the study of its technical and social accomplishments.'

What is striking in these definitions is not so much the variety of meanings in each entry (the task of a dictionary is, after all, to register variety in usage) as the discrepancies between one dictionary and another. The Garzanti is vague and at times tautological, the Zingarelli is more up-to-date, while the Devoto is deeply permeated by idealist terminology, yet it is striking that in all of them the ethnological or anthropological meaning is examined but the concept of material culture (manufactures) is treated separately although an integral part of the ethnological notion. Which leads me to wonder whether such uncertainty is not due to a certain resistance in Italian culture towards the ethno-anthropological conception, although the entry in *Webster's New Collegiate Dictionary* is hardly more satisfactory:

Webster. **Culture**: 'The act of cultivating the moral and intellectual faculties especially by education [. . .]. The steady endeavour and excellence of taste acquired by intellectual and aesthetic training [. . .] acquaintance with and taste in fine arts, humanities, and broad aspects of science as distinguished from vocational, technical, or professional skill [. . .] the total pattern of human behaviour and its products embodied in thought, speech, action, and artefacts and dependent upon man's capacity for learning and transmitting knowledge to succeeding generations [. . .] the body of customary beliefs, social forms, and material traits constituting a distinct complex of tradition of a racial, religious, or social group.'

This entry does, however, bring together the anthropological and material aspects, and is a better indication of why newspapers treat culture separately from science, politics or economics, and of how a generic notion of culture and the cultured person emphasizes humanistic and aesthetic knowledge and the organic nature of the higher education received (a feature also present in the first definition in Devoto).

So let us see whether, on the basis of those cited above, it is possible to formulate three definitions of our concept (sifted and ranked in the manner of an encyclopedia rather than a dictionary). I propose therefore that the current meanings of culture be divided into three broad categories: aesthetics, ethics and anthropology. It should be evident that the first two closely interrelated categories are ideological and class-based. The third, far from being 'objective', does nonetheless answer to the requirements of a scientific approach – scientific in the sense of allowing a cautious structural descriptiveness. The pages that follow will then attempt to introduce an element of *evaluation* into this descriptive model.

Culture 1 is counterposed to science, politics, economics and practical/productive activities. It privileges the formation of aesthetic taste, according to the standards of the dominant class of course (Beethoven is culture, while appreciating the singing of drunks is not, unless in the form of ethnological study, nostalgia, or the snob research of kitsch). It is a notion of merchandise turned upside down: culture is what is not useful; it is art or play, not technique. It is the mark of the person who has managed to achieve a state of thoughtful idleness (the Aristotelian idea of the philosopher). It is not possible for everyone, for reasons of class, income and innate ability. It is a sign of distinction. This conception is to be found in newspapers, magazines or publishers' catalogues, in all of which the 'culture' section is kept separate from those devoted to society, production and the economy.

'Counter-culture' may in such circumstances be a political or civic act that challenges the model of the cultured and refined individual dedicated to the cult of the useless. It is counter-cultural to propound a popular or primitive art, or to emphasize the value of political and economic discussion in humanistic contexts. In this sense the student revolt of '68 – which introduced into universities the problems of the working class, political issues, respect for instinctive and 'untamed' creativity – was undoubtedly an expression of counter-culture. However, it remained so only inasmuch as it opposed the dominant philosophy of the humanities faculties.

Culture 2 defines itself as a superior attitude of mind set against the bestiality, ignorance and idolatry typical of the masses (we might recall the polemics of Ortega y Gasset or Adorno[2]). It does not necessarily privilege the 'humanities' and whatever is useless: a bank manager and a customs officer are equally men of culture. Yet the more they manage to free themselves from the requirements of their jobs in order to cultivate the humanities, the more they will be men of culture. In the final analysis, culture is the possession of knowledge in every sense. In this respect, it is a characteristic of men of power (Clausewitz, who knew about strategy, was a man of culture; hence he knew how to win[3]). In its democratic aspects this idea gives rise to appeals for the diffusion of culture among the lower classes. But precisely because practical and manual knowledge are excluded from it. A car mechanic is not a cultured man. The knowledge that goes by the name of culture in this sense is theoretical knowledge that demands a certain detachment from immediate necessities and from action with a direct practical purpose. Therefore this idea of culture also entails a measure of idleness as a necessary condition for cultural growth.

This conception perceives its opposite as negative. So counter-culture is identified as the undiscerning pseudo-culture of mass man, slave to his myths and rituals. Yet such an idea may also be opposed by a counter-culture that accepts its own limits as a challenge, a search for a new human dimension. Look at dissident groups, dropouts, underground communities, people who experience discrimination on the grounds of sex or power, income or luck. A counter-culture of this type proudly adopts a separate language and is identified by expressions of frustrated and anyway uncontrolled impulses and desires. It rejects power and integration. The representatives of this counter-culture today are those who practise absenteeism, the *autori-duttori*, Metropolitan Indians, draft dodgers[4] . . . and so on, right up to the extremes of rejection embodied by the mystics of the P.38,[5] terrorists, the homeless and stateless. We might even say that this idea of counter-culture has come about and sometimes takes such extreme, abnormal forms because bourgeois society has insistently propounded a selective model of culture consisting of technical competence, knowledge directed towards the conquest of power, class exclusivity. Both conceptions are victims of their radicalness: both are ideological. The attitude of the 'cultured' man who does not acknowledge the fertility and ideals of marginal cultures is ideological, as is the attitude of the drop-out who confuses repressive power with power *tout court* and declines to exercise power over reality in order to transform it, refusing to accept the role played by knowledge in changing things. A typical manifestation of dogmatic counter-culture is the claim of some student protest groups that study should be rejected because science contributes to the expansion of power (either of capital or of bourgeois society). And all this when power can get on quite well today without universities (simply employing them as parking lots), precisely because not all knowledge is useful for the achievement of its ends. And when there are some forms of critical knowledge that question the repressive exercise of power, the profit-based society, and the application of technology (and of science) for exploitative purposes.

Culture 3 is the anthropological definition. It comprises the complex of institutions, myths, rites, laws, beliefs, codified everyday behaviour, value systems and material techniques elaborated by a group of humans. Compared to the two preceding concepts, this has an apparently neutral character. In fact, people who speak of culture in either of the above two senses anyway always ascribe to it positive connotations. However, people who talk of culture in the anthropological sense do not necessarily have to approve of a given cultural model in order to describe it. They simply recognize its existence and the fact that it is self-sustaining, or capable of reproducing itself. Another characteristic of culture in the anthropological sense is the fact that it does not necessarily need to be made explicit in order to function: a group may live according to its own cultural model without knowing it. In this sense, there are only two cases in which culture becomes explicit: 1) when confronted with a critical analysis that demonstrates the way it functions, or 2) when a competing model arises (either from within the culture or from outside). In a certain sense, the critique too may only be developed in relation to an alternative model which functions as a metalinguistic point of reference. Those cultures whose experience of other, different cultures has not been traumatic do not identify themselves as a culture, but as the model of humanity pure and simple. For them, anything else is 'barbaric' or non-culture. It is only when the barbarians insinuate themselves into the actual body of the culture in question that that culture learns to recognize different models of cultural organization and simultaneously to define itself and the culture of others.

In this context, there are no counter-cultures, just *other cultural models*. At most, a counter-culture might be identified as an alternative model which the dominant culture is unable to absorb. Imperial Rome saw just such a phenomenon with the penetration of Christianity. Christianity was *another* model compared to the Roman and pagan one, but it came in the long run to be seen as an intolerable deviation. Several centuries had to pass before the two cultures acknowledged each other and were able to coexist in some way. The Christian model naturally absorbed the pagan one and won. There are innumerable reasons why one model prevails over another and this is not the place to examine them; let's just say that there is no such thing as a meta-rule for defining victorious cultures; as we shall see later, the most that can be said is that a rule does exist for defining losing cultures, or cultures that are incapable of perpetuating themselves.

OPPOSITION TO THE ANTHROPOLOGICAL CONCEPT OF CULTURE

The anthropological concept of culture is for obvious reasons among the most difficult to accept. On the one hand it forces us to question our ethnocentricity and the confidence we have that *our* way of living and thinking is the only valid one. On the other hand, for the lexical reasons already mentioned, every time a culture refers to a different model as a 'cultural phenomenon' the threatened culture uses the expression in senses 1) and 2), in the belief that the *other* is being held up as the only positive model. Those peoples who practise cannibalism may be said to share a culture, but to acknowledge cannibalism as a culture does not mean that one is putting it forward as a valid model for other cultures. And yet anyone who speaks of cannibal culture will encounter the hostility of those who suspect that speaking of 'culture' in such a case means singing the praises of cannibalism.

These reflections take on a particular significance if we think of the events of the last few months in which violent demonstrations have broken out on the streets of Italy. Every time somebody tried to ask what were the ideals, values, rationale and rules governing the behaviour of these 'subversive groups', and then translated the question into terms of 'cultural or anthropological phenomenon', they have met a wave of protest from those feeling threatened by such behaviour who regarded the designation 'cultural phenomenon' as a blanket justification.

The present writer has found himself at the centre of a series of polemics which are worth summarizing briefly since they reveal the opposition and prejudices surrounding the anthropological notion of culture.

Some months ago, in an article entitled 'Bacchants and Cannibals' published in *Il Corriere della Sera*, I wrote about a phenomenon that public opinion finds disturbing: the terrorist exercise of political violence. And I said that it was necessary to understand how certain events pointed to the crisis of our model of culture. As an example of alternative 'culture' I used the metaphor (indeed the metonymy) of the P.38. I thought I'd made myself quite clear: while obviously condemning the politics of the P.38, I said that it was possible politically to reject terrorist insurgency without thereby shirking one's (scientific and political) duty to ask oneself about social developments that call for investigation, not facile dismissal.

I was also very explicit in my use of the term 'culture': I used it in the sense in which it has been used by the human sciences for at least a hundred years, to refer to a body of knowledge, beliefs, moral codes, law, custom and 'any other ability and habit man acquires as member of a society' (Tylor[6]).

If culture is understood in this way, it is clear that there are organized and dominant cultures and that there are alternative, often peripheral cultural models. The latter are not always destined for success, but may be acknowledged when they present such characteristics as continuity, organic unity, and correspondence (albeit incomplete) between ways of behaving and theoretical (philosophical or mythological) justifications of actions. Finally, I repeated that talking about drug culture, for instance, does not mean one wishes drugs on one's own children. Rather it means identifying the tendencies within society that could one day lead our children to inject themselves with heroin, allowing us therefore to take corrective action.

When we encounter a cultural phenomenon, we must avoid labelling it as individual deviancy, an accident that can be righted by the strong arm of the law. No doubt the strategists of tension will find recruits among those involved in the new forms of political violence, but what interests me is the increase of such recruitable 'material'. These groups are not reducible to 'a few isolated violent individuals'. Their gesture of revolt is no longer an emanation of the Marxist revolutionary model but harks back to the historic model of millenarian communism that preceded the birth of 'scientific' socialism. But as in its historical forerunners, behind this choice is an economic reality, a 'religiosity', a psychology. And values too (or principles believed to be 'valuable'). Are these values extraneous to our society or are they its counterpoint, reaction, underbelly? To what extent is the ideology of reappropriation directly produced by the ideology of consumerism and prosperity? Is the proposed reappropriation of life (especially when this has connotations of violent expropriation, perhaps even of other people's lives) a product of nineteenth-century revolutionary ideologies or is it a product of late-capitalist ideology which for decades has been repeating that 'we are living in the age of plenty, everybody can have everything'? If such questions are not asked, the belief grows that a few repressive measures will be enough to isolate an underground society of widespread dissent which will then continue to survive and to explode over many years at times when the consensus society is least expecting it. There have been two types of negative reaction to my proposal for a cultural-anthropological inquiry (what is a culture of dissent? where does it originate? what are its economic causes, what its ideology, what political and cultural responses does it force us to consider, and on what scale?).

The first reaction was to use irony (but laced with vicious sarcasm) against those intellectuals who granted the status of 'culture' to these displays of violence. Some even went as far as to say that I had defined the P.38 as a cultural event, using the quotation out of context and distorting it in such a way as to turn it into an insinuation, a piece of moral blackmail. Yet an insinuation of this type could have hit its mark, for our cultural world has not yet shaken itself free of the taboos with which idealist philosophy saddled the word 'culture'. Cultural anthropology apart, even a humanist like Adorno taught his readers to distinguish between individual formation (or *Bildung*) and culture as a social phenomenon (*Kultur*). And even if he didn't like the idea of *Kultur*, in sketching an identi-kit for the 'semi-culture' of mass society he was in effect pursuing good (and serious) cultural anthropology, or at least he was supplying the materials for it.

But there was a second type of reaction which was just as equivocal. I was asked whether I disapproved of Salvemini or Gramsci for not having 'described and justified' the phenomenon of Fascism with cultural anthropology. The answer is no. I blame my critics for having extremely gloomy or over-'American' visions of cultural anthropology. As far as I know, Salvemini and Gramsci both made earnest studies of new 'cultural' models (even if their cultural formation prevented them from using such a term). And I blame those who believe, *à la* Croce, that an explanation is always and necessarily a justification. I have never thought that History was 'justificatory'. It is a mistake to resort to Croce's concept of history (and historiography) in order to discuss questions of new cultural anthropology.[7] Naturally, I am then asked provocatively whether the present is always right. No, there's a difference between saying that the present is always right and saying that it is reasonable to acknowledge the present as a given fact which has to be confronted and explained (as I put it in my article, 'calling cancer by another name will not turn it into a cold'). Only a profound understanding of what is currently happening can produce the political decision to transform the present according to the values we wish to see prevail.

SELF-REPRODUCING CULTURES AND DEPENDENT CULTURES

A good anthropological inquiry does not surrender the concept of value. Even if one's reasoning is carried out in purely structural terms, one has first to discriminate between cultures that are a) *self-sufficient*, b) *self-destructive*, and c) *parasitic* or *dependent*. Liberal bourgeois culture is undoubtedly a model of self-sufficiency: competition is a value that can include everyone, and even those who are defeated or excluded from the outset are a part of the model and contribute to its perpetuation (even if this might not be palatable). Nazi culture was a culture in every respect, with its own rituals, myths, values, customs and cast-iron rules. But it was a culture that contained the seeds of its own destruction: racism prevented the hybridization which is a prerequisite for the health of any race, and the burning of books prevented the development of the scientific discussion which is a prerequisite for the continuous process of adaptation necessary in a dynamic culture. And lastly, 'drug culture', complete with its own values and its own rituals, can survive only as a tolerated alternative within a much larger cultural model that does not itself propound the spread of the drugs principle. In a world made up exclusively of junkies there would be nobody left to run the international drug trafficking business: drug culture presupposes a commercial framework for the buying and selling of drugs and this in turn presupposes a free enterprise culture. Those hippies who artificially recreate an idealized culture of the past in which to live can only do so thanks to the existence of General Motors or the Pentagon, which allow them to languish on the periphery of their model of repressive tolerance.

The same problem arises today with the cultures of absenteeism, proletarian expropriation, happiness and desire. The danger here is not in these cultures' inability to express their own system of values and behaviour, but in their failure to acknowledge their dependency on the dominant bourgeois model. They expropriate what others have produced, or rather what the dispossessed proletarian has produced, accepting the logic of productivity. A culture of desire which claims to be the only dominant model no longer produces the objects to be desired and expropriated. It must therefore transform itself into another cultural model which acknowledges the need within itself for productivity, social consensus and (some form of) state organization.

That is why any rejection of the political in favour of a total, liberating return to the private cannot claim to be anything other than a parasitic model: in order to become a self-perpetuating model, a counter-culture of the private has to find its own internal political dimension.

THE FOURTH DEFINITION OF CULTURE

So there are cultures and there are cultures, and in order to survive, a culture must be able to recognize and criticize itself. Such a critique of one's own cultural model and that of others constitutes the fourth accepted meaning of culture. It feeds upon the third but at a slightly higher metalinguistic level. It is culture as a critical definition of the dominant culture and critical acknowledgment of emerging counter-cultures. When

Marx wrote *Das Kapital* he was creating culture in this fourth sense. A member of an archaic culture who acknowledges the limits of his own model and compares it to the one that is being formed as an alternative, from inside or outside his model, is creating culture in this fourth sense. This fourth sense of 'culture' is always, and in a positive sense, 'counter-culture'. Counter-culture is thus the active critique or transformation of the existing social, scientific or aesthetic paradigm. It is religious reform. It is the heresy of whoever confers a licence upon himself and prefigures another church. It is the only cultural manifestation that a dominant culture is unable to acknowledge and accept. The dominant culture tolerates parasitic counter-cultures as more or less innocuous deviations, but it cannot accept critical manifestations which call it into question. Counter-culture comes about when those who transform the culture in which they live become critically conscious of what they are doing and elaborate a theory of their deviation from the dominant model, *offering a model that is capable of sustaining itself*.

THE ROLE OF THE INTELLECTUAL

At this point it is possible to define another category, and one which is just as ambiguous as those of culture or counter-culture: the category of the intellectual. Let us say right away that an intellectual may be described as being a person who makes it his job to carry out the critical activity described as culture in sense number 4. In other words, the intellectual is always engaged in a counter-cultural critique, independent of whether he is literate or illiterate, humanist or non-humanist, working in isolation or 'politically committed', a *cane sciolto*[8] or an 'organic' intellectual.[9]

Like 'culture', the term 'intellectual' also presents quite a few lexical ambiguities. But I'd like to start by deliberately not consulting the Italian dictionaries for a definition of the term intellectual, since they cannot but reflect the philosophical ideas propounded by Italian culture on the subject. Let me try with a dictionary of English – Webster's – because it's my impression that in America they don't speak about intellectuals in terms of a well-defined politico-social category, as we do here, or at least have done from Gramsci onwards. I find: 'intellectual person', and that's all. Then I see that intellectual is not defined as a noun but as an adjective, so I proceed to the adjective and find: 'being pre-eminently guided by the intellect as distinguished from emotion or experience.' This is no use to me since it's a psychological characterization, and anyway it would exclude Galileo and that seems wrong somehow. I also find: 'given to study, reflection, and speculation', which would exclude the editor of a newspaper who spends his evenings with the type-setters. Then I come across: 'engaged in an activity requiring the creative use of the intellect.' That's more like it, I think. Not that I want to play the xenophile, but the definition provided by the Devoto-Oli is much more perplexing: 'a person gifted with a real or presumed spiritual or cultural superiority; and destined furthermore to play a leading or critical role in a political organization or an ideological tendency', and 'objectively: one who cultivates studies associated with modern humanistic values.' All right, let's go back to the Webster definition. The use of the intellect seems to cause embarrassment, whereas creative use of the intellect is looked upon favourably. But 'creative' is a vague term. The Classical, Medieval, Renaissance and Baroque worlds all distinguished between the liberal arts (intellectual) and the technical arts (manual). According to this distinction, a bad poet is engaging in the liberal arts while Michelangelo and Bernini are engaged in the technical arts, so you see it doesn't work. Today we know that it's possible to think with the hands; if we were to judge Picasso by his utterances he might not seem so very impressive, and yet he 'thought up' some great works.

Shall we say, then, that a person is engaging in intellectual activity when, by wielding a pen or working certain materials, or simply picking up a telephone, he forces others to think and to experience emotions and tastes in a different way?

Confusions arise at this point. For if an intellectual is a person who doesn't work with his hands (this being anyway the most widely-held opinion), then a painter – unless he's a conceptual artist – is not an intellectual, while a director of such and such a section of the Bank of Commerce is. Which would be true of the latter but unfair on the former, for, after all, society looks upon both, albeit in different ways, as 'respectable' people (in the sense that they are not engaged in manual work).

So I think we need to make a distinction between *intellectual work* and *intellectual role*. Intellectual work is work that uses the head more than the hands. It's considered to be less tiring (which is often but not always true), and anyway, society being what it is, it's better paid. That's why so many people want to go to university. Clean hands earn more money than dirty ones. This is only true up to a point because usually a butcher is better off than a Latin teacher. So let's put it this way: one of them is more 'respected'. Very true: the Latin teacher is so happy at being more respected than the butcher that he resigns himself to eating vegetables five days a week. That's why intellectuals look down on non-intellectuals who make money: they are people who have preferred steak to an educational qualification.

Now for the problem of intellectual work: this is carried out by town clerks, bank clerks, big industrialists, professors of Romance Philology and their assistants. Let's say that people such as sculptors, who are engaged in quality manual work and whose products generate intellectual activity, are also engaged in intellectual work (if it wasn't for the fact that their work is discussed by critics and the public, sculptors would make objects for sale by weight, putting themselves on a par with furniture makers). Priests and bishops also do intellectual work. So do the Pope and the union leader. But what about people who perform an intellectual role or function? Here the problem is more difficult. Perhaps at this point we can attempt a typology of the historical meanings of the term 'intellectual', just as we did with 'culture'.

1. *Trade unionist description*: the intellectual as professional, or the pen-wielding intellectual. He who works with his mind. In antiquity, and during the Middle Ages and Renaissance 'technicians' who worked with their hands were not included in this definition. Dante was an intellectual, Masaccio was not. And even more seriously, the Renaissance technicians who had invented new machines and breathed fresh life into scientific theory were not recognized as intellectuals.

2. *Sacred definition*: the intellectual as shaman or holy man. In contemporary terms, the 'piper'[10] to the state or the revolution. The defender of the dominant culture. The repository of values. Superficially, he would appear to have no connection with Benda's *clercs*[11] because these exclude the politically committed and 'organic' intellectual, but basically it's the same thing: he is the conveyor-belt of cultural values (already or yet to be established). At any rate, as in the preceding definition, he has an elitist function, he is one of the chosen ones.

3. *Middle-class definition*: the intellectual with the mandola, the jester. The creative genius who can get away with anything, the bohemian, just so long as he doesn't upset the social order or question it, unless in the laboratory of his creative imagination. He is a clerk who would never carry out a true betrayal. The Academy has been created to accommodate him.

4. *Paleomarxist definition*: the intellectual as the man who puts back on its feet what previously walked on its head. The transformer of the world. In this sense, even the unknown craftsman who invents the mechanical loom can be an intellectual; as can the merchant who invents the cheque; the explorer. But so too can anonymous and collective creativity, and dispossessed working-class inventiveness . . . This would appear to be the most all-encompassing definition were it not for the fact that it begs the question of why dispossessed inventiveness was dispossessible in the first place. Why has the anonymous

culture of proletarian groups, buskers and peripatetic critics of power never manifested itself as a dominant culture, and why has its acknowledgment as a culture (as is the case today) always come about thanks to the dominant culture and intellectuals in senses 1, 2 and 3 of the term? Questions like these suggest that we should put pressure on definition number 4 until it yields the truth, i.e. definition number 5.

5. *The intellectual as critical spokesman of the great cultural transformations*. In this sense, the intellectual is somebody, whether literate or illiterate, artist or technician, who helps make explicit the problem of defining a counter-culture and reveals it to the world. The intellectual is whoever transforms the situation but at the same time maintains a critical awareness of the repercussions of its transformation. The intellectual (whether writer or illiterate agitator) is the self-proclaimed critic and conscience of his own counter-culture within the dominant culture. While the intellectual as shaman reiterates the incest taboo, the intellectual in the critical sense, at the height of the Victorian era, carries out a critique of the incest taboo, outlining its *raison d'être*, its problems, contradictions and uneliminable conditions of existence. Thus did Freud prepare the way for a redefinition of sex within the framework of individual and social life. The question as to whether a culture should, during its counter-culture phase, have a full-time intellectual as spokesman, or whether everybody involved should take turns to perform the role of intellectual, is another problem. Different cultures are characterized by the solutions they give.

However, if a counter-culture is a critical alternative which, acknowledging its own potential for self-reproduction, means to assume power, then the intellectual is the engineer of this power. There is no place for moralism, illusions of innocence, or aesthetic anarchism. The problem of counter-culture and of its intellectuals is, once again, a problem of power.

1983

CHAPTER 2

The New Forms of Expression

1. The question we are asking ourselves today is this: to what extent has literary activity changed due to the presence of other communication systems, and especially of the various phenomena of mass communication? Actually, this question gives rise to a host of other questions:

a) Has literature been forced to break new ground in order to withstand the spread of the so-called mass-standardized languages? (This question would imply that our discourse should be conducted along the lines of Clement Greenberg's thesis as defined in his 'Avant-Garde and Kitsch'[1]: that in the face of an invasion by mass media which concentrate on effects, literature has tended increasingly to establish itself as an *activity that makes a public show of its own production processes*.)

b) Has literature been forced into a compromise with the mass media?

c) Could it be that literature has become the research sector of a communications industry which adopts the stylistic characteristics of literature, while at the same time providing it with new linguistic phenomena on which to conduct its own experiments?

d) in a society dominated by the institutionalized practice of the *multimedia*, does literature still represent a *dignified* activity?

e) What does the practice of literature mean to young people today?

We shall be attempting to answer the last three questions.

2. These three questions would seem to cast doubt on the institution of literature as a *dignified and privileged* activity. One can thus readily appreciate the foolhardiness of attempting to formulate an answer that is theoretically organic, rhetorically convincing, and comprehensive of all the sociological and philological phenomena which should support it. This essay, then, should be understood as the enunciation of some questions, if not for discussion, then at least for disquieting reflection. So that rather than unravelling certain questions, we shall limit ourselves to airing some suspicions, to reading, if you like, the signs in the sky. We shall act not as astrologers (diviners of the future) but as employees in a meteorological office whose job is to make announcements regardless of the effect these will have on society: theirs is not to wonder whether the announcement of a blizzard or of an increase in sunspots will provoke fits of depression and panic suicides among the more physically fragile viewers.

3. I should like to begin by relating my experience as a university teacher and as an editor in a publishing house: it has always been the lot of these two types of functionaries of humanity (to borrow Husserl's flattering expression) to be accosted by young people who pull their latest aesthetic parturition from a pocket or plastic folder in the hope of advice or a publisher's contract. Now, until the mid-1960s these young people would present you with a bundle of poems: at first these were hermetic, then *Linea lombarda*,[2] and later avant-garde. Alternatively, it would be the first chapter of a novel and sometimes (on bad days) the whole novel, in 400 single-spaced pages. I will not recount to all of you (us) veteran liquidators of immature (and sometimes also mature) talents how one wriggled out of such situations. Obviously, when it comes to that we could teach the devil a thing or two. But the fact is, since the

mid-60s, those same young people have been approaching me with two different types of texts: sometimes it's a political manifesto for which they request my sanction (frequently of a pecuniary kind), in the commendable attempt to compromise me in the eyes of the system and help me discover in myself the comrade I didn't know I was; others present large sheets of paper half covered with drawings and with a minimum sprinkling of graphemes, in the manner of a Jules Feiffer comic-strip, the drawing style by turns essential, by turns floral, but always restive and accentuated, irascible and irritated (even when lyrical and elegiac), angry and intense, and in which the phrase, the quip, the semantic scribble does not always have meaning, but represents rather a sort of free roving of language, not unlike that once found in poetry: they are texts which demand concentration and love, generate perplexity and anguish and, as is appropriate to the message with a poetic function, are both ambiguous and self-searching. Yet the context within which they operate is twofold, for the text relates both to itself and to the drawing of which it is a phylactery or reminder, and in any case it is never totally an end unto itself but always in some way bound to everyday life, to politics, to social mores, even when both drawing and *versiculi* take the form of the impartial arabesque.

This means that today there are at least two ways in which young people can make literature: one way is to write politically about politics in a language that belongs exclusively to politics, and which it is the linguist's and the historian's task to study in its 'becoming' and in its play of linguistic dependency and opposition with respect to the language of parliamentary politics; the other is to use the page for a combined exercise in graphics and poetry. This is not to say that some young people aren't still attempting to write poetry and short stories, but in my opinion these (at least the ones who come to me) are the least interesting; the others duplicate or print their poetic texts directly, at their own expense, distributing them on circuits other than those of the culture industry proper: the *ultima Thule*, the underground. And in a country like the United States there is no need to remark on how deeply the new forms of production, distribution and consumption of the literary product have also made their mark and continue to make their mark on style, on content – in a word, on the new linguistic norms that are currently taking shape. The same sort of observation applies to another literary genre which has now achieved a high degree of respectability: the poetic text written to accompany the music of non-commercial singer song-writers, or folk musicians as they are known in America, the most sophisticated of them being Joan Baez and Bob Dylan.

4. This said, we have by no means exhausted the list of different ways in which a young person today can make literature. I shall list a few more, and I would ask that you resist the initial temptation to reject these as 'non-literary'.

The first example is a bogus sociological questionnaire distributed by a group of architectural students in Florence called 'Gruppo Ufo'.[3] I have put this text at the end but it can be consulted at random. There is nothing to stop us considering the questionnaire as a questionnaire, because in fact it asks to be filled in. It isn't clear whether the text is the questionnaire itself (which has an identifiable author), the various completed versions (including answers from unidentified authors, and no known results), or the very experience of distributing and completing the questionnaire (or the refusal to do so).

The second example concerns something known in America as guerrilla television groups (and now emerging in Italy). These are groups that aim to produce and show, either on the screen or on closed-circuit TV, audiovisual happenings in which the image is matched to the discourse – discourse encompassing not only the presenter of the image but those reacting to it. Happenings of this sort are intended for group experience; sometimes the record of the discussions that ensue, from tape recordings to typewritten pages, forms the basis for yet another production, this time of cyclostyled material: the result is an exchange, a verbal and visual provocation that turns into theatre, debate, and constitutes the sole method by which certain groups express themselves and produce culture. Often the audiovisual material, which is a mixture of cinema, slides, posters and debates in progress, comes out of a previous study – of the press or of television production, let's say – and these in turn become the objects of a political critique, stimulating what are known as 'counter-information' activities. If *The Encomium of Helen*[4] read on the Athens *agora* was literature, then it is difficult to see why the extraparliamentary anti-eulogy of that Paris, Giovanni Agnelli of Fiat, referred to affectionately on the Turin assembly lines as the *Avvocato*, shouldn't also be literature (by reason of generic classification if not of specific excellence).

Sometimes the happening takes the form of exhibitions of counter-information: a theme (the predicament faced by a certain urban neighbourhood, the distribution of green space in the city, the right to housing) is chosen as the subject of an exhibition in which different media are employed, such as posters, slogans, argumentation by syllogism, photographs, press cuttings or official documents, pinball or the juke box, and in the end involving the local production in a discussion that sometimes lasts for days.

I have seen students, before they even set about writing their texts, posing themselves rhetorical problems of *kairos* – evaluating the likely reactions of their audience, the linguistic level of the target group, techniques of non-hypnotic persuasion, and organizing images and text according to the dictates of argumentation technique. For me, this is *writing*: giving a dialectal tone to the *act* by means of the *ornate*, rediscovering the rules of a new *cursus*; giving expression to *endoxa* with *edysmata*, constructing *callidissimae juncturae* . . .

The desire to be a 'true historian' that inspires these new writers is no different from the desire of the Romantics to give a stylistic response to a problem of political pedagogy. I wonder if Tommaso Grossi or Cesare Cantù[5] will outlive these exhibitions of counter-information just because they were astute enough to entrust their labours to the long-lived book form and did not, as the authors of exhibitions do, dismantle their 'text' after a week in order to recover the materials.

I could also cite the wall posters on *tazebaos* which adorn our universities when not destroyed by the rectors. Not that I want to claim that *tazeboas* are usually examples of good graphics and good political literature (indeed, sadly I take the opposite view). Not because they are visually revolting or stylistically dissimilar from a good *feuilleton* in *Il Corriere della Sera*; in fact, it is precisely this which allows them to be classed as specimens of a *new genre*, to be valued chiefly for its morphological characteristics and not according to some model of perfection. The reason is rather that such exercises are often not consistent with the poetics they express, and are hence both abortive and politically and literarily negative. A less ethnocentric and paleohumanist reading might lead us to see them as examples of a new mode of voicing our thoughts, a mode whose rules and underlying structures have yet to be grasped in order to be adequately judged.

5. These and other examples of how young people use the word and other sign systems could, however, be seen simply to show that literature is 'elsewhere', or rather, is dead. If it weren't that an implicit semiology underlies these exercises, albeit one that is introjected unconsciously: the certainty that the rules of signification are in large measure the same whether they produce a text with words or a sequence of images and sounds, making the use of several registers worthwhile. In other words, in texts judged by the man of letters not to be 'writing' a praxis of *subverting writing* exists which produces

subversive writings. It is no longer important whether these writings tread the paths of *grammata* or icons, or even of semiotic clusters in which different canons interacting among themselves produce *formosae deformitates et deformes formositates* – incredible multimedia syntagma which allude to a new aesthetic paradigm of the functional, the conditions of a new *apta coordinatio signorum*.

Nor can we forget, moreover, that new critical practices have been developed which sustain this new signifying practice. Even in our universities the more traditional courses of philology are today supplemented by texts on the language of advertising, on the relationships between verbal and visual registers in the new forms of communication, on the rules governing title composition in newspapers, on the structures and the narrative functions of the comic strip. In this new critique of the multimedia language, the ideological critique of content adopts, in the best cases, the methods of a formal critique of the sign-clusters. It is here more than in those practices anchored to venerable traditions that the salvation required by formalism is found, and semiotics is revealed as the new form of cultural anthropology, sociology, criticism of ideas, and aesthetics.

6. We must now take a step backwards. Because this situation – that is to say, the new ways of conceiving of the practice of the sign and of the 'deviant' forms of literature of which I am speaking – has been made possible only because it was preceded by other phenomena. There was a moment in which contemporary literature believed it could provide an alternative in opposition to the language of the mass media, the scleroticized languages of bourgeois everyday life flattered by so much literature priding itself on the size of its print runs and on tourist-season literary prizes. This radicalization of the opposition came about with the advent of the neo-avant-garde, and however great one's distaste it must be credited with the

invention of a cult of provocative incomprehensibility.

Then suddenly it all came to an end with a development that the neo-avant-garde[6] had itself foreseen: society showed itself capable of swallowing even this unacceptable way of speaking.

The excerpts I should like to read are taken from a collection which Lamberto Pignotti put together some years ago in an article in the Italo-Yugoslav magazine *la Battana*, combining lines by the poets Pagliarani, Cesarano, Sanguineti and Balestrini with ads.

Allow me to read to you some of these 'poetic' passages:

> Relassez vous è l'ultima parola della scienza
> contro i mali moderni, aggiorna aggiorna i due
>   comandamenti

> Relassez vous is science's last word
> against modern maladies, update update the two
>   commandments
>
> (Pagliarani)

> Non dobbiamo più
> partire di febbraio: la nebbia è più nebbia
> febbraio più febbraio

> We must no longer
> depart in February: fog is more fog
> February more February
>
> (Cesarano)

> Il mondo è tutto
> alla rovescia
> La porta è sopra il tetto
> il cane cammina sul cielo
> il lago galleggia
> sul battello di gomma

The world is all
topsy turvy
The door is on the roof
the dog walks in the sky
the lake floats
on the rubber ferry

(Pirelli)

È come una carezza, una lieve
silenziosa carezza
che sfiora il vostro viso

It's like a caress, a soft
silent caress
that lightly touches your face

(Gillette)

L'orizzonte è veramente orizzonte
il paesaggio è paesaggio il mundus sensibilis è mundus
    sensibilis
la coniunctio è coniunctio il coitus il coitus

The horizon is truly horizon
the landscape is landscape and the mundus sensibilis is
    mundus sensibilis
the coniunctio is coniunctio coitus coitus

(Sanguineti)

Cominciò come un gioco poi l'idea prese forma
uno due tre elementi con molte composizioni a scelta
[. . .]
nelle vetrine quelli che volgono
oppure gli oggetti più nostri o il servizio buono

It began as a game then the idea took shape
one two three elements with several compositions to
   choose from
[. . .]
the ones turning in the shop windows
or the objects most bearing our mark or the good dinner
   service

                               (Mobili Elam)

      quelle luci! molli!
      miseramente vidi lei, ancora in quella nebbia

      those lights! soft!
      unhappily I saw her, in that fog still

                              (Sanguineti)

      Una sola ombra offusca quei giorni
      la sensazione che essi scorrano troppo presto
      Una sola amarezza: lasciare la
      nave al termine del viaggio

      One shadow alone casts gloom over those days
      the feeling that they are passing too quickly
      One sorrow alone: leaving
      the ship at the end of the voyage

                            (Compagnie Italia)

tutto tace nella bocca piena di sangue lo sgombero della
   neve
su tutta la strada i passi necessari perché non entrino i leoni
si libra ad ali tese sull'erba fuori l'estate fu calda

all's quiet in the blood-filled mouth the snow plough
all over the street the steps necessary so that the lions don't
   get in

it hovers with outspread wings over the grass outside the
    summer was hot

(Tape Mark I)

The little game I've played on you does not mean, bearing in
mind context and circumstances, that the avant-garde passages
have had the same impact and force as the advertising copy
and vice versa. It just served to show the voracity with which
society overtakes literature, making use of its creative impact
to castrate and steal its power, as in any cannibalistic rite worth
its salt. Not one line of the Novissimi[7] poets loses validity
just because some clever advertising copywriter changes its
outward stylemes. Yet understandably, faced with the possible
standardization of language and the disappearance of the
'Otherness of the Same', a new generation decided that writing
had to become something else: maybe not even writing, but
putting up posters, scrawling provocative messages on walls –
and even the writings on walls have been subjected to a rhetoric
analysis in order to demonstrate that a slogan may sometimes possess the same intensity as a satyrical couplet in an
anthology. I will not cite the well-worn Sorbonne slogans,
but a phrase that appeared on the walls of the Faculty of Architecture of the University of Milan: 'Workers, do you want
your children to go to university? Enrol them in the police
force.' Maybe I'm jumping to conclusions but perhaps this is
a new way of saying, 'Your Excellency who scowls upon me'.[8]
It's certainly more concise, but no less tragic for that and, at
the end of the day, no less permeated with human and ferocious
compassion.

7. Making up a good slogan does not mean giving up using
words in favour of pure action. However, it may mean that
provocation is no longer purely identified with deviations
from the verbal norm, but rather with deviations from the
conceptual norm. On the other hand, the neo-avant-garde had

already attempted a critique of the content but had itself taken on these contents in the scleroticized forms that they assumed in mass society (which is why the need arose to carry out a critique of the contents by means of a multimedia fusion or rather a combination of poetry and visual-verbal material, a collage of the various forms in which mass society enunciates and confirms its ideology).

I am here referring to those experiments with visual poetry which had their first (but not their last) centre in the Florentine Gruppo 70:[9] it is difficult to say at what point visual treatment began and verbal treatment ended. It was the first symptom of a literature that no longer recognized itself in its canonical forms (and which, moreover, began again to create words-in-freedom works on the Futurist model, but this time in such a way as to place more emphasis on content than on form).

8. Neo-avant-garde methods included: cuts-outs and montage, tape-recordings, free use of language spoken by others and (in the ultra-paternalistic mass media) against others. Remember Nanni Balestrini's verbal collages.[10] But with his recent novel *Vogliamo tutto*, Balestrini, who after '68 became an extra-parliamentary political activist, gives us what for me is a fine example of a literary use of expressions that were then burgeoning in factories and mass meetings, caught between student unrest and worker fury.

Glancing through the newspapers of the political groups we come across attempts (often ingenuous) to *invent* a 'national-popular' language.

With its lyrical demagogism whose stylemes partly flow from bad translations from the Chinese and partly from the corrupting example of neorealistic mannerism, the choice of language produces results like these in *Servire il popolo*, the organ of the Union of Marxist-Leninists:

> They put up the price of bread and meat and all the
> while the price of furs and jewels for the squalid mis-
> tresses of the bosses and political crooks remains the
> same.

An alternative to this revolutionary kitsch is seen in the
attempt made by the weekly *Lotta Continua* to elaborate a
spoken Italian interwoven with everyday, technical or dialect
terms, some of them obscene. Here, the defect is not in being
over-vulgar, but if anything in being too cultured, resulting in
something more reminiscent of Testori or Gadda than of the
assembly line:

> Workers' pay-packets are one big swindle and nobody
> can make them out.
>   Some of my mates are welders who get a pension
> for being deaf 'cos it's like this, you're welding, say,
> and along comes a beveller and takes his chisel to your
> welding and it drives you mad.

What interests us, however, is not just that a political newspaper attempts to reproduce (and promote) the language of
workers, but the fact that this workers' language exists and has
its own *texts*: factory discussions and leaflets or speeches at
mass meetings.

These texts are *texts* for two reasons: a) they are recorded
word for word either on paper or on tape; b) they are conceived
as *texts*, i.e. as discourses constructed for persuading, agitating,
arousing, setting out the facts.

The fact that these texts are created *spontaneously,* from
below, does not mean that no consideration is given to their
communicative power. And it is this consideration that makes
them objects of critical interest (otherwise their only value
would be as linguistic documents).

9. The extent to which they constitute *texts* may be seen when

a writer takes them on, as in the case of Balestrini's *Vogliamo tutto*. Here are two examples. In the first example, we have the taped record (in which manipulation is carried out not on the lexical or syntactical level, but rather in the clever juxtaposition of the narrative units, or the macrosyntagmatic) of a worker's discourse before the advent of class consciousness, all anger, indignation and ferocity:

So I go off home. At home I never washed my finger and it was all covered in that black grease. I never washed it nor even moved it and I made sure not to rest it on anything. After six days it had swollen up a bit. That's why I never moved it, to make it swell up. If you move your fingers, they lose the swelling. But if your finger gets hurt and then you never move it, it really swells up and gets bigger than the others. Not that it swells much, but you can see that it's a bit bigger. And it's smoother as well, because you haven't used it to touch anything.

I go back after six days and say: Look this finger has swollen up. It still seems to hurt. But can't you work with it like that? No, because we work with our hands. If I have to pick up a bolt or use the gun, that thing for screwing on the bolts – it's called a gun – I have to use my hands. Now, either I'm careful about what I'm doing, the bolts I pick up, or I'm careful about my finger and don't let it touch anything. This means I have to watch what I'm doing and keep an eye on my finger as well. There's no way I can do that. Because after three hours of banging away on something it ends up getting on my nerves, I go crazy and hit someone over the head with something. I can't do it.

The doctor guesses that I'm having him on and so he makes me a proposal: Would you rather go back to work or be admitted to hospital? I thinks to myself: I've gotta stand my ground here, because it costs them more to take me into hospital. He can't justify sending a worker to hospital for a finger, no way. He was bluffing, he was thinking: this guy wants to have another three or four days holiday so I'll threaten him. And he'll go back to the factory rather than go to hospital. You're fucked in hospital, you can't have any fun in there, you just have to lie there and that's it.

So I say: No, I'll go to hospital then. Because as far as I can see my finger is still hurting, and it's no better. So he turns and says to someone: Get the hospital form for this man. I was hopping mad, I thought: He's got me, the bastard.

The second part of the book marks the worker-protagonist's passage from apolitical absenteeism to class consciousness by assembling sequences of argument from agit-prop leaflets and turning them into narrative sequences:

What do we workers want? We've said it over and over again, with all-out strikes at the Mirafiori foundries in the North and South. We want a 200 lire an hour increase on basic pay, or wage parity with the steel workers. That means a rise of 30,000 lire on the monthly basic wage, and not the paltry sum offered by the boss. On the production lines, we want a 50 lire increase on basic pay. Regrading for all workers after six months in the factory. We want it all now. No bargaining. Nothing in lieu of agreements. We don't want the bosses' line-speeds. What we say to the owner and the unions is this: the shop steward is no use to us. What we need is a meeting of the sections and workshop committees to organize a permanent struggle against the boss, his line-speeds, his henchmen. Let's organize, let everyone be a delegate.

> Workers, when we are in struggle, the boss is weak,
> now is the moment to attack. We have to organize
> ourselves, workshop by workshop, and spread our
> struggle further.

Although it is presented and operates as a means of political
engagement, *Vogliamo tutto* is still a book, a literary exercise.
Vogliamo tutto is literature because, through the use of montage
techniques (that make reality 'strange'), we are allowed to discover discourses as if listening to them for the first time; or
they are presented to us for the first time in the pages of a
book although already in existence outside literature and
maybe already literature before Balestrini incorporated them
into literature – literature meaning the ability to articulate ver-
bally, the means to discover, if not reality, then a novel and
rich way of interpreting and experiencing it.

10. What is happening here is that there is a blurring of the
distinction between the aesthetics and the practical, the birth
of new aesthetic parameters, and lastly the collapse of a dialectic
of distinctions. As we have seen, it is not only the distinction
between genres that is lost, so that on the one hand the discourse of literature is linked with that of sectoral and technical
languages, and on the other with that of music and the visual
arts. The distinction is lost between 'poetry' and 'literature',
and thus the distinction of the forms of the spirit, at the very
moment in which the aesthetic can no longer be pursued as a
preferential and autonomous sphere but is reabsorbed in the
practical and the economic, as well as the theoretical. So that
the task of literature (or of art) ceases to be that of producing
Beauty in isolation, and returns to being what it was in Ancient
Greece, before idealist Romanticism and before the Renaissance: one aspect of that wider range of activity going under
the terms of *techne* or *ars*. This entails an *act* of making whose
purposes are less restricted, and whose aesthetic value, if one

exists to be recognized, is displayed only as the quality of an achievement definable by other parameters.

According to Jacobson, language may have various functions: referential, expressive, conative, metalinguistic, of which the aesthetic or poetic function is only one.[11] A discourse is rarely articulated in such a way that only one function is operative. It is rather that one function overshadows the others, without the others disappearing into the background. Literature in the traditional sense of the term allowed the aesthetic function to prevail overpoweringly to the detriment of the others. Now once again, an idea of literature is emerging as signifying practice in which the aesthetic function is no longer privileged. The 'Forms of the Spirit', to evoke those ghosts still known to some of us, are vanishing as distinctions because the Forms of Communication are changing. Nor can one see how the ghostly Spirit can be anything but a mode of communication and part of culture.

Today we are beginning to recognize that there has been a change in the purposes of communication. In this perspective, it may be that the institution of Literature has to be reformed along with the university institution by which it has been defended: Literature should no longer be a Faculty – a place for cultivating specific and exclusive vocations – but a centre or crossroads at the service of many vocations.

APPENDIX

Elements of Territorial Proxemics (Questionnaire distributed by Gruppo UFO, Florence)

have you ever noticed that certain repressive insti-   yes   no
tutions of the bourgeois state such as *prisons, con-*

vents, army barracks, secret bases, police stations (even local ones) are permanently surrounded by a kind of protective psychological ring, a special type of magnetic field that is determined by singularly strange circumstances?

do you think that the sentries, who are obviously there on guard, have something to do with this? yes no

do you think that these emissions are given out by some kind of cryptopower? yes no

do the occurrences and the things connected with these sorts of institutions seem to you to form a single entity of a symbolic type? yes no

if yes, have you ever seen a building that is active? yes no

and a car? yes no

have you ever experienced an apparition involving events, people and things, when you had the vague feeling, but unwillingness to admit the possibility, that there was a connection (subsequently verified) with what is described above? yes no

have you ever, while in the vicinity of these institutions, been subjected to psychological, bodily or any other sort of violence? yes no

on the part of whom? ....

have the emissaries of these hidden powers ever spoken to you on some pretext or other, or because you had committed actions which in any other part of the territory, probably just beyond that magnetic ring or whatever, wouldn't even have been noticed? yes no

describe ....

are you prepared to describe more generally one (or more) experiences you've had of this type?   yes   no

describe..

once over this adventure, did you catch yourself thinking that it might have been [*a dream / a joke / a conspiracy*]?

thinking you'd passed through a place bewitched so that less personal freedom existed there than in other parts of the territory?   yes   no

did you think that it might have been what is commonly known as 'a figment of the imagination'?   yes   no

have you recently noticed any sudden disappearances or occurrences, persons or things while in the vicinity of said institutions, especially allied military bases?   yes   no

describe..

attempt by means of a diagram to describe the topography of the place, providing exact points of reference:

have you ever noticed morphological transformations of the territory due to camouflaged prostheses of entrances, exits, secret hatchways?   yes   no

do you believe in the existence of UFOs?   yes   no

have you ever had contact with beings from other worlds?   yes   no

which..

can you readily distinguish the fields of influence exerted by different institutions upon the area?   yes   no

can you painstakingly follow, find them again and connect them, even during a journey?	yes	no
when you leave the city?		
no! I meant to say, when do you stupidly get the idea you're leaving the city?		
do you think it depends on the signposts of bour-geois geography?	yes	no
or the newness of the buildings?	yes	no
or unlet shops?	yes	no
or the sudden appearance of a gardener running away?		
do you believe in the existence of the perfection of the periphery?	yes	no
do you think it's just a source of big profits for some people?		
for whom?..		
did you know that a burglar who escapes into the periphery is nabbed immediately?	yes	no
why is it that in the city or the country, the same burglar can get away with it?		
can he get away with it?	yes	no
have you decided now how to behave at university?	yes	no
and at home?	yes	no
could you deduce (guess) from the preceding evi-dence the activities of the inhabitants, the time of day, their education, their habits?	yes	no

on a trip abroad can you instantly recognize the institutions similar to the ones you are so familiar with at home?	yes	no

(This area of observation includes motorways, ANAS houses, state railways, children's institutions and more generally *industry-agriculture-service sectors*).

	yes	no

Note: Given the importance of this point, a case by case analysis would be preferable, except for overlaps; in this regard it is important to place oneself in a privileged and completely subordinate vantage point. Anyway give precedence to those aims that are truly aims with a crudely realist bias, i.e. the evidence.

did you know that cars are public property?	yes	no
would it therefore be sensible to interrupt motorways every 100km with 200 metres of deciduous woodland?	yes	no
do you think that these walks in order to change cars may be good for people?	yes	no
even in America?	yes	no
would you like it?	yes	no
in your observation of and search for the evidence, do you feel conditioned by the segregation that the city imposes?	yes	no
do you feel yourself to be truly a part of the life of the area with all its infinite secrets?	yes	no
have you ever thought that every act of segregation or camouflage increases the hidden power of those responsible for it?	yes	no

have you ever, in the vicinity of these institutions,   yes   no
seen people from windows?

and shot from cannons?   yes   no

where ....

have you ever watched a race run in laps and wit-   yes   no
nessed a hijacking from the track?

reconstruct in the heat and cold of the moment, if
you happen to possess any means whatsoever of
gathering information, the circumstances in which
you found yourself:

(Photographs of buildings, topographical dia-
grams, magnetic tapes, film, microfilms, occasional
opinions of witnesses, interviews, telephone
numbers, aerial photos, photos of the area, video-
tapes, account books, *real solid evidence*, and anything else that might be of use in providing
information on the case in question.)

have you ever tried to gain an insight into a police-   yes   no
man's brain taking his uniform as your starting
point?

you are standing in front of a building, the head-   yes   no
quarters of one of the aforementioned institutions:
do you observe its formal characteristics, try to see
what is going on inside it, pausing to consider
apparently insignificant details, do you think that
you are on the edge of a world completely
extraneous to you, to your hopes for the future,
do you try to guess the complex of habits that
regulate its inner workings, do you think you find
yourself in front of a kind of unknown monster of
enormous dimensions which is eating, ruminating,
spitting flames, shitting, and busying itself solely
with things that have to do with itself, sending its

emissaries and executors throughout the whole of
the surrounding area?

have you ever been a member of a clandestine   yes   no
organization, or a secret sect?

which?...

have you taken part in initiation rites?
where? (describe the exact places and circum-
stances): ....
what do you think of Freemasonry?

do you think that it has anything to do with the   yes   no
current political situation?

and with the situation in which schools find them-   yes   no
selves?

how many times a day do you make love with your
wife (or girlfriend or lover etc.)?...........................

do you think that drugs are a way of ruling the
world?...

in what way?..

are you willing to pardon these digressions?   yes   no

do you excuse their banality?   yes   no

at what level do you think that secret organizations
intervene (if they do intervene) in controlling
schools (universities):
janitors?...
students? ....
demonstrators? ....
junior lecturers?...
senior lecturers?...
higher grades? ....

what strategy do you intend to adopt in order to have a family?..

would you know how to shoot at a B-52?	yes	no
and at an F-104?	yes	no
do you think you'd win or be overwhelmed by forces more powerful than your own?	yes	no
secret ones?	yes	no

if somebody told you that to obtain an official (or non-official) post as ass-licker you'll have to sell yours, what would your reply be? ....

(In answering this last question remember that you are free to cite actual examples that have taken place, complete with names, occasions, people, things, etc.)

if these questions seem too peculiar and limiting (too individualistic) do you think that class consciousness could help you to resolve your problem?	yes	no

through which parties?...

do you think this questionnaire isn't objective?	yes	no
so you'd be willing to found a new mass movement?	yes	no

what do you think of the technicians' crisis? ....

have you ever seen an unemployed technician?	yes	no

if so, where?...

was he seeking work?	yes	no

was he taken on?	yes	no

at how much per month?.....................................

where?..

by whom? ....

tel. no. ....

is it important to you to get good marks?	yes	no
to do well in your exam?	yes	no
to do a good piece of research?	yes	no
to have a good political line?	yes	no

which of the four?   I   II   III   IV

why? ....

you'd like to hold a conference in the Vatican on the subject of

....	yes	no
and in China?	yes	no
can you give the names of 10 people who think as you do on a number of counts?	yes	no

and 100 that don't think like you?........................

excuse me, but do you think these questions are *brainteasers*, the product of a sick imagination?	yes	no
would you be willing to take part in a serious investigation into *cryptopowers*, to uncover the evidence?	yes	no

   so, tell me:

have you ever been questioned by the police? by the barman of 'Ordine Nuovo?'	yes	no

have you ever realized that you're not in the same place and same mental situation from casual evidence such as the heat difference between one zone and another of the city, a sudden swoop of birds, different sounds relative to the main activities of a place, strange smells perceived olfactorily with a quasi-erotic taste, something that comes over you all of a sudden, a strange indefinite feeling of disquiet, an emptiness inside, suspicious presences in the full light of day?   yes no

have you ever seen particular signs of life – thick vegetation, flights of birds, presence of animals, motionless coleoptera, bats hunting in the morning – in the vicinity of the institutions under examination?   yes no

let's start with you: yes no
are you guilty or not guilty?

cyclostyled edition, supplement to *Rheinische Zeitung*, editor Karl Marx

1973

CHAPTER 3

On Chinese Comic Strips: Counter-information and alternative information

THE IDEA OF counter-information encompasses two distinct types of communication: alternative information, and counter-information in the strict meaning of the term. Even if the two phenomena fall under a single sociological definition, meaning that both can be described as another way of using the circuit of mass communications, their difference lies in the fact that alternative information is defined as such for ideological reasons, and its shifts are at the level of *content* in the articulation of messages, while counter-information is designated as such for technical reasons and because of its specific stance in relation to the *channel* and the *codes* of the receiver, even if ultimately it brings about a change in the content of the message. To be more precise, let's say that alternative information acts on the message as a *signifying form*, while counter-information acts on the message as an existing *signified*.

By *alternative information* we mean all the messages which, within a given society (or when comparing two societies), aim to reformulate their content in a different way from the one typical of the official circuit of mass communications. Examples of alternative information within a single social context are political tracts or newspapers such as *L'idiot international, La*

Cause du Peuple, Il Manifesto or the underground press. This type of information uses the same channels as mass communications (or else alternative channels that are structurally homologous) and ultimately it experiences the same problems as official information, since the transmitter knows what message is being transmitted and by which code he would like it to be decoded, but he doesn't really know whether all the receivers will decode it in the same way.

Counter-information, on the other hand, has a *parasitic* relation to the official message at its point of reception and it operates so as to encourage the receiver to: a) read the message using other codes; b) identify the codes by which the transmitter wanted the message to be read in order to infer their ideological intentions; c) analyse the message so as to draw attention to the transmitter's manipulations of the signifiers, in order to achieve a given response from the receiver, whose decoding is fixed in the desired way or to whom unexpected decodings are suggested at the level of emotive connotations. Counter-information takes place, for example, when: 1) school pupils reread their set books in a critical way; 2) Berlin students stop people in the street to persuade them to think about the content and the presentation of news items published in the newspapers of the Springer group; 3) listener groups organize television audiences in such a way that news or television shows are received and discussed from a conscious and critical perspective; and so on.

We can see, then, that counter-information uses the already transmitted message to alter the response of the receiver. The result is that, by comparison with alternative information, it has the advantage of effecting a *face-to-face control* of the communication instead of transmitting other messages in competition with those of official information of which the decoding is quite aleatory.

On the basis of these observations, the comic strips published in China by the government of the People's Republic constitute examples of *alternative information* (at the level of opposition between two societies) and not counter-information (we shall return to this later).

What is interesting about these comic strips is not primarily the act that they are (as one could expect) the vehicle for a different ideology from that of Western comic strips. Their interest for us has more to do with another question: whether modalities of communication similar to those in the West can in reality be the vehicle for a different ideology, or whether the form of the mass communication process does not already imply a fixed ideologization of the product. And there is also the question: on the basis of which signifying strategies and which formulation is the different ideology actually presented?

First, though, it is worth including some background information on these *media*.

THE ORIGINS, NATURE AND IDEOLOGY OF CHINESE COMIC STRIPS

Around the middle of the nineteenth century there appeared in Chinese newspapers illustrations with long captions in the main body of the drawing (this was not unprecedented: Chinese paintings have always had commentaries or even poems by their author in one of the corners). The illustrations represented scenes from daily life – exemplary punishments for those lacking in filial respect as decreed by Confucian morality, weddings, condemnations of opium abuse; later, they included modern innovations – the bicycle, the sewing machine as adopted by the ladies of Shanghai.

They were not complete stories; they were rather concise annotations from which the illustrations were independent.

Foreign comic strips first began circulating in a number of Chinese cities on the Pacific coast (in particular in Shanghai, Canton, and Tien-Tsin) during the 1930s and 40s. *Mickey*

Mouse, Flash Gordon, Mandrake, The Phantom, etc. These were fairly well translated, and had a distribution that did not extend beyond the children of the comfortable 'comprador' middle class who attended schools run by Westerners, or beyond the large cities where there was an active Western presence. In the rest of China, beyond the coastal strip, comic strips did not exist.

After the Liberation (1949) the Communists began producing comic strips. And it was no accident that the first publishing houses to put out comic strips were located in Shanghai, the most 'Western' city in China. To begin with, the narratives were mere entertainment for an audience of young people: war stories with patriotic undertones but low in ideological content. Photonovellas, put together using film stills, were more commonplace and already more ideologized, given that Sino-Communist cinema has from the outset, with rare exceptions, been used as a tool of politicization.

It was probably some time between 1958 and 1960 that the Chinese comic strip took an independent direction. In any case, in his study on 'Chinese comic strips as counter-culture', Jean Chesnaux locates the origins of this type of popular culture, a longstanding figurative tradition and Western influences aside, in a very clear political decision made in Yanan, the Chinese guerrilla capital during the struggle against the Kuo-Min-Tang (1937–49).

> Out of patriotism, out of concern to get closer to the people, out of sympathy for the Communist struggle, a great many intellectuals and artists had in fact left the cities at that period, to join up with guerrilla bases and lead the harsh life of the partisans. But they were not so wholly won over to new ideas; they often retained an elitist conception of culture and art. In May 1942 a large meeting was held in Yanan during which several hundred of them debated with Commu-

nist leaders, soldiers and peasants. In his opening speech, Mao stated: '*The presence of these writers and artists in Yanan in the heartland of the resistance bases does not in itself mean that they have achieved a total fusion with the popular masses of these bases. Now, a fusion of this kind is indispensable if we wish to advance our revolutionary work. The conference which we are opening today must help us truly to transform literature and art so that they become an integral part of the general motor of revolution, a powerful means of rallying and educating the people, a fearsome weapon enabling us to defeat and wipe out the enemy, a tool capable of helping the people in their unanimous struggle against the enemy.*'

Two fundamental questions were debated at the meeting. First, 'In whose service must our literature and our art exist?' The answer given was: the people. This implied a renunciation of elitist ways, a denunciation of culture as an end in itself, a definition of art and literature as activities that were part and parcel of the life of the community.

The answer to the first question itself prompts the formulation of the second question: 'How should we serve the great popular masses?'

Discussion around this second question seems to have been more complex. For some it was primarily an issue of maintaining and above all raising the cultural 'level' of works destined for the people. Whereas for others what mattered most was to make literature and artistic works accessible to all. In his conclusion, Mao did not skirt this dilemma. He acknowledged that the question of standards was a serious one but he intimated that reaching a wide audience was more important than the raising of standards as – yet again – an end in itself, regardless of the social environment of the works: 'broadly accessible means accessible to the people; the raising of standards means the raising of standards for the people.'

In his closing speech, Mao put particular emphasis on the need for writers and artists not to confine themselves to the areas of 'aristocratic' culture (classical theatre, the novel, poetic conventions, painting on silk) and not to scorn popular artistic and literary forms: 'Our masters of the pen must give their attention to the wall newspapers published by the masses, and to letters from military units at the front; our master playwrights to the small companies working among military units and in the villages' ...

This same 'line on the masses', the same concern to make intimate connections between cultural life and political struggle, is expressed in the famous woodcuts of the Yanan period. These peasant prints, easily understood and appreciated by peasants many of whom could not read, expressed the harshness of work in the fields, the severity of oppression by landowners and the Japanese, the strength of the peasant movement. A peasant dance like the *yangke*, which was very popular in the guerrilla bases around 1940 (and whose simplicity impressed the Western journalists visiting these areas), also expresses the priority of collective imperatives, the strength of the people here being almost physically united in a single movement. No couples alone or embracing, no individual performances, but the whole village in a circle, singing and performing very simple rhythmic movements.

The simple, communal, politicized, easy-going culture of Yanan thus represented a version of the Chinese Communist that was very different from the image given by even the most unequivocal revolutionary intellectuals during the 1920s when the great faceless cities like Shanghai were the centre of Communist struggles. At Yanan it was possible for the intellectual to connect with the people; in Shanghai, it was very difficult. In the history of Chinese Communism, Shanghai man is in opposition to Yanan man (an opposition which was to reach its apotheosis in the 1960s with the 'struggle between the two lines' and the conflict between Mao Zedong and Liu Shaoqi).

Chinese comic strips belong to the cultural patrimony of Yanan man.

IDENTIFYING SOME FORMAL ELEMENTS

These comic strips seem to take their cue from a graphic mode that is somewhat traditional, static and a long way from the enervated stylization of the American comic strip (cf. for example Gould's *Dick Tracy*, *The Fantastic Four*, *Joe Palooka* or *Little Orphan Annie*). We might ask whether: a) the graphics derive from the popular Chinese tradition; b) they are imbued with distant Western influences; c) they conform to a need for total realism. While hypothesis (c) is not at odds with the first two, hypotheses (a) and (b) are opposed and complementary. The graphic mode of these stories draws on the one that became commonplace in the iconography of the revolution's propaganda and in many textbooks currently used in Chinese schools (where there also appear illustrations derived from traditional Chinese art). Nevertheless there is a quite definite graphic connection between the Chinese comic strip and the British comic strip of the 1930s, and one can posit a direct influence if one bears in mind political and economic relationships between China and Great Britain before the revolution. Figures 1 and 2 allow a comparison between a British comic strip of the 1930s and a Chinese comic strip of today. We can note the same scrupulous realism, the enthusiasm for detail, the

Fig. 1 Thirties English comic strip by W. Booth

very precise delineation of perspective, the fine-lined pen-work which harks back to the eighteenth-century engraving rather than looking to the American comic strip. Figures 3 and 4 compare a British comic strip of today (where you can see the link with the tradition of the previous decade) and another Chinese comic strip. One of the typical characteristics of these Chinese comic strips, their lack of humour (which by contrast abounds in the American tradition), can be attributed not just to motives of 'revolutionary seriousness', but precisely to the influence of the English schools, where humour is indeed lacking.

Figures 5 to 9 illustrate some aspects of the 'grammar' and 'syntax' consciously employed by the Chinese illustrators.

In figures 5 and 6 we can note that the stylized use of *flashback* in a photonovella, with a very specific cinematographic derivation.

In figure 7 the foot sticking out of the frame displays a degree of the graphic sophistication that is to be found in the European comic strip.

Figures 8 and 9 show two examples of a wide shot where the primary scene is re-presented with architectural features or trees as its frame; yet another mannered element which,

Fig. 2 Frame of the Chinese comic strip *Following the Trail*

particularly in figure 8, is used also to give the background scenes a total realism, its technique recalling Hergé's *Tintin*.

This precision, particularly in its description of peasant scenes, I'd say derives from the function fulfilled by the image.

These comic strips can be classified as belonging to the category of *verbal diegesis*. The fact is that the story here, unlike other types of comic strip, does not have its momentum in the images. If we look at the images without reading the text we have no understanding of the story. The story is therefore *led* by the text. The image functions connotatively and as an iconic complement to the information, and it serves above all to facilitate the reader's identification with the narrative through a realistic evocation of his or her daily life.

The 'bubble' fulfils a specific function. Let's look at figure number 10. If we read the bubble without reading the caption we do not understand what has happened. But if we read the

Top: Fig. 3 Frame of a contemporary English comic strip, *Tiffany Jones* by P. Tourret and J. Butterworth (Courtesy of Associated Newspapers Limited)
Bottom: Fig. 4 Frame of the Chinese comic strip *Letter from South Vietnam*

caption without reading the bubble (and without looking at the illustration) we are unable to proceed to the next frame. The reading sequence is therefore as follows: 1) caption, 2) image, 3) bubble. The bubble makes it possible to proceed from the caption to the image and from one frame to the next, producing a close fusion between visual information and verbal information. The images in figure 11 reveal an additional curious feature. In the story titled 'The Opium War' the Chinese are represented according to the customary rules of perspective, while the English invaders are pictured like 'Epinal' toy soldiers, stylized and two-dimensional. This is the opposite of what Panofsky observed about Egyptian painting, where two-dimensional representations, exclusive to images of pharaohs and priests conferred a hieratic character, while slaves could be represented with foreshortening.[1] Here, however, two-dimensionality connotes the *extraneous* and is exclusive to the enemy.

We could pursue other details, but the ones we have cited are enough to demonstrate the existence of precise rules of grammar and syntax, besides those of semantics, and to dispel the impression of 'naivety' which burdens these stories at first sight.

TWO MASS CULTURES

Another series of observations brings us to the problem of alternative communication and the possibility of a mass culture in a socialist society. If it were true that 'the medium is the message' there would be no point in changing ideological content, since the very form of communication would constitute an implicit ideology.

Chinese comic strips are produced from above, for a very broad mass of consumers, their pre-packaged message surrendered into the hands of the recipient and unable to benefit from the feedback or the reinforcements and corrections of

210 · *Apocalypse Postponed*

Top: Figs. 5 and 6 Frames from *Lei Feng*: the protagonist remembers a scene from his childhood
Bottom: Fig. 7 *Following the Trail*: graphic suppression of the frameline's metalinguistic function

Figs 8 and 9 Two frames from *Following the Trail*

Top: Fig. 10 Frame from *Following the Trail*
Bottom: Fig. 11 Frame from *The Opium War*

communication which take place in an interpersonal relationship. Likewise, they have to rely on certain strategies that will attempt to guarantee their widespread comprehensibility. The characters are inevitably *stereotyped*, standardized, either good guys or bad guys; psychology must be *reduced to a minimum*; problems must be stated simply, *with none of the fundamental ambiguity* they have in daily life; solutions must correspond to widespread expectations. There can be no introduction of new, contentious, unknown values, since these are products read for entertainment and therefore in contexts inappropriate to problematizing doubts. The drawing itself must follow recognizable iconographic rules and therefore, yet again, be standardized. In this respect there is a great difference between Chairman Mao's *Little Red Book* and comic strips, even if apparently their content is the same. The former is an occasion for interpretation, an *open form* applicable to different contexts, whereas the comic strips constitute a kind of one-way pedagogical orientation rather like: 'In the event of such and such this is what to do.' However, the *Little Red Book* says: 'Here are some general rules which will enable you to mobilize all your experience in the manner which circumstances present as the most fitting and *correct*, the most in keeping, that is, with the demands of the people and the revolution.'

It would seem therefore that some general laws of mass culture remain immutable in all conceivable contexts, and that the best revolutionary will cannot prevent those instruments based on a stereotype from being stereotyped, and therefore anti-democratic and authoritarian.

The simplest response would be this: Mao, or whoever is acting in his place, knows very well that the problem of the neutrality of technical instruments is resolved at the level of revolutionary practice; for instance, the atomic bomb is not a neutral fact, it depends on who possesses it and the use that is made of it. Comic strips may therefore be used without prejudice for the ends of revolutionary education; the static, conservative element that vitiates them from within remains a small price to pay in relation to the pedagogical outcome. But I think there is a more subtle answer, one which renders this choice 'correct' precisely when we bear in mind the enormous efforts made by Chinese Communism to educate and culturally unify the huge masses emerging from sub-proletarian illiteracy.

Who is it that attacks Western comic strips (independent of the specific ideology they carry)? Usually it is the humanist-inspired intellectual, who sees in them an impoverishment of the educational possibilities which would otherwise be realized by books, schooling, and the theatre. Since in theory every citizen of bourgeois society has the right to go to school, to read Stendhal and Goethe and to listen to Bach, the fact of seeing them reading 'Superman' or listening to Tino Rossi's pop songs highlights the fraud perpetrated by mass culture at their expense, whereby they are prevented by 'easy' messages from having access to other more nourishing experiences. If citizens have been discriminated against since childhood so that they do not go to school, or if, even doing so, they are unable to achieve an understanding of Goethe and Bach, or if, in the end, having understood them, they have neither the necessary time nor energy to pursue them – well, that's another problem.

But Chinese revolutionary pedagogy obviously must have worked things out differently. The huge masses which it had to educate were barely on the threshold of literacy; the culture that had preceded them developed in such a way that it was completely foreign to them. As a result, the kind of culture transmitted by and embodied in comic strips is, albeit at the lowest level, the only culture both possible and realizable. It does not constitute a loss in relation to something that already existed, but a stage of transition, a phase which has to be gone through. The publication and distribution of comic strips ceases, then, to appear as the result of a purely empirical and unavoidable decision to use all possible means, even negative ones, through which the basic ideology can be transmitted. It is instead an awareness of the fact that, where necessary, to think 'through comic strips' is a positive phase for a people who can no longer think 'as the mandarins did'.

History through comic strips ceases, then, to be the degradation of the Word as something already well established; it constitutes the primary foundation for an Alphabet.

In this task even humour would be an injurious sophistication. When you are still teaching that A is A, doubting sarcasm has no place on the page. And besides it is well known that the humour of mass bourgeois culture is a surrogate for a happiness that is in fact denied. If instead society, at least in principle, has to allow happiness, peace and joy, the sneering pretence of escapism is superfluous. People laugh in earnest, or not at all.

SKETCH FOR A SUBSTITUTIONAL ANALYSIS OF CHARACTER VALUES

The final series of observations concerns a widely distributed and highly successful photonovella, the story of Lei Feng. This is a hagiography which appears very similar to those of saints or 'model pupils' common in Western schools. Lei Feng spares nothing of himself for the people and dies helping the peasants of a flooded rural area. He is thereby offered as an example of the perfect Chinese soldier who serves the people in peacetime as in wartime. The purpose of the story is therefore educational and propagandist and both its structure and its content can be likened to a number of Western wartime propaganda comic strips. Nonetheless its ideological distinctness is made plain, if not at the level of graphic form, then at the level of the substitutional *structures* which are set against clearly defined *value-bearing characters*. This becomes clear if we compare a Western comic with the story of Lei Feng. The Western comic is a page, now famous in the history of American comics, by Milton Caniff. The page is part of the series *Terry and the Pirates* and is dated 17 October 1942. It is an example of wartime propaganda in comic-strip form and as such was widely distributed among the combat troops in the Pacific. We must therefore assume that the superficial similarities between the two pages are not accidental and that the Chinese author had somewhere in mind this very well-known model. What we shall now compare is the eleven frames on the Terry page and thirteen frames (from 32 to 45) from the story of Lei Feng (which is taken from a film).

Past histories and present situations are largely identical. Terry is a young adventurer who has made a speciality of the war against the pirates in the China seas, and who, with the entry of the United States into the war, joins the Air Force. He is keen to get into combat when one night Colonel Corkin comes up to him and gives him a pep talk about team spirit. Lei Feng is a young Chinese whose family fell victim to the Japanese and the landowners, and who, now a soldier in the People's Army, asks to be sent on a mission against the traitors of Formosa. During the night his unit instructor comes up to him and gives him a pep talk about his duties in terms of collectivity.

TERRY

1. Double frame with title inset. In the middle of the airfield the colonel approaches and says: 'Let's take a walk.'

2. The colonel tells Terry he has a speech to make. The last of its kind. He's to give it all his attention.

3. The colonel draws Terry's attention to the meaning of the wings on his uniform, and his responsibility as a US officer. He's going to tell him something he's not to forget.

4. The colonel reminds Terry that the USA is the country which has contributed most to the development of aviation.

5. The colonel tells Terry it will be his job to defend his country with the very weapons it has itself provided. Behind aviation technology is a host of brave young men whose test flights produced the know-how that Terry now has at his disposal.

Fig. 12 Milton Caniff's page of 17 October 1942

Fig. 13 Frames from *Lei Feng* (dir. Dong Zhaoqi, 1st August Studio, 1964)

6. The colonel goes on with his list of those who have come before Terry. He will be a combat pilot and he should be proud of it, but . . .

7. He should not forget that every bullet and every gallon of fuel was brought in by other pilots, on transport assignments. Terry will get the glory but others put the lift in his balloon.

8. The colonel shows him the mechanics who are working through the night on the aircraft engines. These grease monkeys will be right there with him in the cockpit when he takes off.

9. The colonel tells Terry things won't always go smoothly in the army. But sooner or later, the old American eagle has ended up as the winner in every game since 1776 . . .

10. The colonel winds up his speech, reminding Terry one more time that there are

thousands of young American guys all over the world who are behind him and counting on him. *Terry stands to attention and salutes.*

11. Terry goes off into the night. An inscription on a stockade wall says: 'This way to Tokyo! Next stop USA.'

LEI FENG

32. Lei Feng is outside the door of the command post when the instructor approaches him. Lei Feng asks him if he has requested new combat missions.

33. When the instructor tells him that they have clear assignments already, Lei Feng shows his impatience. The instructor calls him back for a chat.

34. The instructor reproaches him for his impatience. It makes no difference that he has suffered a lot, combat isn't to be sought out for its own sake.

35. The instructor takes Lei Feng into his room and looks in Mao's works for a solution to his ideological problem.

36. Lei Feng fails to understand why he has to return to a text he knows by heart.

37. The instructor prompts Lei Feng to remember that the essay 'In the service of the people' was written by Mao in memory of the soldier Zhang Side.

38. The instructor asks Lei Feng if Zhang Side died in the course of legendary wartime actions. Lei Feng answers that he died because a coal mine collapsed while he was working in Shensi.

39. The instructor's prompting makes Lei Feng understand that Zhang Side was a great hero because he died for the sake of the people. The instructor says that many people imagine, however, that to be heroes it is necessary to be involved in frontline action against the enemy ...

40. The instructor asks whether Lei Feng would humbly accept the same works as Zhang Side. Then Lei Feng understands the nature of his error.

41. Lei Feng says he will obey whatever orders he is given: he'll face machine guns or he'll mine coal but either way he will be at the service of the people.

42. The instructor tells Lei Feng that this conversation has been an act of self-criticism for him too, since he himself had committed the same error to start with and had gone to headquarters asking for a combat mission. So they will study together to improve their ideological formation.

43. The instructor gives Lei Feng the four volumes of Mao's selected works so that he can

study them. *Lei Feng stands to attention and salutes*.

44. Lei Feng promises to study.

45. On the flyleaf of Mao's book he writes four solemn promises: 'Study the writings of Chairman Mao every day. Study the words of Chairman Mao. Follow the directives of Chairman Mao. Be a good soldier of Chairman Mao.'

The parallels between the two sequences (with three surplus frames in the Chinese story) are so striking that the idea of a deliberate copy is not unwarranted. In literary terms the model in question is 'late-night discussion between a superior and a recruit on the theme of team spirit'. But the analogy ends there. And not just because these are obviously different wars, fought for different motives, and because two different literary styles are used – Colonel Corkin's speech is utterly colloquial, slangy, full of college boy references; the dialogue between Lei Feng and the instructor is thoroughly didactic from start to finish. The differences are deeper, and they are so exemplary that it is worth summing them up in a series of paired oppositions which, despite appearing to be oppositions between characters-actors, are in fact oppositions between *substitutes*, abstract ideological elements in a cultural drama.

I *Monologue* vs *Dialogue*
Colonel Corkin is the only speaker and Terry listens respectfully to his superior. The instructor, on the other hand, has a discussion with Lei Feng.

II *Authoritarian transmission vs Maieutic*
Corkin spells out the principles to which Terry must adhere. The instructor guides Lei Feng to his own elaboration of them and finally points out that he too has experienced the same error and that they must improve themselves together. Corkin says 'Listen to me', while the instructor says 'Listen to yourself!'

III *Asymmetry* vs *Symmetry*
In the one instance from the leader to the subordinate, in the other instance leader and subordinate in an equal relationship.

IV *Digest* vs *Research*
Corkin tells Terry things once and for all, summing up conclusive principles. The instructor exhorts Lei Feng to embark on personal study.

V *The language of leadership* vs *The language of the masses*
Corkin teaches a lieutenant about soldiers. The instructor teaches a soldier what he must be.

VI *War* vs *Peace*
Corkin teaches Terry that he must go to war in a state of mind compatible with team spirit, while giving him promises of victory. The instructor tells Lei Feng what his state of mind should be in order to devote himself to peacetime missions, because war is not an absolute value.

VII *The Individual* vs *Collectivity*
Corkin speaks to Terry as an individual, with a specific function – a wartime pilot – urging him to bear in mind that he has need of collectivity. The instructor speaks to Lei Feng as a member of a collectivity, urging him to serve his collectivity. Put another way, Corkin explains to Terry the merits of the grease-monkey mechanics working for him but he does not tell him that he too must become a mechanic and work alongside them. The instructor tells Lei Feng that the heroic soldier's task is to mine coal for the people and not just to silence enemy machine guns. Terry is told 'Everyone is working for you'; Lei Feng is told 'You must work for everyone.'

VIII *Division of labour* vs *Global intervention*
The very images that show in turn sections of a plane, mech-

anics at work, and the words successively naming the transport pilots, the mechanics, the test pilots, give the impression of a society built on Taylorism. Instead Lei Feng is given models constituted through alternating tasks. Terry learns that 'everyone has a specific job to do', Lei Feng that 'everyone has to do everything.'

IX *Technological organization* vs *Human organization*

The notion of unity given to Terry is that of a perfect technological machine where everything has its place and the outcome is a flawless war machine; if it is used correctly there can be no defeat.

The notion of unity given to Lei Feng is that of a relationship with the people which gives meaning to the soldier's situation. The solution to each problem is placed in the study of theoretical principles applicable to each instance according to the needs of the people. Terry now knows what he must do at any given time. Lei Feng begins studying because he has received only general directions on the ideological stance with which he must confront problems to be resolved.

The switching of our analysis onto the ideological values in the two pages has probably told us what we already knew: namely, that both comic strips are ideological vehicles and that the two ideologies are different. So has the painstaking formulation of oppositions and the reduction of content itself to forms amenable to analysis been a futile exercise?

We do not think so. In the first place, it is only in this way that it becomes clear where the difference is located, thereby enabling it to be spelled out in other than general terms. And moreover it has thereby been possible to see how, through the articulation of the same formal structures and the same ideological unities in a different way, the formulation of two different messages becomes possible.

Finally, we have seen that the comic-strip form is not an

ideological cul de sac. It allows for multiple manipulations and articulations and ultimately even a narrative model very probably borrowed from Western culture has lent itself to opposing communicative aims. It is untrue that the medium is always and utterly the message. Sometimes *the message becomes the medium*.

1971

CHAPTER 4

Independent Radio in Italy

IN SPEAKING ABOUT the 'free' radio stations in Italy my objective is not to propound a semiological theory of radios but rather to contribute some information for a further discussion of this phenomenon as well as to try to convey the atmosphere created by these radios.

It is said that at present there are over a thousand independent radio stations in Italy. It is, however, almost impossible to come by any reliable statistics concerning this phenomenon because there are radios which are born and die in the space of a day. Since only a handful of stations are able to programme their broadcasts two weeks ahead of time, the specialized publications which contain future programmes can give only a summary idea of the number of independent radios broadcasting in Italy today. It is nonetheless evident that a great cultural and political diversification has been achieved. In fact commercial stations broadcasting rock music and advertisements exist alongside the politicized radio stations. Diversification is also found among the politicized stations since there are radios which represent the extreme left, the New Left, the communists, the socialists and the labour unions, as well as radios on the opposite side of the political spectrum such as the *Comunione e Liberazione* station (a rightist Catholic movement) or Radio University (which is connected to the neo-fascist party, MSI).

The proliferation of radio stations is such that anyone

driving from the centre of Milan to Florence, along the 'Auto-strada del Sol', will discover that the car radio picks up and loses stations, mixing them up and superimposing them so as to create a constant soundscape. While driving through the centre of Milan the listener does not even notice that the car radio is constantly tuning in to different radio stations because most independent radios broadcast the same kind of music. The continuous succession of stations does not present a problem when a song of Gloria Gaynor is replaced by one of Esther Phillips. But if you think you are listening to *Canale 96* (a more or less New Left radio) and are actually tuned in to Radio University (neo-fascist) the listener will experience a feeling of great disorientation. There are times when the subject matter of broadcasts are politically 'clear' and other times when they are not. The mistakes do not really come about because of the similarity of the music broadcast but also because of the homogeneity of the language used by all the independent radios.

Once the listener drives his car onto the highway his relationship with the radio is simplified. For some thirty kilometers (or approximately a quarter of an hour) the radio will stay tuned to the same station. The new stations picked up during the trip can be distinguished by the regional accents of the speakers and by references to local news. The young Communists of the Emilia are replaced by the *Vitelloni* of the Adriatic coast who speak of their summer conquests of German girls. Then the distinctive voice of Radio Alice comes through, broadcasting under the sign of the Anti-Oedipus, soon to be replaced by the soft-spoken voice of a Catholic station that introduces a song of Joan Baez as if she were the Virgin of Carmel.

The variety of styles and content transmitted by the independent radios in Italy must be pointed out. These radios are not part of McLuhan's world since they do not exemplify his belief that the medium is the message. In Italy today the medium is a vehicle for a great variety of messages. Furthermore it is not just by chance that Radio Alice was closed down while other radios continue broadcasting songs of the resistance or folk protest music in a calmer and more museum-like atmosphere.

STATE MONOPOLY AND INDEPENDENT RADIO

Before continuing this report on the independent radios in Italy, I would like to describe the characteristics that distinguish them from the state monopoly radios. The first item on the list is language. The independent radios have replaced the standard Italian of the state radio with local accents. The result is that the audience is surprised. Announcers speaking the same way as the inhabitants of your town or city destroy the feeling of the radio as being a kind of 'official' voice. But these broadcasts are not only phonetically distinct, in fact, they are also syntactically and semantically different. For the first time since the beginning of Italian radio, everyday words are used and often those spoken at night too. Events are described by those who have just experienced them, causing a non-observance of *consecutio temporum*. One has the distinct feeling that someone has come running into the studio to speak at top speed about what he just saw. One has the impression that there is a total lack of selection and censorship. I stress the word 'impression' because, of course, the ideological outlook of the radio station is responsible for the selection of its spontaneous contributors. It would be quite naive to speak of a total lack of censorship but, on the other hand, the selection criteria of independent stations are very different from those of the state radio. In fact, when the former first began broadcasting people in Milan turned their radio sets on and, thinking they were listening to the RAI (the state monopoly radio), heard a debate of homosexuals who were engaging in explicit propaganda. The listeners began to ask themselves whether the RAI had gone mad because they felt the lack of a certain type of censorship.

The above-mentioned characteristics of the independent radios once differentiated them from the RAI, but since the reorganization of the state monopoly radio in 1976 the differences have been somewhat eroded. The RAI has adopted some of the stylistic and thematic aspects of the independent radios. The result is that today one hears long conversations in local accents in which the participants use some cliché expressions of the left.

THE LANGUAGE OF ITALIAN INDEPENDENT RADIO

An analysis of the language used by the independent radios reveals what one may call a 'rhetoric of the immediate', of the present and its clichés. In fact the practice of being in contact with the immediate develops a specific rhetoric and its own hackneyed phrases. Of course the clichés change from one radio to another. Commercial radios indulge in broadcasting a mixture of pseudo-proletarian spontaneity, disc jockeys' fake joviality, and clichés taken from the repertoire of the mass media. A whole generation speaks through these radios, unveiling either its creativity or the hackneyed ideas it was fed upon. Sometimes the hackneyed statements are capitalist and sometimes they are New Left. Yet some radios, the case of Radio Alice being extraordinary in every respect, have broken away from all clichés. During the first months of Radio Alice's broadcasts even people who were not sympathetic to the radio's political outlook could not fail to recognize its radical renewal of radio broadcasting. Since then the Italian political situation has become such that Radio Alice has been subject to blackmail on moral and theoretical grounds. Many people have become extremely cautious with respect to the independent radios.

The new radio language creates an impression of an uncontrolled message not unlike a psychodrama. This is especially true if the listener keeps changing stations, which happens automatically when he drives through Italian cities. The radio broadcasts have become a continued psychodrama, a stream of consciousness and an interiorized dialogue which unfurls in the listener's ears.

The first constituent element of the psychodrama is the ever-present and invasive music. Independent radios broadcast music that is appreciated by the young, music that is quite different from that broadcast by the RAI. The violent melodies one hears are interspersed with well-balanced intervals of speech. Of course the amount of speaking increases under special circumstances, such as the Bologna riots in March 1977 when the politicized radios reduced the music to a minimum in order to concentrate on incoming telephone calls, announcements and spoken tracts. The second element of the psychodrama is the speaker (whose language is everyday speech which omits the niceties of stylistics). In the case of the commercial stations the speakers indulge in disc-jockey language or dialogues based on silly exchanges. In the case of the politicized radios one hears debates and commentaries that come to the radio from the third participant, the public. In fact the independent radios have inaugurated the practice of having the public continually intervene via telephone. Listeners criticize the radio they are speaking through. In some cases the radios engage in dialogue, or even in polemics, with the caller whereas others, as was the case with Radio Alice, are nothing more than a transparent filter for the voices coming from outside.

The RAI has recently adopted this characteristic of the independent radio stations. The result is not the same, however, since it seems that only old ladies call up the state monopoly radio.

The fourth element of the psychodrama, the 'token reporter', is the most interesting and important invention of the independent radios. The 'token reporter' has evolved because these stations cannot afford to hire correspondents. Even the radio studio is manned by volunteers who take turns playing records, speaking to the public, and reading the news (which at times is nothing more than the first page of a newspaper that has just been printed). The lack of correspondents has been easily resolved since any friend, sympathizer or collaborator can become a reporter. During an event the 'token reporter' observes the situation, goes to the nearest public phone booth, calls the radio and is put on the air; he thus automatically becomes a reporter. This practice is an important innovation despite the fact that it has given rise to accusations against leftish stations which are criticized for broadcasting 'the voice from outside' without taking responsibility for what is said on such occasions.

However, it would be wrong to think that the independent radios have only changed the linguistic aspects of broadcasting or the workings of the mass media; they have also raised social, political and juridical problems. In order to introduce these problems we should first look at the brief history of these radios and examine some of the broadcasts which have been under attack.

INDEPENDENT BROADCASTING

The breakdown of the state monopoly on broadcasting began with cable television. This first venture did not have much success but it paved the way for independent broadcasting: in fact the era of pirate radios began shortly after the first failure of independent television.

It must be pointed out that there is an enormous difference between independent TV and independent radio. The differences are basically of an economic nature but they also have repercussions on social and political levels. Private TV stations need a great amount of funding, even though cable television has cut these costs significantly. The price of the equipment does not allow small groups to benefit from the liberalization of this medium. On the other hand modern technology has reduced the costs of radio broadcasting to such an extent that any small group can buy the equipment needed to go on the air. The result of these material difficulties is that many Italians support the rights of independent radios, and even the need for them, while still maintaining a very cautious attitude towards independent TV.

Until a year ago (1976) the independent radio stations were illegal but tolerated. From time to time one or another was closed down for technical reasons, such as interference with the broadcasts of the state monopoly radio. The verdict of the Constitutional Court finally gave independent radios a legal status. The last step of this liberalization, the drawing up of regulations, has not yet been accomplished.

THE EXAMPLE OF RADIO ALICE

Radio Alice is probably the most interesting new radio in Italy and is worth examining more closely. It began broadcasting in January 1976 as one of the outgrowths of the A/traverso/ collective.[1] Their first broadcast began with:

> Radio Alice broadcasts: music, news, gardens in flower, pointless conversations, inventions, discoveries, recipes, horoscopes, magic philtres, love, war bulletins, photographs, messages, massages, and lies.

As you see, this kind of manifesto is a mixture of *Finnegans Wake* and McLuhan.

The films they like best are, without any doubt, those with the greatest political commitment: *Yellow Submarine* and *Lassie* . . .

The stylistic climate is quite distinct. When speaking of a strike which took place in spring the statement is: 'April is the cruellest month.' The enemy is attacked with '*Toi, hypocrite lecteur, mon semblable, mon frère*'. The citations used by Radio

Alice do not hesitate to mix Sade, Mayakovsky, Mandrake (the comic strip), Artaud, and the hero Guattareuze (as they call the Anti-Oedipus authors, Deleuze and Guattari).

The philosophic statements which intersperse their broadcasts also have a particular style: 'Desire assumes its own voice', 'Transversal writing that frees desire', 'Refusal of sense, morality, politics, and the political', 'Revolutionary desire in the life of young proletarians, absentee workers, and both cultural and sexual minorities', 'Speak the irrational that is under the skin of everyone', 'Paint the form of life red' (Mayakovsky).

Their definition of the *Movimento* (a variety of heterogeneous protest groups left of the Communist Party) is 'Mao-dadaism'.

Radio Alice is made up of literary citations, classical music, political songs, non-structured dialogues, free-wheeling language, and direct reporting of such varied events as strikes, squatting, demonstrations and fêtes. The result is that a typical broadcast is made up of five minutes of highly politicized talk about an ongoing strike followed by a conversation with a pseudo-drug-addict who speaks of his personal problems, very 'American' music, and dialogues that must be qualified as being 'Alician' (from Lewis Carroll), celebrating nonsense and the nonsensical.

Of course this collage does not permit us to understand the position of Radio Alice. This is true, above all, because they refuse to assume the clearly defined position expected of them by traditional parties of the left. Radio Alice's refusal of the traditional leftist parties (not only on account of a clearly defined position) comes from the fact that problems of the body, of pleasure and of desire are being submitted as politically significant entities. The other reason Alice does not take on a clearly defined position can be attributed to the collective's particular mixture of aesthetic values, its utopian vision of an aesthetic society, its vitality, and its elaborated Dadaist trend.

The characteristic note (which makes it important for the

study of what is happening today in the new Italian generation and its 'Movimento') is the language used by the group of extremely talented people at its head who speak with quotations. What is significant is that the language they use is received and adopted by young, subproletarian masses who have no particular personal culture and who identify with this kind of language. In other words the new generation is speaking a language formerly used only by the avant-garde, thus applying and using what had once been nothing more than a laboratory language. However, these masses have adopted an avant-garde language without knowing its history. The people behind Radio Alice, who, as I said, are very informed and who subscribe to the 'right' reviews and journals, manage to break through to a mass public. The result is that one can no longer tell whether it is someone connected to the radio who is speaking (those who know it all) or whether it is someone from outside who is speaking (those who know nothing). Syntax, semantics, phonetics and ideas are all the same.

In order to understand Radio Alice's role in a situation of urban guerrilla activity one must examine the broadcasts made during the Bologna riots on 11, 12 and 13 March 1977. Before giving an extract of a broadcast made during the riots it must be pointed out that Radio Alice, as well as some of the other stations, became a very powerful source of information because it informed the public of the events in the city almost while they were happening. The Italian independent radios played much the same role as Europe 1 and RTL during the May 1968 unrest in Paris: detailed information was given, so that anyone listening to the radio could join the demonstrators or avoid them. In the case of the independent radios another problem arose. The informal 'token reporters' did not always limit themselves to the strict task of reporting but at times suggested what actions should be undertaken. The concrete example which follows was broadcast on 11 March 1977. The Radio Alice news was interrupted by a telephone call from Bonvi (a well-known Italian cartoonist), whose office on the main street of Bologna was well situated to observe the skirmishes between students and police.

> . . . wait a minute . . . something important . . . god-damn it, my head . . . hey, the telephone cut off . . . do you still hear us? . . . do you still hear us? . . . Now the police just shot tear gas and Via Rizzoli is full of it . . . My office is full of people taking refuge . . . the situation is still fluid but the amazing thing is that the city is reacting very well to the provocation . . . I'm giving the phone back to Gabriele . . .

I choose this example because it shows that even a person like Bonvi, who is not connected with any group in particular and who was not participating in the street fighting, became so excited as to become a propagandist. In the heat of the situation his voice incited participation and the radio provided a vehicle for his message. The Communist city officials and the police concluded that Radio Alice constituted an intolerable threat and decided to close it down. The telephone call quoted above was featured among the evidence presented against the radio station.

The following excerpts are from a recording of the last minutes of Radio Alice. It is not only an exciting recording but also a good example of the particular way in which they broadcast. You will notice that the speaker describes the situation as if it were a film and says that what is happening reminds him of the German film *Katharina Blum*. This is quite typical of Radio Alice: they literarize situations and . . . situationalize literature.

> Anyway the situation hasn't changed . . . the police are trying to get their bullet-proof vests on and pistols pointed . . . they say they'll knock the door down . . . anyway we're asking all comrades who know our

lawyers to get in touch with them and tell them we're under siege . . . have you seen the film? . . . what the hell was it called? . . . the *Case of* . . . *the Case of Katharina Blum* . . . well the helmets, the bullet-proof vests, the pistols pointed and things like that . . . really absurd, really incredible, the kind of stuff for a film and if they weren't knocking at the door just outside I'd think I were watching a film.

Thirty seconds later the situation is even more dramatic:

Come on, give me a record so we can listen to some music for Christ's sake. (Noises) Here's some Beethoven, if you like it fine, if you don't well . . . just fuck off. (Noises and Beethoven in the background.) OK, so the police have started up again . . . Hey, watch out, keep down . . . (Police yelling in the background.) Just five minutes, the lawyers are coming, they are on their way . . . no, look, I am not Matteo and the police are at the door . . . (another voice in the background) they're coming in! . . . (speaker) they're in, they're in, we've got our hands up, they're in, we've got our hands up (noises), the mike, we got our hands up (noises and shouts) . . . (dead silence).

POLITICAL, SOCIAL AND JURIDICAL PROBLEMS

Having looked at the history and some examples of independent radio broadcasts, we must also examine most of the political and juridical problems that have arisen. The most important of these problems is certainly the active role played by independent radios in Italy. There is no denying the fact that these radios are like a third eye on someone's fingertip. With such an eye it is impossible to look everywhere and at everything in a society like ours. The regulations governing its use are extremely complicated. In theory one can even discuss whether or not it is right that a radio should report on police movements, but as we all know anyone can buy a walkie-talkie or other radio equipment and tune into any frequency, including those used by the police. Thus today we are in an electronic world that makes it impossible to enforce certain rules and regulations. Furthermore, even experts in constitutional law admit that it is impossible to cope with this new situation.

The second problem presented by the independent radios is the attribution of responsibilities. As we pointed out above, the journalism of independent radios is such that the radio is only a vehicle for voices coming from outside the studio. Under such conditions it is very hard to attribute responsibilities to anyone in particular. In fact, direct reporting on radio is very different from the case of newspapers, where there is a time-lag between the arrival of news and its being written in article form, printed, and finally sold at a newsstand. The editor of the paper thus has the opportunity to look at the news being printed, which makes him responsible for what the newspaper says. In the case of the independent radios this time-lag is annihilated because the news is spoken directly by the large amorphous body of 'token reporters'. Once there is an agreement on the principle that anyone calling the radio may speak through it, it becomes impossible to attribute responsibility to anyone in particular.

The third problem raised by independent radio practice is the difficulty involved in collecting evidence for incrimination. In fact it is quite impossible to prove that a radio has engaged in illegal information or, as was the alleged case of Radio Alice, that it incited the public to carry out seditious activities. Tape recordings cannot be used as evidence because they are too easily manipulated. Falling back on ear-witnesses is equally impossible because of the frenetic activity of radios which pour out streams of information, and because ear-witnesses may not remember the context of a statement. There is a difference between the statement being an official communiqué or just a comment made by a person interviewed by the radio.

These three points suffice to help us understand how confused the relationship is between independent radios and the law.

Banning direct radio or regulating its usage is much the same as registering guns and giving gun permits. As we all know, gun permits do not top some people from shooting. The accessibility of electronics permits anyone to start broadcasting during a riot. Hence the only sure fact in this maze of problems is that it is virtually impossible to effectively control radio broadcasting.

Radios have existed for some seventy-five years, but they were not owned by almost the entire population until the 1970s. The profit logic of the electronics industry is also involved in this democratization of the medium, but it would be wrong to give this aspect undue importance. Independent radios are principally the result of new sectors of the population acquiring the possibility of stating their opinions and views. This liberalization is at the very root of what is nothing short of a crisis of social consensus in Italy today.

Independent radios have changed the very notion of information and even of public order. They have created social problems that cannot be solved by calling in the police, in the same way that censorship was not a solution for the invention of the printing press nor embargo measures for the invention of gunpowder. I once suggested, during a debate, that maybe a society has to recognize that radios have become a kind of drug. It is said that drugs expand consciousness, but it is also true that they cause social problems. Maybe a society should decide, rightly or wrongly, that it is better to forbid the use of drugs and that, as far as the expansion of consciousness is concerned, watching television should suffice. Maybe the same thing should be done with radios, but if this is to be so all radios must disappear. Clearly the proposition is unacceptable.

The other solution would be to forbid broadcasting to groups which do not supply sufficient guarantees. But this creates the same problem as granting gun licences: *quis custodiet ipsos custodes*? And who will decide which groups supply sufficient guarantees?

Another solution would be to apply a new form of control to a situation in which information and the influence of the individual have been enormously expanded by electronic means. One might even say that Hyde Park's Speakers Corner now travels with the aid of electromagnetic waves. Mounted policemen once controlled pedestrian rioters. Today, it would seem, everyone is on horseback. The problem presented by independent radios is no more momentous than when our society found itself faced with the problem of thieves using cars.

In any case, a satisfactory solution must be found, since freedom of speech itself is at stake. Even those who do not agree with Radio Alice or with the phenomenon of independent radios must nevertheless recognize that we are faced with an important new development in the realm of freedom of information. We are entering a new era in the history of communications and a new era in the history of man as a communicating being. Furthermore, the experience of independent radio in Italy contradicts many media writers who still assert that the mass media are always manipulated by the powers that be and that they inevitably encourage social integration.

1978

CHAPTER 5

Striking at the Heart of the State?

THE SPASMODIC WAIT for a new communiqué from the Red Brigades on the fate of Aldo Moro and the frantic discussion on how one might behave in that eventuality have led the press into contradictory reactions. Some papers didn't reproduce the communiqué at all, but were unable to refrain from publicizing it in huge headlines; others reproduced it, but in letters so small that only readers with 20/20 vision could decipher it (a clear case of unacceptable discrimination). As for the content, here again the reaction was embarrassed, because everyone was awaiting a text strewn with 'Ach so!' and words with five consonants in a row, revealing the hand of the German terrorist or Czech agent, and instead we found ourselves confronted with a long passage of political argument.

That what was being put forward was an argument was generally recognized, and the more alert commentators also noticed that it was an argument directed not towards the 'enemy' but towards potential friends, to demonstrate that the Red Brigades are not a bunch of desperadoes firing off in all directions but deserve to be seen as the vanguard of a movement whose rationale is determined by the international situation.

If this is true, it is wrong simply to dismiss the communiqué as off the wall, crazy, empty, nonsensical. It has to be analysed calmly and attentively; only in this way can one locate the point at which the communiqué, which starts off from reasonably clear-headed premises, reveals the fatal theoretical and practical weakness of the Red Brigades' position.

We must have the courage to admit that this 'crazy' message contains an eminently acceptable premise and expresses, in a clumsy and muddled form, a thesis which has been widely taken up in Europe and America for some time, whether by the students of '68, by the theoreticians of *Monthly Review*, or by the left political parties. So if there is 'paranoia' it is not in the premises but, as we shall see, in the practical conclusions drawn from them.

There is no reason to laugh at the crazy notion of a so-called MIS or Multinational Imperialist State. Maybe the description they give of it is a bit quaint, but nobody now can be unaware that international politics on this planet is no longer determined by individual governments but by a network of productive interests (call it the Multinational Corporation network, why not?) which acts as arbiter of local policy, of peace and war, and delimits the relations between the capitalist world, China, the Soviet Union, and the Third World.

What is interesting is that the Red Brigades have abandoned their Disneyesque mythology according to which on the one side there was one big capitalist called Uncle Scrooge and on the other there were the Beagle Boys, cheats and ruffians in their own way but nice guys really because they took the mean and selfish old capitalist to the cleaners in the name of the working class.

The role of the Beagle Boys was played by the Tupamaros in Uruguay, who were convinced that the Scrooges of Brazil and Argentina would get irked and would turn Uruguay into a second Vietnam, while the citizenry would take their side and turn themselves into thousands of Vietcong. The plot didn't work because Brazil didn't react and the multinationals, who had business to do in that part of Latin America, let Peron return to Argentina, divided the revolutionary and guerrilla forces, and then allowed Peron and his successors to sink up to their necks in the shit, at which point the smarter Montoneros legged it to Spain and the more idealistic were caught and killed.

It is precisely because the power of the multinationals exists (remember Chile) that the idea of a Che Guevara-style revolution has become an impossibility. The revolution took place in Russia while all the European nations were engaged in a world war. The long march was organized in China while the rest of the world had its eyes elsewhere ... But when one lives in a universe where a system of productive interests takes advantage of nuclear parity to impose a peace which suits everybody, and sends satellites up into the sky for each side to spy on the other, at that point national revolutions can no longer happen, because everything is decided somewhere else.

The historical compromise[1] on the one side and terrorism on the other represent two opposite responses to this situation. The idea which, in a confused way, underlies terrorist action is a very modern and very capitalistic principle (which classical Marxism has not yet come to terms with) derived from Systems Theory. The great systems do not have a head, they do not have protagonists, and they are not even motivated by individual egotism. Therefore the way to strike at them is not to kill their King but to make them unstable by means of acts of disturbance based on the system's own logic. Where there is a completely automated factory, it will not be disturbed by the death of the owner but only by the insertion into its processes of items of aberrant information which will confuse the operation of the computers regulating it.

Modern terrorism claims to have drawn lessons from Marx. The claim may be genuine, but in reality it has drawn its lessons, albeit indirectly, from Norbert Wiener on the one hand and science fiction on the other. The problem is that it has not drawn profound enough lessons, nor has it studied cybernetics with sufficient care. Thus in all their propaganda until now the Red Brigades have kept on talking about 'striking at the heart of the state', cultivating on the one hand a nineteenth-century notion of the state and on the other the notion of an enemy with a heart or a head – as in battles of old, where, if the king was struck down as he rode at the head of his troops, the enemy army was demoralized and destroyed.

In their latest leaflet the Red Brigades have ditched the idea of heart, of state, of wicked capitalist, of politician as 'butcher'. Now the adversary is the system of the multinationals, of which Moro is a clerk or at best a carrier of information.

So what then is the error of reasoning (theoretical and practical) which the Red Brigades are now making, particularly when they appeal, against the multinational of capital, to a multinational of terror?

First sign of naiveté. Once the idea of great systems has been grasped it is instantly remythologized with the claim that they have 'secret plans' of which Moro was a bearer. In reality the great systems have nothing secret about them and everyone knows perfectly well how they work. If the multinational equilibrium makes the formation of a left government in Italy something to be avoided, it is childish to imagine someone sending Moro a letter explaining to him how to defeat the working class. All that is needed, say, is to provoke some event in South Africa, wreak havoc in the Amsterdam diamond market, affect the exchange rate of the US dollar, and there will instantly be a run on the Italian lira.

Second sign of naiveté. Terrorism is not the enemy of the great systems. On the contrary it is their natural, accepted, taken-for-granted counterpart.

The system of the multinationals cannot live in a world-war economy (and nuclear war at that) but it knows equally well that it cannot reduce the natural pressures of biological aggression or the refusal of peoples or groups simply to buckle under. It therefore accepts small local wars, which it controls and keeps in check as required with the aid of shrewd international interventions; and it also accepts terrorism. A factory here or a factory there stopped from producing by some act of sabotage, and the system still continues to function. The odd plane hijacked, and the airline companies are in trouble for a week or two, but in recompense press and television interests will do well. Furthermore terrorism helps justify the existence of armies and police forces which are otherwise left idle and need to be given something more active to get on with. Finally terrorism provides a justification for disciplinary interventions in circumstances where an excess of democracy is making a situation ungovernable.

The 'national' capitalist *à la* Uncle Scrooge is afraid of revolt, theft and revolution which threaten to take away his means of production. Modern capitalism, which invests in a number of countries, has always enough room for manoeuvre to cope with terrorist attacks in one isolated place or another.

Because it has neither head nor heart, the system displays an incredible capacity for restabilizing itself and its boundaries. Wherever it is hit, that place will always be at the margin. If the head of the German employers' organization should happen to be a victim, this is a statistically acceptable risk, like the level of motorway accidents. Meanwhile, as has been noted for some time, there is a reversion to a medieval division of territory – with fortified castles and residential blocks protected by private guards and electronic surveillance devices.

The only serious danger would be a simultaneous worldwide terrorist insurgency, mass terrorism on a global sale (such as the Red Brigades seem to argue for); but the multinational system 'knows' (in so far as a system can 'know' anything) that this will never happen. The multinational system does not send children down the mines. The terrorist is someone who has nothing to lose but his chains, but the system runs things in such a way that everybody, apart from an inevitable marginalized minority, has something to lose in a situation of generalized terrorist uprising. It knows that when terrorism ceases just to carry out the odd picturesque activity and begins seriously to disturb the everyday quiet life of the masses, those masses will unite to form a barrier against terrorism.

So what does recent experience show that the multinational system really views with disquiet? The answer is the rise to power in, say, Spain, Italy and France simultaneously of political parties which have the backing of working-class organizations. However 'corruptible' these parties may be, the fact is that it is when mass organizations start getting their fingers on the international management of capital that the system could be in trouble. It is not that the multinationals would collapse if Georges Marchais and the French Communist Party took over from Giscard d'Estaing, but their life would become that bit more difficult.

The worry that if the Communists came to power they would be privy to NATO secrets is a mere smokescreen. NATO secrets are an open book. The multinational system's real worry (and I say this with complete detachment, having no sympathy for the 'historical compromise' in the form in which it is being put forward at the moment) is that party political control would interfere with a form of power management which is impatient of any process of mass consultation.

Terrorism on the other hand is much less of a worry, because it is a natural biological consequence of the multinationals' rule, just as a day of feverishness is a reasonable price to pay for an effective vaccine.

If the Red Brigades are right in their analysis of a world government by the multinationals, then they must recognize that they themselves are its natural and taken-for-granted counterpart. They must recognize that they are acting out a script already written by their supposed enemies. Instead, having stumbled, albeit crudely, on an important principle of the logic of systems, the Brigades respond in the style of a nine-teenth-century serial novel full of brave and implacable avengers and executioners like the Count of Monte Cristo. This would be a joke, if the novel were not written in blood.

The struggle is between powerful forces, not between demons and heroes. Unlucky the people that is struck with these 'heroes',[2] especially if they still think in religious terms and involve the people in their bloody storming of an uninhabited paradise.

1983

PART FOUR

In Search of Italian Genius

CHAPTER 1

Phenomena of This Sort Must Also be Included in Any Panorama of Italian Design

1. We are surrounded by artificial objects, or artefacts. The notion of artefact covers a wide range of things, from the house to the screw. A great Italian architect and theorist of architecture, Ernesto Rogers, formulated the following slogan as the designer's ideal: *from the spoon to the city*. Artefacts are *designed*. The English term 'design' is richer and more comprehensive than the Italian term *disegno*, and indeed an expression such as 'industrial design' cannot be exactly translated by what would appear to be the Italian synonym *disegno industriale*. *Disegno* in Italian gives the idea of a profile, an outline, something that has more to do with the outer shape than with the organic form of an object. *Disegnare* is the verb you would use to describe what a draughtsman does when he draws (in English it would be better to say 'sketches') the shape of a horse, but a horse is really designed inasmuch as it is an object of nature, that is to say, it is designed according to a relationship between the inside and the outside, between form and function.

Let us talk then about design, but not only about industrial design: between the second half of the last century and the first half of the present one various thinkers came to the conclusion that design already existed before the industrial world did, indeed before the time of the eighteenth-century mechanical looms. Neolithic woman (apparently it was a woman: men went out hunting, and women invented objects in the village), when she dampened the clay and turned it on a wheel to produce a vase (the perfect, functional, revolutionary shape), was acting as a designer.

We have thus established two points: design concerns the vase as much as it does the city; and design is a form of human activity that precedes the industrial revolution.

2. However, we still have to distinguish three types of design:

a) Identified Design, which is the outcome of an expressed theory and of a practice in which the object aims to exemplify explicitly its author's theory; the Seagram Building and Pininfarina's belong to this category, but so do the submarine and the war machine designed by Leonardo da Vinci.

b) Anonymous Design (or design that does not seem to have an author that anyone can remember, even if there was one originally); design of this sort has no explicit theory, or if it does, it does not claim to exemplify it; the author, famous or anonymous, only wanted to resolve a practical problem; this category includes the various coffee machines that can be seen in Italy, those produced industrially for coffee bars and the hand-made ones once used in people's homes.

c) Non-conscious Design: I use this term in order to avoid the term 'savage' or *selvaggio* currently used in Italian, which does not seem quite right; this category includes farmers' and blacksmiths' tools and many other devices that can be found in industrial society; the people who made these objects did not think of themselves as designers, were not aware of demonstrating any theory and certainly did not think their names

would be handed down to posterity: their concern was only
to produce an object that would work; this is how the inventor
of the first plough or rudder worked; this is how the anonymous inventors of many (perhaps hundreds) of different kinds
of pasta used in the Italian peninsula approached their task;
let us, then, not talk about savage design, even in Lévi-Strauss's
sense of the 'savage mind', because these objects rely on technical knowledge that is very similar to that of anyone who con-
ceives of and constructs an industrial object today.

These three types of design are present in any civilization: in
archaic society, we can think of a pyramid or the sarcophagus
of a mummy as examples of identified design, weapons of war
as an example of anonymous design, and agricultural tools as
an example of non-conscious design. In the United States, the
Seagram Building is identified design, a gas station is anonymous design, and a lollipop is non-conscious design. New
York's Towers are identified design; uptown apartment buildings are anonymous design; Manhattan and especially Wall
Street as an almost casual result of 'savage' planning are non-
conscious design and, seen from the sea, Manhattan is more
beautiful than the Statue of Liberty, which is an example of
identified design.

3. In each of the three cases that we have given the person
who designs an object does so for three reasons:

a) First of all the object is meant to be *useful*, in the sense that
whoever uses it should be able to make it work the right way.
The idea seems elementary, and certainly whoever built the
first plough had an idea of this sort in mind.

In this sense we could say that the first theorists of design
included thinkers of the past who posed the problem of the
relationship between beauty and utility. For example,
St Thomas Aquinas wondered if a saw made of crystal could
be considered beautiful and answered in the negative because

a crystal saw cannot perform the function proper to a saw. Thus Sullivan's formula 'form follows function' must refer not only to the shape of objects but also to the choice of materials. An object must be shaped so that it serves the purpose it was conceived for; this condition is necessary for the concept of design, but it is not sufficient.

b) Indeed, an object should show what its purpose is and how it should be used. In a word, the object has a *communicative* aspect, and this is part of its design. A pair of scissors is a perfect example: the shape makes it quite clear where the fingers go, even to someone who has never seen scissors before. Scissors are a masterpiece of design: not only do they cut, but they show how they have to be handled. This aspect of design is fundamental, although it is not always borne in mind. Indeed, there is no denying that non-conscious 'savage' design is often considerably wiser than identified design, because the latter often bows to 'aesthetic' demands and comes up with new forms that tell the user nothing useful at all.

c) Finally, design has *symbolic* functions: by this I do not mean those primary functions that the object must allow for, but a host of further meanings that allow the object to be used as a mark of social status, power, and so on. These symbolic functions should not be thought of as something extraneous to the object; far from it, they are part of its functions, and it would be wrong to imagine that, if 'form follows function', the form should not follow symbolic functions as well. The clearest example is the Rolls-Royce. Obviously, if the purpose of a car is to cover a certain distance at a certain speed, then we can buy a Fiat or a Ford rather than a Rolls-Royce. But if the ornamental and symbolic aspects of the Rolls-Royce have an important social function, one that is as important as its mechanical functions, so that even in the case of the Rolls it can be said that form follows function, then the form is exactly what it should be if the Rolls-Royce is to be used as a Rolls-Royce.

The Rolls-Royce continues to perform its social functions when it is parked motionless outside the office or the Hilton Hotel.

4. It would be interesting to write a history of Italian design from the time of the Roman Empire to the present. We would discover marvellous examples of identified design, of anonymous design (think of the aqueducts) and of non-conscious design. And we would find some marvellous examples of objects that serve their purpose, that declare and communicate their functions and at the same time communicate symbolic meanings: the first thing that comes to mind is something you can still see in Italian trattorias, the wine flask. It serves its purpose because it holds wine and stands upright on the table; it clearly communicates how it has to be held and how the wine is to be poured, and if the wine drips down the side it is absorbed by the straw covering and does not stain the table; it also communicates ideas and feelings of authenticity, happiness, and simple living. But this analysis would take us too far, and it is probably better to begin our history with the industrial era, when Italian design became well known in America, where it is represented by objects in the Museum of Modern Art in New York (for example, the Olivetti Lettera 22 typewriter). We will start out with this type of 'high' design, because Italy is perhaps the country in which the idea of design has been most highly cultivated even in connection with political and social problems. If other countries have had a theory of design, Italy has had a philosophy of design, maybe even an ideology.

In 1972 MOMA in New York organized an exhibition of Italian design that differed from this one because it stressed identified design and its philosophy. It was a good opportunity, even for Italians, to review the entire history of the dreams, the utopias and the crises of the design idea. Let us try to identify the most interesting period in the history of 'high' design in Italy. I would place it between the 1950s and the 1960s, in the climate of economic, political and civic rebirth after the end of the war, although some of the problems discussed had already been faced before the war. During the course of the 1950s architects (and designers) were in a privileged position in Italy: they personified a Leonardesque dream, that is, they tried to give new life to a renaissance image of man interested in all aspects of life.

While Italy was industrializing and distinct specializations developed in all sectors, the architect tried to be a sort of intellectual interested in politics, art, literature, philosophy and sociology. The architect wanted to produce a way of living by means of the objects he built, and he wanted these to reflect the ideas and the ideals that were being worked out in literature, art, politics and philosophy, and sociology. In those days, at the centre of Italian design, that is to say, in Milan (for centuries a centre of European culture, a crossroads between France, Germany, Switzerland, the Slavic countries and Italy), it was easy to come across architects talking about contemporary philosophy, the psychology of perception, aesthetics, the organization of labour, social planning or the economy. When Rogers said, as already mentioned, that designers should concern themselves with everything from spoons to cities, he meant that the modern architect's dream was to influence life in all its aspects through his proposals. Designing meant being engaged in politics and helping to solve social problems. It was a time when an industrialist of great culture and sensitivity to social problems, such as Adriano Olivetti, would gather researchers from various disciplines around him, and in particular the best designers; not only to produce functioning objects that would sell, but also to project through industry itself a more just and humane society. I am not trying to give my political judgment of that project here; I am just registering a fact that should make understandable the atmosphere in which design developed in those years (basically industrial design, of course). Architects and designers wanted to 'build society'. The great ideas of Walter Gropius and Frank Lloyd Wright found a new climate in which to grow and develop. Designers expressed faith in culture as an independent power that could influence politics. The crisis of that ideal came in the years when architects and designers realized that this was not at all possible, because the laws of economy and politics often frustrated their good intentions.

To summarize, we might say that the drama of the designer was that of an intellectual who had decided to use the power of industry to educate the masses for a better life and to do so had decided to leave the artist's or thinker's ivory tower and to make compromises with economic power. These intellectuals suddenly realized that they had modified the form and several of the technical functions of radios, watches, typewriters (and sometimes even buildings) and had certainly invented more beautiful objects, but had in no way modified or conditioned political or economic power.

I am not saying that this utopia turned out to be a failure or that designers have completely abandoned those ideas; I am saying that the utopia of the 1950s has been cut down to size and that designers now tend to have a more critical and prudent attitude. In some cases this utopia generated cynicism (and the designers produced what industry asked for); in others, designers answered the crisis with ironic and provocative programmes (radical design).

5. But what is interesting in this exhibition is that it shows how many of the projects of identified design have produced a civilization of anonymous design over and above the crisis and disillusionment of the defeat of utopia. This civilization of anonymous design is contradictory, in that it includes kitsch objects and objects that are useless or that do not serve their purpose as well as modest ones that look good and work well, that do what they are supposed to do and make it quite clear

how they should be used, that tell symbolically how the average Italian lives, works or amuses himself.

This is an interesting outcome, one that would seem to indicate that in Italy there is a widespread style which is expressed in the anonymous work of small industries and artisans and helps to maintain a certain 'quality of daily life' despite political and economic crises. We shall not be so naive as to think that the 'average' beauty of Italian objects can save Italians from other and far more serious problems. But when we say that good anonymous (or non-conscious) design is still present in our country, we are not saying only that it is still full of minor and unknown 'artists' who continue to produce even as economic crisis knocks at the door or terrorists shoot in the street. We are also drawing attention to a phenomenon that helps explain how it is that economic crisis, terrorism and bad government do not reduce Italy to a state of ruin. There is a term used in our country, 'submerged economy'. The term refers to a wide range of economic activities involving small and medium industry that flourish in every small Italian city and that prosper, even when large national industries face periods of crisis. This submerged economy is said to be what saves Italy. Well, anonymous and non-conscious design is the external facade of this submerged economy. Behind the 'good' form of a coffee machine, of a pair of shoes, of an article of clothing, there is human labour, creative intelligence and economic productivity that are never completely in a state of crisis.

And this is why an exhibition that includes anonymous and non-conscious design alongside identified design does not tell two different stories or merely deal with a purely 'aesthetic' history that has little to do with the real life of the country. They are not different stories, because there are influences and adaptations that connect identified design to the success of anonymous design (just as non-conscious design has often inspired identified design). This is not a purely 'aesthetic' history because, as I have said, behind these objects there is the creativity and optimism of a society that continues to produce and produce efficiently.

6. One aspect of the exhibition that may surprise visitors is the large number of objects related to leisure time. All things considered, even the Italian bar with its coffee machines, glasses and sugar bowls is a fundamental aspect of free time in Italy. Italians do not go away for long weekends, but they interrupt the working day (or continue to work) by going to the bar, and the bar is a social mechanism of great importance. The list of leisure-time objects also includes sports cars, seaside and mountain holiday equipment, sports equipment, even the bicycle.

It would be wrong to suggest that all this only concerns free time. In fact, behind this phenomenon there is a civilization of work time, and it is the liveliest and sanest part of an economy.

7. Finally I would like to say that anonymous design often corrects the errors made by identified design. Indeed, among the causes of the crisis of the design utopia during the 1950s was undoubtedly an unconscious betrayal of the true functions of objects. Paradoxically, in aiming to make functional objects, designers tried to accentuate the communicative functions of these objects; and instead of producing objects that communicated the way they could be used, they produced objects that communicated the design philosophy. That is, the object did not say, 'I can be used like this', but rather said, 'I am a perfect design object.' Let me try to give a very simple example. In anonymous designed Italian cutlery there is the long-pronged fork. It is a fine object, it looks like a hand, and Bruno Munari once did a whole book in which the forks 'talked' by moving their prongs as though they were the fingers of a hand. (Italian forks can do this sort of thing because, as everyone knows, the Italians often express themselves with hand movements.)

At a certain point designers sought to make more beautiful, more functional forks that were inspired by the ones designed by the Danes, and they produced beautiful forks with short prongs. For many people, buying these forks meant being up-to-date. The fork said 'I am a modern fork.'

Unfortunately the Italians eat spaghetti, whereas the Danes eat a lot of peas. Now short-pronged forks also work as spoons, that is, they can be used for spearing meat as well as for scooping up peas. But this kind of fork is no good for eating spaghetti, because spaghetti can only be twirled around a long-pronged fork, which the eater plunges into the spaghetti perpendicularly to the surface of the dish and then rotates in such a way as to roll up the spaghetti. So the designers' forks were all right in rich people's houses where more meat and less spaghetti were eaten, but not in poor people's houses. What's more, they weren't even any good in restaurants, because even rich people usually eat spaghetti in restaurants, because each restaurant has its own speciality.

I imagine that some designers made this choice on purpose, in that they tried to introduce new feeding habits into a more affluent society through the design of forks. But it wasn't up to the designer to decide who should eat more meat, so he ended up by producing fine museum pieces but terrible ones for restaurants.

In this sense anonymous design has taken its revenge, has corrected the errors of the identified designer utopia and has repopulated the country with good 'normal' forks. Normal means more efficient, more understandable, and thus more beautiful and more human.

8. I think that the history of Italian design should not be seen as a linear history, but as a development that contains these contradictions, that arises from a trial-and-error process, and in this sense it is an interesting story even for non-Italians. And I believe that this exhibition can supply the elements

necessary for reading the history of Italian design in this way; a way that is free, I hope, in which everyone will try to compose his or her own story.

This aspect of Italian life may call for some further observations. These observations may appear to have little to do with design and more with ways of living. In a highly departmentalized university they wouldn't concern the Department of Architecture but the Department of Cultural Anthropology. This would be a mistake: the only way to understand the needs of non-conscious design in a given society is to understand the needs that this society expresses. We were on the subject of coffee bars. In Paris a bar is a *café terrasse*, an easygoing meeting place where people sit at tables, where Sartre wrote, where lovers decide on their adulteries, where cinema producers meet actors. In New York bars like this don't exist. There are places where you can drink an orange juice standing up beside a cocaine pusher and a tramp, and there are cosy little coffee shops where you can eat and talk in peace. The Italian bar is something different again, perhaps more like a French café than an American coffee shop, but that is not all. In Italian bars most people stand up. You can sit down too if you want to, but you don't have to. You go in, you order a coffee and get it in two minutes, you drink it and you go out. But in this space of time, standing up at the bar, all sorts of things get done. Business is discussed, real estate is bought and sold, the candidacy of politicians or the end of a love affair is decided. You drink a coffee, an aperitif, you eat a croissant, a toasted sandwich, maybe even a steak.

The bar no more belongs to work than it does to leisure time; it's a no man's land, halfway between leisure and the job. People go there to fill out football pool coupons, so it's also a sort of gambling saloon where people discuss sport. It's a classless place: except for a few areas of the city (there are blue-collar bars and white-collar bars), the bar is a place where the chairman of a corporation discusses the fate of ten thousand workers alongside an accountant who chats with a friend about what he's going to do at the weekend.

This is cultural anthropology, and it has its effects on design. The bar is a place where you order something but where you also *choose* or *take* something with your hands (a sandwich, a lottery ticket, a packet of chewing gum). So everything in the bar has to be 'legible'. Each object has to be so designed that it can be quickly, immediately, easily and independently used. Without an anthropological background of this sort, even the espresso coffee machine would be hard to understand. Espresso coffee is a symbol of Italianness throughout the world, but real Italian coffee is Neapolitan coffee, and this is made in a little handmade machine with religious care and love: there is no haste and the balance between water, flame and time has to be perfect. In a wonderful scene in Eduardo De Filippo's play *Questi fantasmi*, the rite of coffee-making is described to perfection. Thus the espresso coffee machines you find in bars are Italian in the sense meant by Malinowski when he said that certain bicycles, used in African countries but manufactured in Japan for the African market, were no longer objects of European civilization but were new autochthonous objects of African civilization. Espresso coffee is coffee plus the civilization of the bar. And the same can be said of the cups, the sugar bowls and the glass cupboards with their sliding doors where the pastries are kept.

The second subject is the bicycle. Do Italians use bicycles for work or for sport? It's hard to say where one begins and the other ends. Of course, in 1940 the bicycle was a work tool. In the 50s and 60s, with the automobile boom, the bicycle practically disappeared. I remember Rogers back in 1962 seeing a mutual friend, a rich industrialist, arrive one evening by bicycle and saying: 'He's a lucky man to be able to come by bike!' In those days going by bicycle was a luxury, or worse, an oddity, like going by balloon, an oddity that only a millionaire could allow himself. Nowadays, what with the oil crisis, ecology and urban overcrowding, bicycles have come back as a means of transport. But those who use them not only aim at getting around quickly. All right, they're moving around for work, but they're also getting the same sort of exercise that Americans get by jogging. It's a question of cholesterol. This has influenced the shape of bicycles. Before the war bicycles came in two shapes: normal and racing models. The normal ones were for normal people, straight up and down jobs without extra bits and pieces; the racing ones were for those who had to get everything possible out of a bike. Today the bicycle is a centaur, a thing that is both functional and symbolic at the same time; it's used for getting around on, for keeping muscles in tone and for showing everyone that its rider has chosen the ecological option (the bicycle is thus a vehicle and a philosophical declaration). And what does the bicycle look like? Its shape becomes ambiguous, functional elements unite with symbolic elements, and it's no longer clear which bits are supposed to make the wheels go round (to lessen the effort), which are supposed to keep the legs moving (to increase the effort), and which bits are supposed to keep the mind and the imagination going. What does 'form follows function' mean for a bicycle nowadays? What is its function? These questions have to be borne in mind if we are to understand the design of the contemporary Italian bicycle.

Another important aspect of Italian life is the concept of space. Proxemics scholars studying the social meaning of spatial distance have distinguished between centripetal spaces and centrifugal ones. Centripetal spaces tend to put people in contact, centrifugal ones to separate them. The classic Italian city, with its houses surrounding the square and its network of roads converging towards the square in diminishing circles, is the sort of space that deliberately encourages people to meet each other (whether to socialize or fight is neither here nor there). The structure of the American city, with its main street lined with shops and its residential areas away from the city centre deliberately ensures individual privacy and thus tends to separate. Much has already been said about the structure of urban space. But these problems have to be taken into consideration when thinking about the structure of a restaurant or a café in Italy. They're centripetal structures that tend to promote contact between people.

Suffice it to think of the typical structure of train compartments in Italy. The American train is like a bus, a long corridor with seats one behind the other so that each person can see only the back of whoever is sitting in front: this train defends privacy. Compartments in Italian trains on the other hand are divided up like little sitting-rooms in which passengers have to sit *facing* each other. This sort of compartment favours socialization and conversation. In an American train the most important thing is to have a little pull-down table in front of you, as in planes, so that you can put something to eat or drink down on it (what else is there do do?). Italian trains have few of these pulldown tables, not one per passenger, because this isn't considered to be an important problem. In American trains the lights are usually individual spots, as they are in planes, whereas in Italian trains the lights help create a collective ambience. In American trains the colours are dark and isolating, in Italian trains they are light and conducive to socializing.

Understanding this Italian conception of space means being able to understand not only the design of small objects but also certain recent decisions regarding the restructuring of space in cities. During recent years Italy has suffered from a phenomenon that has grown widespread in large industrial civilizations: urban violence, and the temptation that people then feel to stay home or stick to a few suitably 'fortified' places where everyone is checked at the entrance. In many American cities there are public spaces that are only open for a few hours in the day for a whole range of activities: Washington Square, for instance, or Central Park in New York, for as long as there's daylight. As soon as it's dark the city is deserted, except for the part of town where the shows are (Broadway). Italy began to move in this same direction a few years ago, but the structure of Italian cities simply couldn't cope with temporal and spatial divisions of this sort. The Italian city was built to be lived in *all* day and *centrally*.

In recent years many interesting proposals have been made for the revival of the historic old centres of towns by means of festivals, collective shows, events of one sort and another; these amounted to attempts to rescue the city as a place for 'living in together'. These efforts have involved design, particularly the design of amusements (processions, shows, masquerades) and the revival of objects and situations (archaic design such as the sweetmeats stall, the soft drinks kiosk, temporary sales points). These are not new inventions but the recovery of old traditions that once belonged to country fêtes and have now turned up again in the city. They cannot be said to be purely commercial attractions but part of an overall policy (much discussed and perhaps questionable, but nevertheless interesting and important). Phenomena of this sort must also be included in any panorama of Italian design. Otherwise it is hard to grasp the idea of Italy itself or of design.

1982

CHAPTER 2

A Dollar for a Deputy: La Cicciolina

ANYONE WHO CHALLENGES the election of Miss Ilona Staller, currently running for deputy in the Italian parliament,[1] must risk appearing bigoted, reactionary and intolerant. However, there is one argument that cannot be dismissed and it supports the position of those who object. What is it? And how can it be countered by the would-be deputy?

There are six arguments designed to deprecate the elevation of Miss Staller to the post of parliamentarian and all are vulnerable to sharp but disinterested criticism. The first is that it is inappropriate to send a 'porno-star' to parliament. Personally I find the use of the term shows lack of knowledge because in Greek *porne* means whore whereas good taste now obliges us to say *lucciola* (firefly). If she had stood as a candidate for 'Women of the Red Light District' and won, would you have objected? Would you have questioned that fundamental principle of an open society, namely that no one profession is less honourable than another? If so, you would have committed an error because this principle has a social function. Were there professions condemned as less honourable, everyone would want only to follow those considered honourable and we would have the classic *bellum omnia contra omnes* (war of all against all).

The second argument goes as follows: if one has to have a striptease artist in parliament, then one should choose someone of talent and originality, a Rita Renoir or a Lily Niagara[2] (if they were Italian) or at least a Rosa Fumetto. Instead, we have ended up with a practitioner who calls her act 'Perversion' but hasn't a clue about the art of lighting the fuse of desire with a mere nothing. The Right Honourable Ilona Staller doesn't deconstruct her sex in pure *écriture*, she doesn't tease to the limits of endurance through an elusive play of shady and decadent illusion. Rather she offers it up to her customers for tactile inspection, as happens with those stars of the burlesque you can admire at very close quarters, in the area around Broadway, for only three or four dollars, or in places with booths for a mere twenty-five cents. Blissfully unaware of Swinburne, D'Annunzio and Peledan, innocent of the way the Flesh goes with Death and the Devil,[3] and of fire's beauty, she ends up (thanks also perhaps to her foreign origins) confusing seduction with micturition, and eroticism with exoticism.

But look how discriminatory the argument is. It would be impossible to have a Gassman or an Olivier on all the lists of candidates and we would risk making second-class citizens out of those represented by the likes of Pippo Franco.[4] If that were so, and God does not will it, Aesthetics would intrude upon Ethics or produce some other unthinkable admixture of the different forms of the Spirit. The next step would then be to limit the right to vote to citizens with wealth and education, and to exclude labourers, to enfranchise the stroller in Central Park but not the visitor to a Theme Park. The voyeurs of *The Three Penny Opera* would vote but not the players of the three-card trick. Hardly very democratic.

Third argument: Ilona Staller ran an election campaign based on the generous exhibition of her intimate parts. We've had campaigns based on bringing along the left shoe,[5] and others on the promise of posts as ministerial door-keepers, to say nothing of Mafia fund-raising or votes extorted from patients in coma. As far as immorality goes, worse has been seen.

And this brings us to the fourth argument, according to which it isn't right to have as a member of parliament someone who belongs to a profession said to be offensive to a good third of the electorate. The Right Honourable Ilona Staller has already answered this hypothetical objection by asserting that it is surely better to see on those venerable seats someone who has broken the sixth commandment and not the fifth, seventh and eighth. True enough. Two wrongs don't make a right and if a plebeian bankrupt was introduced into an aristocratic club the standards wouldn't be raised by making a retailer in ecological fertilizers into a member. However, since the candidature and election of the Right Honourable Staller were designed as a premeditated insult to the parliamentary institution, one has to admit that, if insults are a weapon in the battle for higher moral standards, the whole question makes sense and has therefore to be judged accordingly.

The fifth argument collapses as well – the one which plays on the suspicion that Miss Staller may find herself the victim of frequent lapses of memory when the debate is dealing with questions of the economy, law or public administration. Apart from the fact that it isn't yet a given and everyone has the right to prove themselves, let's not forget that a good many elected representatives (if they were made to do their school examinations again) might reveal equally unsatisfactory levels of education.

The sixth (and utterly specious) argument has already been answered by the Radical Party spokesman, Giovanni Negri, when he reminded a petulant journalist on television that his party isn't criticized for having Leonardo Sciascia as a senator or Rita Levi Montalcini as a deputy. Negri's point completely undermined the notion that, sadly, when it comes to public opinion Gresham's Law prevails; if, as happened about ten years ago, a distinguished theologian (cardinal in fact) is caught in a house of ill-repute, people conclude that the churchman frequents dubious places, not that a papal edict has given the house the status of the Sistine Chapel. In this instance, Negri's case holds water since Rita Levi Montalcini is a woman of such style, seductive intelligence, undefinable allure and exquisite nobility as to be able single-handedly to save even a party that had recruited all of Maison Tellier. Similarly, Sciascia is a man of such lucidity, sobriety and forbearance as to be capable of civilizing a gathering of Liverpool football fans. However, it is a sorry sight to see two public figures of such stature reduced to being disinfectants.

Now that all these lightweight arguments have been dismissed, a seventh objection remains and I see no way of faulting it. The Right Honourable Ilona Staller has during the course of the electoral campaign announced her intention of entering parliament in order, whatever the resistance, to provoke and artfully beguile the representatives of the major parties, thereby upholding (with deeds rather than words) the right to control one's own sexuality – although, be it said, she affirms this right in words while denying it to her scopophiliac devotees by her actions.

And here's the pitfall. Parliamentarians are also elected thanks to the esteem they have earned from professional and artistic merits, but they enter parliament in order to dedicate themselves to the common good, not to display these merits. There's nothing wrong with electing a fire-eater as a deputy; it would be wrong if he were then to do nothing but eat fire. The next thing we'd have Paolo Villagio[6] elected and coming along to debates dressed as Mickey Mouse, Giorgio Strehler in rags as 'Harlequin the servant of two masters' or, worse still, as a theatre director who'd make honourable members do somersaults and marionette movements saying 'Yes, sir. No, sir.'

Even worse scenarios are imaginable.[7] The famous neurosurgeon might want to subject the Right Honourable Bettino Craxi to a lobotomy, a trainer might make Senator Fanfani play basketball, an ear-nose-and-throat specialist might force stones down De Mita's throat, a hair-stylist might shave off Occhetto's moustache and turn De Michelis's shock of hair into a mohican, the osteopath might subject Andreotti to painful and useless therapy, and that's to say nothing of the tasks that might have fallen to a funeral director. Imagine what would have happened when Galeazzi Lisi was papal embalmer.

This is certainly not what we expect of the people's representatives. We elect them to represent the people as a whole, whether they be chromolithographists, surveyors, legal experts, bakers, Eugubines, acupuncturists, Premonstratensians or taxidermists, not to exercise their specialist (and limited) skills.

Of course the Right Honourable Ilona Staller could deviate from her initial plan. A surgeon wouldn't present himself in a white coat, hands dripping blood, a fakir would avoid going round in chains distributing bits of broken glass to colleagues, Villaggio would desist from throwing himself on the ground muttering about monstrous mega-galactic plots. Likewise, the Right Honourable Ilona Staller could come wearing a severe Chanel outfit and propose bills for the protection of reptiles or the conservation of the environment, even if it meant losing some of her 'appeal' and some of her earnings, seeing that (voluntary) service of the Fatherland requires sacrifices.

And were this to happen, all the other objections to her election would be null and void. Moreover, she would triumph over all those who, in voting for her, sought to humiliate, treating her not just as an instrument but as a blunt instrument.

1987

CHAPTER 3

For Grace Received

HERE ARE some of the innumerable titles that constitute what we might call the 'thaumaturgic underground': *Sorriso di Pargoli, Dalle api alle rose, Primavera missionaria, Aiutiamo gli orfani, Il perché della vita, Araldo di S. Antonio, Domenica del corriere, Papa Giovanni, Celeste Consolatore, La voce della Madonna, Pax et Bonum, Primavera missionaria, Il santo taumaturgico*, and the list could go on. These are publications of varying format and size, many printed daily, that are sent free of charge by a range of orphanages, missionary societies and sanctuaries, and circulated throughout the country. Despite differences in approach, all these magazines have one feature in common: the publication is a kind of outer wrapping for the payments slip. Each offering has a 'mediated' and an 'immediate' objective. The mediated objective is the support of orphans, the acquisition of an altar for a mission in the Congo and so on. The immediate objective is the future attainment of grace or recompense for grace received. Kant would have said that these publications were based not on categorical imperatives (do good for the sake of good) but on hypothetical imperatives (do good if you want your boil to be cured).

THAUMATURGIC ADVERTISING

If you go into a church in a town and ask for information about this type of publication, you will end up convinced that it is something quite insignificant. The priest will generally shrug his shoulders in irritation, like the vice chancellor of a university who has been asked about photo-novels for house-wives: 'It's all silly nonsense. After the conciliar reforms of the 1960s the Church has nothing more to do with such things, and none of this stuff is to be found in this parish.' And yet the question is not of such marginal importance. It raises both financial and ideological issues, and should, moreover, be the subject of a key chapter in any book about the press in Italy for the simple reason that it represents the biggest publishing business in the land. Faced with the circulation figures of the *Araldo di S. Antonio* or the *Domenica del corriere*, photo-novels look like the most arcane of avant-garde poetry.

No press yearbook or handbook for advertisers even mentions these magazines. However, in a city like Milan an esti-mated one in three families receives a copy a week. Often the same family gets more than one copy, even if not regularly. Perhaps as many as one million copies are distributed in Lom-bardy alone. If we take regions especially prone to thaumatur-gic advertising, in the South for instance, the figures would increase dramatically. Naturally what the publishers make from this enterprise is veiled in mystery and they constantly harp on about the hard-heartedness of their readers in the hope of inducing further donations, keeping computerized records.

A quick calculation of donations can be made on the basis of a random sample. Take the May 1969 edition of *Missioni della Consolata*. Add up the donations for new scholarships, for the beautification of Giuseppe Allamano, Servant of God, and donations for missions, and it comes to about five million lire.

IN THE DIARY OF THE SAINT

Nonetheless these are serious publications that are mindful of their accountability to their benefactors. Usually our magazines don't publish complete lists of donations but restrict themselves to the occasional edifying example on the letters page. Nor should one forget the slow non-stop flow of donations for the celebration of Mass. For instance, *Papa Giovanni* of Andria warns: 'The benefactors who join us in our Good Works by donating at least 5,000 lire (even in instalments) partake in the Holy Mass that the Congregation celebrates in perpetuity. Lesser offerings can also enjoy such benefits in proportion to the amount given.' Other magazines fix a miminum sum of 1,000 lire per Mass, pointing out that smaller offerings are seen as acts of pure charity.

In fact the minority of donations are made by tens of thousands of humble people who send in tiny sums, often to several different organizations. An interesting insight is provided by a story printed in the *Celeste Consolatore* of Messina concerning Battista, a carpenter who 'made a good living and managed to feed five children'. It was an ideal family because it was moved by 'fear of God, love of work and moderation of desire'. His desires had to be moderate, for Battista, on his carpenter's wage, had to find a way of simultaneously sending three sets of donations to the three different magazines taken by himself, his wife and one of his sons. One thousand lire to each publication, while mama, busy at the store, secretly wiped away a tear, happy to have a husband so good. People like Battista are found in their thousands, and one of the first tasks of every reader is to send the magazine to as many of their addresses as possible.

This is how a web of collaboration is woven between readers and magazines. It is also what enlarges the address list, whose size needs to be considerable for any thaumaturgic saint worth his salt. The public is continuously called upon to participate actively – procuring new friends, setting up little votive altars with alms boxes in their own homes, spiritually adopting orphans and young missionaries in the Third World, dedicating benches and holding funeral services for deceased persons, paying for the construction of sanctuaries (500 lire per brick, 1,000 lire for tufa, 1,500 lire per hundredweight of cement, 3,000 lire for a day's labour – these are the prices cited in *La voce della Madonna* in 1969; the cost in 1954 of 100 bricks for a similar building was just 1,000 lire).

DEVOTIONS ON THE MOTORWAY

So much for the questions of finance and circulation. As for the ideological influence of this thaumaturgic press, it would be easy to suggest that the majority of recipients put the publications in the bin or send a donation just to salve their consciences without bothering to read them. However, even allowing for the fact that a tiny percentage actually read the contents, we still have hundreds of thousands of readers, as indicated by the letters page, by the declarations of grace received, and by the reasons given for making donations, which are never vague but indicate attentive perusal of the propagandist material. Let's now look a little closer at the cultural, political and moral world of the thaumaturgic press and its regular readers, noting that a single issue of these 7 × 12 cm magazines would reach more readers than a year's worth of *L'Espresso*.

The main commodity offered by the thaumaturgic press is grace received. Donations for grace to be received are rare. Usually it is payment on delivery, and the recipients prove remarkably honest in declaring the receipt of grace. Moreover, it is reasonable to suppose that payment is often made for acts of grace of which the protector saint remains blissfully unaware. The acts of grace on the motorway are a case in point and depend on a glaring sophism. A typical letter goes as follows: 'I was with my family on the motorway and we were involved in a terrible accident. The people in the other car were all killed and yet we escaped without a scratch. Thanks be to the Madonna of Fatima, Santa Rita, San Gaspare del Bufalo etc. We are sending 10,000 lire.' If the act of grace were genuine one would have to infer that Santa Rita or San Gaspare are directly responsible, from either carelessness or malice, for the death of the travellers in the other car (and they should therefore pay the 10,000 lire to the family of the unfortunates).

THE CHASTE IMPREGNATOR

The second type of act of grace entails underestimating secondary causes, to use the theological jargon. As is known, God acts upon earthly things through secondary causes (for example, the punishment of sinful mankind through floods takes place as a result of atmospheric changes and rainfall). The problem of identifying a miracle (hence the extreme caution of the ecclesiastical authorities) consists precisely in establishing whether the secondary causes have taken their course in the normal way, in which case there is no miracle, or whether they took extraordinary forms. Another of the typical formulations found in letters concerning grace received is the following: 'I was affected by a gastric ulcer that was unbearably painful. I entrusted myself to our patron saint and immediately, after an operation, the pain vanished.' A more theologically sophisticated letter writer spells out that the saint 'guided the hand and the brain of the surgeon'.

A fairly singular case is that of San Domenico Savio, a saint with influence over childbirth, as shown by the *Bollettino Salesiano*. The specialism is odd because, as we know, Domenico Savio was a young man of such absolute chastity – his thoughts never even strayed to sexual objects – that compared to him San Luigi Gonzaga comes across as an old libertine. Well, among the acts of grace attributed to Savio in just one issue are some six successful conceptions. One might hazard a guess that the saint intervened to help couples long troubled by infertility. But no, 'Giuseppe and Maria Zanchetta (from Bivio di Frossasco) declared that, overcoming serious difficulties and well-grounded fears, they saw their family filled with happiness for the fourth time with the joyous birth of little Franco. They all express their gratitude to San Domenico Savio for this very special act of grace.'

SAN GIUSEPPE, LET ME PASS THE EXAM

Once again thanks is given: 'Michele and Olimpia Ferrero (Piassasco) through the intercession of S.D.S. have seen their union made joyful once again with the birth of a dear little boy. As a sign of true gratitude they have named him Domenico.' No doubt a saint so successful in promoting births in the same family bears serious responsibilities when confronted with the question of global overpopulation. A unique way of making up for a life dedicated to abstinence!

A typical example of underestimation of secondary causes is provided by the acts of grace of San Giuseppe of Copertino, patron saint of exam candidates. Copertino, described as a 'saint especially beloved of students, who was distinguished by an eventful life and for ecstasy and levitation' (*Pax et Bonum* of Osimo), chose an easy field in which to work. While it is relatively rare to have malignant tumours and rarer still to be cured of them (in which case it is a matter for Santa Rita, 'saint of the impossible'), examinations are a normal feature of life and it is equally normal to get reasonable results (particularly in the wake of the 1968 student protest). And yet every successful exam paper is attributed to the hand of Copertino by his devotees, who never think for a moment of holding him responsible for poor results.

TWO THOUSAND LIRE FOR TONSILS

Frequently, gratitude for acts of grace scarcely conceals the lack of confidence parents have in their children: 'My daughter passed her diploma. I give thanks to the saint for obviously affording protection' (*Dalle api alle rose*, February 1970); or 'I am a fervent devotee of the saint of examinees and I received two acts of grace. I called upon him to help my son graduate and my call was answered. Last year another son had to take a diploma and has so far passed all three university examinations' (*Pax et Bonum*). Thanks to his specialization, Copertino can therefore count on a continuous inflow of donations of between 1,000 and 5,000 lire, which swells with the onset of the examinations season and the subsequent re-sit period.

Sometimes a patron saint's job is plain sailing; the 2,000 lire received by the Madonna of Fatima for a successful tonsil operation represents a good return given the ease of the task. Equally easy are the acts of grace attributed to God's Servant, Canon Allamano: 'My brother suffered from a boil in his throat. I turned with trust to God's Servant and, the very same evening, after a small operation, he recovered and the pain ceased.' As can be deduced, 'operation' stands for 'surgical operation'. A topical manifestation of grace (this was the time of the Hot Autumn strikes) is reported in the November 1969 issue of *La voce dell'orfano*, a publication of the followers of Sant'Antonio of Padua; a young policeman was accused of being overzealous in dealing with presumed villains and was suspended from duty following a court ruling. Sant'Antonio interceded and the young upholder of law and order resumed his normal duties. The magazine prints a photo of him. Evidently it is the wish of every recipient of acts of grace to see their photograph in print, or at least to see a picture of whoever interceded on their behalf. Magazines cannot always oblige and *La voce dell'orfano* gives a perceptive and mystical explanation as to why not: 'Could I please be allowed a little joke?', someone writes, 'Tell Sant'Antonio to obtain fewer acts of grace from God as this is the only way you and many others could be guaranteed a turn.' The explanation also functions as an advertisement, a recurrent feature of the thaumaturgic magazines as a whole.

MIRACULOUS POWDERS

If our calculations are accurate it can be said that there are too many thaumaturgic magazines in circulation. As a result the editorial bodies have to face up to strong competition. They have to compete by offering a wide range of services and by organizing timely advertising campaigns, to say nothing of improving their product. Anyone in a position to offer unhoped for cures does so; those with lesser powers can rely on pass marks in economics or accounting exams. In terms of services many sanctuaries and charity organizations have already developed a commendable inventiveness. The sanctuary church of Santa Rita of Cascia offers miraculous powders which, when swallowed or rubbed onto the painful spot, promise instant relief from a variety of conditions. In the Salesian area of influence, San Domenico Savio even intervenes through a garment with thaumaturgic properties which is meant to be worn in moments of extreme pain. The *Bollettino Salesiano* reports that Giovanni Levicotti from Verzuolo used to suffer from calculus and that he was advised to have an operation and to entrust himself to the intercession of S.D.S. by putting on this garment. Instant cure.

The Josephine fathers of the Madonna die Poveri in Milan seem especially well organized in that they offer the faithful a long catalogue of extra services including: twin-coloured gold embossed ball-point pens (500 lire), rosary beads (500 lire), phosphorescent statuettes mounted on plexiglass stand with carillo and lamp (4,500 lire), miniatures in artistic frames (1,500–10,000 lire), magnetic plaques for car dashboards, key-rings with image of the Madonna dei Poveri (150 lire), enamel brooches (100 lire) and, lastly, miners' lamps [*sic*] (3,500 lire). Wishing the poor, in the name of the Madonna and in the light of these brilliant business ideas, that they may not remain so for long, one must acknowledge that neither the quality of the product nor the abundance of services can overcome the competition unless they are sustained by an adequate advertising launch.

IN THE NAME OF POPE JOHN

What is it then that sells? Apart from speed of service, initial thaumaturgic appeal is made on the basis of the prestige of the saint. The simple fact that there are numerous independent editions of the *Araldo di S. Antonio* makes one think that the Paduan saint must be at the top of the best-sellers' list. However, on closer examination it becomes evident that lying in second position and catching up is Pope John ('Papa Giovanni').

Use is freely made of the unfortunate pontiff for ends that would have horrified him both as man and churchman. Quotations of his words pepper the multifarious exhortations to make donations, but the most skilful organization actually appropriated his name for the title of its magazine – *Papa Giovanni* is actually the organ of the missionary society of the Sacro Cuore of Andria (which, if it hadn't been for commercial considerations, would have called the magazine *Il Sacro Cuore*). One of its slogans goes: 'In honour of Pope John give a missionary to the Church. Adopt our aspirant missionary by sending 15,000 lire.' Instalments accepted.

Pope John also provides leverage for *Incontro con gli amici*, the publication of the missionary school of Gesù Bambino di San Antonio Abate, Napes. One of its slogans asks the reader: 'Have you ever given yourself the blessed contentment of having a series of Gregorian Masses celebrated on behalf of your dearest deceased?' The series costs between 35,000 and 40,000 lire and entitles you to a free copy of the Holy Bible. *Pax et Bonum*, on the other hand, proffers two efficacious slogans: 'Charity gains forgiveness for sins', and 'May one hundred lepers turn to you and smile!' (15,000 lire). The service is rendered by our old friend San Giuseppe of Copertino.

THE EXPERTS OF ALBANO LAZIALE

The most outstanding exponent of advertising is undoubtedly the magazine *Primavera Missionaria*, which is a kind of payment slip with an advertising appendix edited by the trainee missionaries of the Preziossimo Sangue of Albano Laziale. The ace up the sleeves of the devilish future missionaries is San Guiseppe del Bufalo, 'the great thaumaturge who daily obtains dramatic acts of grace from the Holy Blood of Christ'. Despite the modest quality of the printing, one finds here a training in advertising that is not a far cry from the world of detergents ('biological washes whiter than white' etc.). The slogans with which he is promoted include the following: 'Let no home be without the image and prayers of this wondrous saint', and 'Adopt a future missionary and you will always have a priest to pray for you.' 'By praying to San Gaspare the sick are healed, the afflicted comforted, tears dried and worries assuaged. All these things are in the power of prayer and charity.' Even acts of grace received thanks to San Gaspare are presented with fine news sense. Here are some of the headlines: 'DRAMATIC ACTS OF GRACE', 'AFTER FOUR YEARS OF HELL!', 'OFF THE DANGER LIST', 'IT SEEMED IMPOSS-IBLE!', 'BETWEEN LIFE AND DEATH', 'TRUE', 'TUMOUR GONE'.

Arcobaleno, published by the Rogationist fathers of Oria near Brindisi, relies instead on speed of service. Prayers to Sant'Antonio 'in order to beseech him for any act of grace whatever' are conceived in the shape of a bureaucratic form with requisite blank spaces: 'Beseech on my behalf for the act of grace that I unceasingly ask of you (tick as required) if that be for the good of my soul. Do so in the name of the innocence of the orphans to whom I promise a donation according to my means.'

Our journey into the small world of thaumaturgic magazines cannot avoid being pitiless; and yet many of these organizations actually help abandoned children and take in orphans. If a suggestible soul is comforted by swallowing miraculous powders and believes himself subject to an act of grace on account of cured tonsillitis, why deny him or her the subtle pleasures of the supernatural?

THE POOR MAN AND THE LITTLE BLACK CHILD

Don't forget that the magazines have a massive circulation and are read with devout trust. The ideological message they convey is therefore important. The thaumaturgic centres represent real pressure groups which it would be foolish to ignore. By giving serious consideration to their social doctrine one comes to realize that the whole of this Catholic 'underground press' remorselessly propounds a discourse that harks back to a time well before the Second Vatican Council. Before the time of Pius IX or even that of Luther. The various mystical-cum-commercial exhortations appear as nothing more than a sale of indulgences.

The majority of the magazines could be dated at random 1970, 1870 or 1770. History is missing from their discourse and the good is presented as a triangular relationship between the devotee, the saint and the orphans. Swimming in pity for the foundling, the pauper child and the sick African boy, none of these magazines ever asks why there exist abandoned children, children in poverty and sickness. The most that is achieved by way of sociological analysis is reference to 'hard-hearted' people who refuse to make donations. The existence of evil and poverty is established as an unchanging background that ultimately makes possible the commercial enterprise which prospers on that basis. The poor appear in three different guises: as objects of charity, as the objects of divine predilection ('Blessed be the poor'), and, finally, as the objects of the specific love that the rich owe them ('Rich men, love the poor!')

An example of the totally ahistorical nature of this discourse is provided by publicity maxims. The Rogationist fathers in Naples compile these under the heading 'Some Words of Advice'. Each piece of advice consists in a verse from the Bible, whether from the Wisdom of Solomon or Ecclesiasticus.

WHAT DOES THIS DON MAZZI WANT?

It is common knowledge (and the Church knows very well) that a verse from the Bible read out of historical or philological context can serve any lunatic purpose. Take this almost comically reactionary piece of advice to the modern person (with appropriately 'modern' photos, albeit showing 1950s fashions): 'He who loves his child does not spare the rod . . . He who admonishes his child shall move his enemies to envy and his friends to praise . . . Yoke his neck in youth and beat his sides while he is a boy so that he may not be hardened and deny you obedience, otherwise he shall bring suffering to your soul . . . Show consideration to the horde of poor people and the humble of heart.'

Naturally not all the publications operate at this level of ahistorical naiveté. Magazines like the *Araldo di S. Antonio* (Desenzano and Rome editions) or *Il santo taumaturgico* of Naples are, by contrast, proudly committed to their views on the problem of our time. They open up with the battle against divorce and follow on with polemics against social protest. While the Naples magazine dedicates many articles to the miraculous powers of Sant'Antonio's tongue, the *Araldo* frankly confronts postconciliar realities and broaches the question raised by a reader concerning a priest involved in protest actions. To the reader's enquiry, 'But what does this Don Mazzi want?', comes the answer: 'One would like to ask him because maybe he doesn't even know himself. In fact he twists and turns too much, and always dances in a leftward direction.' And so on.

THE GENERAL'S SACRED READINGS

Other issues of the day include the defence of church schools, the pre-eminence of the Pope over his bishops, and social equality. As mentioned, the solution to this last problem is always pitched in terms of charity and obedience. First prize must go to the pamphlet *The Whys and Wherefores of Life* of the Sant'Antonio orphanage of Oria. It begins with a letter written by the bishop of Oria which praises the 'clear-cut reply given to those petty questions that are frequently debated'. Among the petty questions passed over let us consider the answer to the question: 'Why must so many social inequalities exist?' It's simple enough. Social inequalities cannot be avoided. Take an engineer who gives orders to a worker. The former has studied for years and years at the cost of hard and unending sacrifices, though 'perhaps helped by his financial circumstances'. What about the employees of a factory, what have they done? 'They have preferred to acquire a skill rather than an educational qualification, perhaps because attracted to a practical life and not one of study.' So why all the protest? Take a general: 'How long is the apprenticeship that he has had to undertake! During the war, which for others brought only grief and suffering, he knew how to plan strategy . . . and for his merits in warfare he was promoted to the rank of general.' After all, 'Some want to study, others don't; some want to work, others don't. One person is happy to become head technician, another wants to pursue his career and become a manager.' It is not clear therefore why people should protest. 'Inequalities, created by nature and human will, will always exist – in every branch of activity there'll be people who give orders and others who obey them . . . Everyone cannot be equal. Society is a ladder – nobody can ever change his nature.' It is necessary to remember that these are not quotations taken from a speech addressed to the counter-revolutionary army of Fra' Diavolo in 1799 but are dated 1955. For the record it should be noted that the author of the pamphlet is Father Tangorra and that, professionally speaking, his work consists in bringing up orphans. In order to carry out his ministry he receives donations from benefactors. The circle is complete – the business of the orphans can only prosper in a world in which generals, through years of tenacious study, learn how to produce them in the first place.

A JET FOR THE HEALER

Refusing to die, thaumaturgic joy seems to get stronger through the medium of mass communications which our technological civilization has put at the service of Father Tangorra and his colleagues. What, then, will be the future of this 'business'?

We should start by dispelling some of the illusions of those convinced that migration, social mobility, the extension of motorways and the increasing use of cars would blow away the dark clouds of obscurantism whose elimination was first entrusted by poor Carducci to the Ministry of Railways run by Satan and Queen Margherita.[1] The sociology of religion (and everyday experience) teaches us that technological development provokes rather than reduces the need for the sacred. Preacher-healers like Billy Graham were not born in Copertino and they travel in private jets like the director of *Playboy*. The future of thaumaturgy in technologically advanced societies may be encapsulated in one of the most developed and flourishing thaumaturgic enterprises in the United States that I have had the good fortune to visit.

I am referring to Oral Roberts University, a huge establishment in Oklahoma, not far from Tulsa, the major centre of the oil industry.

THE TECHNOLOGICAL MINARET

Oral Roberts is a Protestant preacher who is still alive. Like all American founders, he immortalizes his name immediately, before dying. The Oral Roberts soars upwards in a desolate windswept plain and raises skywards science-fiction structures that recall the Osaka Expo. Modern, elegant (an elegance naturally kitsch), combining quotations from space movies with the mannerism of model cities, like Chandigarh or Brasilia, the university complex is dedicated to the formation of upright and God-fearing teachers – teachers predisposed to learn verses of the Bible off by heart but against anything smacking of evolutionary theory. The students have to have short hair, smoking is prohibited and mini-skirts are out. However, visitors are escorted through these buildings (bristling with audio-visual facilities) by pretty hostesses. Lecturers, in order to be employed, must declare that they have 'the gift of tongues', the gift of the Holy Spirit to the Apostles.

At the centre of the campus arises the tower of prayer, a masterpiece of Expo-style architecture, somewhere between a space station tower, a minaret and the tower of Ming, tyrant of Mongo, enemy of Flash Gordon. A computer at the summit of the tower gathers and computes the thousands upon thousands of donations (from a quarter of a dollar upwards) that arrive at the establishment to beseech prayers. The turnover is estimated in millions of dollars per annum.

GENESIS IN TECHNICOLOR

Then prayers are transmitted throughout the world by an independent radio station, from the very same tower. On request, people are invited into a large mystical theatre where they attend a *son et lumière* show on the creation of the world. A mural rises up on the central stage, a vast multi-dimensional panel of coloured plastic that reproduces the hands of God creating the universe in perfect (but unwitting) Pop style. Then the lights go out and while a voice recites the story of the Creation, a clever play of lights brings the panel to life as if one were seeing God at work conjuring up galaxies and planets. Meanwhile sweet music wafts through the air and the faithful are rapt by a vision. In the effulgence of plastic and in the midst of the electronic throb I saw myself in front of an asbestos altar while a celebrant in a diving suit carried out the transubstantiation of Coca Cola. Well, our Father Tangorra has still much to learn – the future of the Italian thaumaturgic press has hardly begun.

1970

CHAPTER 4

The Italian Genius Industry

TWO MONTHS AGO, this advertisement appeared in the 130 lire a word personal columns of the *Giorno*: 'A free copy of my book *Liriche La Casa*, pub. 1969, to anyone purchasing complete set of my thrillers (*L'albero stregato; Quandro si scorge il traguardo; Tre uomini in due barche*). Send 1,000 litre or equivalent sum in postage stamps to the author Angelo Guacci, via Colombo 2, 63100 Ascoli Piceno.' For those who delight in the sociological minutiae of the Italian literary scene such finds are not rare, though they always come as a welcome surprise. With the surprise comes a not unrelated subtle pleasure, renewed every time one leafs through the pages of such precious literary journals as *Il pugnolo verde* of Campobasso, *Calabria nobilissima* of Cosenza, *L'eco del Parnaso* of Naples, *Fiorisce un cenacolo* of Eremo Italico, *Il giornale dei poeti* of Rome, *La disfida* of Corato, *Intervallo* of Modica, *Italia intellettuale* of Reggio Calabria, *Selezione poetica* of Galati Mamertino, not to mention the renowned *Giornale Letterario* published in Milan by Gastaldi.

Such pleasurable activity can also be richly informative: national newspapers and weeklies distributed on a not altogether national basis carry lengthy accounts informing us of, for instance, meetings of the International Poetry Association where, in the presence of famous personalities from the world of literature (one such account mentioned 'Comm. dott. Armando De Santis and signora Velia, prof. Mario Rivosecchi,

Donna Acsa Balella, dottor Nino Pensabene, etc.'), the actress Maria Novella gave a reading of Lorena Berg Fattori's latest poetic works (*Ad ogni ora che passa* [With every passing hour]), described by the official orator as showing certain affinities with the poetry of Leopardi and fulfilling Croce's dictum according to which 'poetry is truth'.

Rarely on such occasions does one come across poetesses with short and commonplace names like Elsa Morante, Anna Banti or Gianna Manzini, nor do they appear in the pages of the journals cited above. Poetesses, like lady teachers of mathematics, always have double-barrelled surnames and are called Alda Mello Caligaris, Antonietta Damiani Ceravolo, Maria Pellegrini Beber, E. Ghezzi Grillini (to cite the most recent additions to the Gastaldi catalogue), or Giselda Cianciola Marciano (authoress of the poetry collection *Polvere di stelle* [Stardust]), Antonietta Brino di Bari (*Azzurro corsiero* [Blue Charger]), Carlotta Ettorè Tabò (*Sinfonia di vita e di morte* [Symphony of Life and Death]), Edvige Pusineri Chiesa (*Mesti palpiti* [Mournful Throbbings]). The men sometimes hear simpler names: they're more likely to be called Emo di Gilio (author of a valuable monograph entitled *L'ascendentismo come l'ismo dei senza ismi* [Ascendantism as the ism of the ism-less], or something out of the last century, when registry offices resounded with surnames like De Gubernatis, De Andreis, De Pretis, De Ambrosiis, De Filippis. All names that seem, for some inexplicable reason, to be absent from the catalogues of major publishers today, names that hark back to an epoch in which it would have been possible for an Arialdo Finzi Contini to write a novel entitled *Il mistero del giardino Bassani*.[1]

These books and the names of the people who write them provide the unsuspecting reader with clues to the secret of what I shall call fourth dimension writers. Let me explain how I arrived at such a term – a term in which evaluative criteria play no part, it being based solely on classificatory criteria of a sociological kind.

There is a literary first dimension. It is that of the manuscript. Were publishers not sworn to secrecy by professional codes of conduct, what tales they could tell us of 400-page manuscripts submitted by retired colonels claiming that the theory of relativity was mistaken, that Newton got his sums wrong, that Pope Pacelli was behind the 25 July coup.[2] Tales of 2,000-page fictionalized autobiographies, of authors who assure them of their novel's unquestionable success, undertaking to buy ten copies themselves, etc.

But as we know, not all manuscripts get published. Those that make it into print are, say, one in a thousand. This one in a thousand enters the second dimension – that of the literary journals and books. The journals may be called *Nuovi argomenti, Paragone, Il Verri* or *Rivista di filosofia*. And the books appear under the names of Mondadori, Rizzoli, Bompiani, Einaudi, etc. There are also smaller publishers and less famous literary journals, but their admittance to the second dimension is ensured by some sort of unspoken convention: it's hard to say how and why it is that a publisher who perhaps set himself up only yesterday and whose name is still unknown nonetheless already forms part of the second dimension. Books published by the small, newly established publishers are reviewed in the major literary journals. This is a society whose members recognize each other. And since we have established that value judgments have no place here, I am unable to say why this is so. That's how it is. The 'couldn't-care-less' response of those excluded from this dimension goes: 'They're all in it together.'

Then there's the third dimension, that of success. The book, whether published by Scheiwiller or Mondadori, becomes famous and is reviewed and translated abroad. At worst it is reprinted and runs to several editions in its country of origin. It makes its mark.

But what of the 999 manuscripts that didn't make it out of

the first dimension into the second? Let's say 900 disappear: the author resigns himself, commits suicide out of desperation, resolves to dedicate his energies to the family firm, goes back to looking after her nice, rather boring husband and the children, enters a convent, toasts the manuscript's destruction with champagne. However, the remaining ninety-nine manuscripts pass into the fourth dimension. The fourth dimension has its own literary journals and its own publishers, its own circle of reviewers (who very rarely write negative reviews), its own roads to success and public recognition. It cuts across the two major dimensions without being noticed, often without noticing them or without being aware that they exist, or sometimes engaging in continual, obstinate (and ignored) polemic with them. Whoever enter the literary fourth dimension can live a happy existence, surrounded by readers, honoured – if not by followers – by devoted friends and relatives, and maintaining a busy emotional and cultural correspondence with their counterparts from one end of Italy to the other. Like an army of 'aliens' come from another planet to live among us as ordinary human beings, they are part of our daily experience: the pensioner sitting in the park, the bank clerk who accepts our cheque, the lady living on the other side of the landing. They outnumber the writers of the second dimension ninety-nine to one. Statistically speaking, they are the backbone of the Italian literary scene.

To be autonomous, a dimension has to have its own independent economic base. The fourth dimension supports itself on the business turnover of the fourth-dimension publisher, to be referred to from now on as 'the FD publisher', and whom I shall attempt to describe using a fictional model synthesizing the actual characteristics of many of his flesh-and-blood colleagues. So, the FD publisher receives the manuscript which has usually been rejected by the second-dimension publisher. However, the manuscript often comes to him in a virgin state, since he is the only publisher the author knows of; indeed, he is thought to actually be the publisher of the second dimension, or the one and only publisher.

Suppose, then, that *cavalier* Evermero Altamura De Gubernatis sends the FD publisher his collection of poems entitled *Cuore dolente* [Aching Heart]. The FD publisher writes back to De Gubernatis to say that his book is of great poetic worth and proves its author to have the stuff of a true writer, that his publishing firm often takes it upon itself to launch new talent, but at present he is weighed down by other commitments and the only way he could publish a thousand copies of the book would be if the author were prepared to contribute financially. Usually, the contribution requested easily covers printing costs (the FD publisher has few overheads, his editorial costs are almost nil since he and his wife do everything, while an accountant cousin keeps the books).

De Gubernatis, who has waited his whole life for the recognition he feels is due, decides to meet the costs, perhaps taking out a mortgage on his pension or assigning a portion of his salary towards it. In exchange, the editor assures him of an impressive critical launch and a hefty discount on the presentation copies he will purchase as gifts for his friends (who are numerous from the outset, and increase in number as De Gubernatis savours the joys of literary renown).

The book comes out, it's well printed and is greeted with a shower of enthusiastic reviews. The reviews appear in a journal published directly by the FD publisher and in numerous associated journals edited by authors published by the same FD publisher, by aspiring authors, and authors published by fellow publishers. Sometimes these contributors get almost as far as the pages of second-dimension literary journals or local newspapers. A copy is even sent to *Il Corriere della Sera* where, if the column is running a few lines short, the title is added to the list of books received; and for a first book, the author can't complain.

Some time later, however, the publisher writes to De Gubernatis that the book remains largely unsold (it's a well-known fact that the stingy, ignorant masses don't care for poets; and for his part the publisher never dreamt for a moment of meeting costs of distribution to bookshops liable to cut deeply into his budget). Pointing to a comma in the contract to which the author hadn't paid due attention, the publisher informs him that he retains the right to pulp the remaining copies (storage costs increase his overheads) unless, and again in accordance with the terms of the contract, the author relieves him of the entire stock at a reasonable discount on the cover price. By this stage De Gubernatis cannot allow the work that has brought him unheard-of fame and happiness, and in which there resides a part of his poet's soul, to disappear into the void of the pulper's yard. He buys. He will be dedicating copies and distributing them to his friends for a long time to come. He'll send them to the young authors he sees blossoming in the second dimension. He'll send another copy to Montale or to Ungaretti, who never acknowledged receipt of the first.

The FD publisher now has a huge advantage over his colleagues in the second dimension. In the first place he has the certainty that he will always sell the very last copy of every book he publishes (a certainty that the publishing giants will surely envy him); in the second place, he only published after his out-of-pocket expenses were covered. As one can see, the fourth dimension is borne on the wings of the national poetic spirit, but flourishes on a solid economic base.

Naturally, as we have said, the FD publisher has a host of accessory activities which, though not profitable, have a public relations function. The industrially based FD publisher doesn't even need to promote them. They flourish unaided, thanks to the initiative of more ingenuous, less profit-minded FD publishers, and to spontaneous creativity. One of these activities is the *Chi è* [Who's Who] or the *Dizionari degli italiani illustri* [Dictionary of Famous Italians]. Naturally, a dictionary of this type is bought chiefly by those people who feature with a fairly lengthy entry, the outline for which they have almost invariably supplied themselves at the request of the dictionary publisher who has contacted all Italians claiming any distinction in the fields of literature and the arts. Naturally, the dictionary also contains entries on Elio Vittorini, Cesare Pavese, Carlo Emilio Gadda and Alberto Moravia. But they were not themselves contacted personally. They are included because of their great renown and so as to authenticate the fame of the others whose names follow or precede theirs in alphabetical order.

All of which requires judgment. A due sense of proportion. Take, for example, Domenico Gugnali's *Dizionario biografico di personaggi contemporanei* [Biographical Dictionary of Contemporary Figures], Gugnali publishers, Modica. Let's look up the entry on 'Cesare Pavese'. It's concise and to the point: 'Pavese, Cesare. Born Santo Stefano Belbo 9.9.1908. Died Turin 27 August 1950. Translator, writer.' A little further on, however, we find: 'Paolizzi, Deodato. Writer and man of letters; presenting Deodato Paolizzi: from earliest childhood he distinguished himself with his spontaneous poetic compositions, but especially with his incisive writings in which one could already sense the lawyer of later years.' This is followed by a brief account of his famous novel *Il destino in marcia* [Destiny on the March] and some remarks about his civic and political activities: 'An Italian by temperament, his heart throbbed with patriotic feeling during the First World War and particularly during the aftermath of the war, when courage and energy both of hand and of mind were sorely needed.'

Continuing in the 'P's', three lines on 'Piovene, Guido' are followed by a long entry on Pusineri Chiesa, Edvige, a primary school teacher from Lodi, poetess and writer, authoress of *Mesti palpiti* [Mournful Throbbings], *Alba serena* [Quiet Dawn], *Cantici* [Canticles], *Il legionario* [The Legionary],

Sussuri lievi [Gentle Murmurs], *Aurei voli* [Golden Flights], *Chiarori nell'ombra* [Faint Lights in the Shadow], *Le avventure di Fuffi* [The Adventures of Fuffi]. She is the Milan editor of the literary journal *Intervallo*, which just so happens to be published by Gugnali, also the publisher of the dictionary in question. The entry includes a photo of Pusineri Chiesa, portraying her in the full glory of her luxuriant maturity, next to which is a photo of the 'delicate Sardinian poetess' Puligheddu, Michelina.

Gugnali's biographical entires reveal a rich and fertile literary universe. Often, a writer's personality is sketched out for us in a few essential strokes: 'Cariddi, Walter. Born 4.2.1930 in San Pietro Vernotico, Brindisi, where he resides (and is known to all).' Poet, critic and journalist, 'he has a vocation for serious studies together with a commitment to the achievement of greater success.' Then there's Arcidiacono, Giovanni, editor of the periodical *Il fauno* and author of *Il giuramento del fauno* [The Oath of the Faun], *L'amore di un fauno* [A Faun's Love], and *Il ritorno del fauno* [The Return of the Faun]. And there's D'Ambrosio, Vincenzo, retired army colonel and *commendatore* of the Italian crown, contributor to literary magazines such as *Controvento, Crociata letteraria, La procellaria, La zagara, Omnia* and *Selva*. Not to mention Leonida Gavazzi, author of *Cromatogramma tridimensionale dell'esistenza* [Three-dimensional Chromatogram of Existence] and *La ragnatela dell'essere* [The Web of Being], and Gargiuto, Gaetano, founder of the poetry movement Armonismo (which even sends numbered editions of typewritten poems to newspapers). There's Maira, Rosangela ('she took part in the "Brava e bella" competition for Sicilian women students held by *Il Progresso Italo-American* . . . and was awarded a prize of a radio'), Montanelli Menicatti, Elena ('one of the most highly regarded poetesses of our time'), Mignemi, Gregorio (author of *Temi svolti* [Written Compositions]), Moscucci, Cittadino ('author of numerous popular songs set to music by *maestro* Cotogni and performed on the radio by the tenor Sernicoli'), and finally, Scarfò, Pasquale (author of *Il signore delle camelie* [The Gentleman of the Camelias], who we are told is 'a chartered accountant with a degree in Economics and Commerce, but who has always preferred army life to his own profession'), not forgetting one Umani, Giorgio, author of *L'ineffabile orgasmo* [The Ineffable Orgasm] as well as *Umani 1937* [Humans 1937], who is, as the biography somewhat pompously informs us, 'a serious scholar of human problems'.

Closer inspection of Gugnali's dictionary reveals the brotherly network of artistic solidarity governing the world of the fourth dimension. The works of authors not published by Gugnali are reviewed in literary journals such as *Il pugnolo verde*, which is produced by authors included in Gugnali's dictionary, who obviously review the works of all the authors published by Gastaldi, while at the same time contributing to the other literary journals listed above. Sometimes, their books are presented abroad by Carlotta Mandel, she being the wife of Roberto Mandel, novelist, author of historical works, war memoirs and poems who was a familiar figure in the market squares of Italy some decades ago, where he ran a stall selling books written and published by himself, his wife and his children, inscribing each copy with a dedication. Those who recall the experience have a vague memory of d'Annunzio-inspired, floral dust jackets, examples of which may still be lurking in many a family library.

What are the books such as those cited in the biographical dictionaries actually about? And how are they reviewed? I shall limit myself to discussing a few examples from my own personal library of the fourth dimension. Here in front of me, for example, I have Carlo Cetti's two-volume work entitled *Difetti e pregi dei Promessi sposi* [Faults and Merits of *The Betrothed*] and *Rifacimento dei Promessi sposi* [*The Betrothed Rewritten*], the latter consisting of the practical application of the critique expounded in the former. Cetti argues that Manzoni would have been well advised to have made one further revision of his novel, lightening the prose by reducing the number of syllables by a third. 'Why say "*lago di Como*" [Lake Como] and "*mezzogiorno*" [an alternative form of 'south'] rather than "*Lario*" [an antique form of Lake Como] and "*sud*" [south]? . . . Instead of saying "*tutto a seni e a golfi*" [all gulfs and bays] it would be better to say "*tutto seni e golfi*", thus avoiding repetition of that *a*.' Proceeding in this way, Cetti manages to rewrite the novel in only 196 pages (published by the author, Como, 1965), from its opening, '*Quel ramo del Lario* . . . ' [That branch of the Lario], to the ending in which, following the death of Father Cristoforo, his text simply reads, '*il povero giovane, sopraffatto da commozione e da gioia, piangeva*' [overcome with emotion and joy, the wretched youth went].[3]

Note that Cetti's is not just a summary of the novel but a full rewrite with excess syllables removed. Manzoni's *The Betrothed* also comes under attack from Vincenzo Costanza (from Agrigento, 'specially admitted to the university teacher's examination by reason of his exceptional scholarship') in a book entitled *Il pecoronismo incantevole in Italia* [The Charms of the Herd Instinct in Italy] where, however, the argument rapidly shifts from Manzoni to the author's belief that Treccàni should instead be pronounced Trèccani.

Of a different nature (and more judiciously normal, with the author giving free rein to his pedagogical inclinations) are the works of Teodosio Capalozza (from Teo da Sepino) published by Teodosio Capalozza in the 'La Diana' series, founded and directed by Teodosio Capalozza. 'La Diana' is a 'collection of eclectic notebooks on universalism'.

Nor should we forget works of scientific divulgation like *Nei misteriosi abissi del sesso* [In the Mysterious Abysses of Sex] by Dr Giuseppe Valenti (published by Castorini Brothers, Catania) and dedicated to young people in need of 'a healthy sex education'. After lengthy explanations of what are almost exclusively sexual perversions – the 'true story of a Calabrian woman who became half-man', a 'typical case of sadism followed by brutality, disembowelling, vampirism and cannibalism' and 'two cases of hypereroticism followed by acts of bestiality (girl copulating with dog)' – there is a description of the movements involved in dancing the twist, which, as the author warns his young readers, represent a dangerous initiation to homosexuality. A different approach is taken by Antonio Germano in his *Guida per amore del sesso* [A Guide for the Love of Sex] (Edizioni Guida d'Amore, Campobasso) in which the tone is more lyrical-mystical. On the other hand, Romualdo Samboco's work, *Ingorda sete dell'oro* [Insatiable Thirst for Gold] is of a moralistic character, its author defining himself as 'interpersonalist, painter, poet and philosopher'.

These and other works, as we were saying, subsequently become the subjects of reviews. The fourth-dimension review undoubtedly constitutes a literary genre in its own right, even though the reviewers are also poets or novelists themselves. The most carefully written are also poets or novelists themselves. The most carefully written are undoubtedly those which appear in Gastaldi's *Giornale Letterario*, their only defect being that they are dedicated exclusively to books published by Gastaldi, giving rise to suspicions of partisanship, even if this is, as we shall see, the result of a precise ideological decision to counter the Marxist filth of official culture. By carefully written reviews meaning judgments that are not excessively laudatory, of the kind: 'Ghezzi Grillini pours forth the fullness of feeling in verse, she sings the cosmos', or, in the case of Clorinda Fontana (*Opera omnia*): 'Her mystical and profane Works bear an unmistakable hallmark, the perfumed breath of an angel transformed into a living spirit, pulsating always . . . a continuous coming and going of green rocks dashed uselessly by the waves of the sea that burst or shatter into the air transforming themselves into gigantic foaming corollas . . . Let us leave her to fly, let us leave her to run, to swarm among mountains and flower-bedecked fields with the mythical spirits of the Naiads, the Napaea, the Oreads . . . Clorinda Fontana . . . a flower blooming in the Milanese fog' (Nino Scalisi).

The same *Giornale Letterario* contains a review by Teresio Raineri of a series of historical novels that is couched in plainer terms, including mention of a *Giardino dei finti [sic] Contini*[4] (a pardonable lapsus) and augmented by tit-bits from the reviewer's own personal memories: 'Quite unique for its transposition of the author who, in the first person, finding himself in the Trentino region, in the Valsugana, so dear to us, due to an accident, during a summer storm' (in which it is unclear whether the Valsugana is dear to Raineri because of an accident, or whether the protagonist of the novel has the accident). Or again: 'I noticed with great pleasure, among the Italian generals of that time, the name of a high-ranking official who comes from a small town not very far from my own.' The review is of *Temporale d'inverno* [Winter Storm] by Wagner Boni, a free copy of which was sent to the reviewer by 'the esteemed publisher Gastaldi': the very least the publisher could do to get a review published in his own literary journal.

Even more interesting is the review in *Mondo nuovissimo* of the novel *Caino nella Luna* [Cain in the Moon] by Enzio di Poppa Vùlture, a writer and man of letters from Lucania whose linguistic daring in this novel of lyrical science fiction is noted by the reviewer: 'Where shall we go for our honeyearth? To enjoy a few beautiful earthlit nights, the balconies of the solar system, funeral pyres migrating through the shadows to stretch our hand out towards the golden robes of the comets . . .' Enzio di Poppa Vùlture is defined as a 'prophet and apostle of a distant horizon' who 'confronts the problem of man's origin and resolves the enternal dualism of good and evil . . .'

However, the most sympathetic and benevolent review I can remember was one in the New York magazine *Supersum* (the Italo-American links of the fourth dimension are many and various – and mysterious) dedicated to the book *Luce sepolta* [Buried Light] by Giovanni Tummolo of Trieste. Tummolo's works are numerous and eclectic in nature. There's the novel *Il divoratore di se stesso* [The Devourer of Himself] (of which I have been unable to find a copy), the stage adaptation of *Sangue romagnolo* [Romagnole Blood] entitled *Meditazioni diaboliche* [Diabolic Meditations], and then the various shorter works in which the author preaches his doctrine of Mystic Atheism, such as *Come evitare la terza guerra* [How to Avoid the Third War], a spirited work full of invective against sceptical fellow-citizens or other authors with whom Tummolo corresponds through the pages of various periodicals (*Il pugnolo verde* of Campobasso, for instance). Of *Luce sepolta* the reviewer writes, 'It is a lyrical and at times superlyrical novel . . . The literature of Tummolo is distinguished above all by its humbleness. A quality which should in theory cause the human heart to feel compassion . . . though in practice the opposite almost always happens . . . It has been shown that almost everybody who, in attempting a narrative synthesis, voluntarily or involuntarily gave *Luce sepolta* a negative review, has revealed himself to be dishonest and incapable of understanding it.' The reviewer's wrath is directed at critics who have mistakenly attempted to summarize the book, yet, as he points out, 'These erroneous interpretations are justified when one considers the enormous literary output of Italy – land of geniuses and heroes – an output of such gigantic proportions that it leaves no time for a careful appraisal.' Although it would be worth wasting a bit more time on the case of Tummolo because, the reviewer remarks, he not only possesses an original style, but an original way of thinking too, while Novalis was but the author of Schelling's philosophy.

The difficulty of getting hold of copies of works like *Il divoratore di se stesso* or *Luce sepolta* is not due to the failings of the commentator. They are hard to come by even in places where they should definitely arrive, like the books sections of newspapers. In fact, it emerges that the fourth dimension's profuse outpourings are shunted off to prisons, hospitals and nursing homes. This allows us to form a very accurate picture of the kind of literary message getting through to the average invalid and prisoner, and echoes of the relentless literary education are to be found in many of the pieces published in another richly insightful publication, *Sotto il faro*, a literary journal 'dedicated to the inmates of Regina Coeli prison'. The inmates themselves contribute (there are even articles by young Potere Operaio[5] theorists who had occasion to reside within its walls). In the absence of contributions from inmates, the prison's medical and religious authorities address the inmates and grip readers consisting of, say, bicycle thieves and cattle-rustlers, with subjects such as 'Metalanguages and Theories', or the (disproved) idea that God is dead.

There may also be a political-pedagogical side to the question of the diffusion of fourth-dimension works if their ideology is taken into account. It is of course difficult, given the unpredictable nature of the contributions, to draw an accurate map of the various strands of thought involved, but I don't think it would be mistaken to suggest that a fourth-dimension culture is a conservative culture. Not just for the (obvious) reason that it shows a 'healthy' stylistic traditionalism, but because, when the fourth-dimension man of letters isn't disregarding the existence of 'official' culture, he is launching Poujadist polemics against it. Not that there isn't a fourth dimension of the Left, though it would have to be sought among semi-literate anarchist groupings (with their own established historical traditions) or among anarcho-fascist malcontents, thereby taking leave of the annals of literature and entering those of politics or psychiatry instead. Not to mention the literature of popular tradition, which itself is part of a separate chapter of custom and language and has vague boundaries that include even semi-commercial ballad-singers. The ideology of fourth-dimension poets and narrators is given coherent expression and a certain stamp of 'authority' by the political style of Gastaldi's *Giornale Letterario*, the tone of which is matched by *Candido* in the North and by *Lo Specchio* in the South.

Mario Gastaldi's editorial in the March issue develops an article by Prezzolini (bewailing the fact that Italy no longer has any spiritual teachers along the lines of a Gentile or a Papini) and, under the title 'The serious and alarming crisis in Italian culture today', points to a series of parallels and contradictions that might be summarized as follows: on one side are those (Gastaldi's authors) who still believe 'in the values of the spirit and . . . in the unbreakable rules of grammar', and, on the other, the bogus culture of 'phoney radio and television broadcasts concocted by Lefties'. On one side the true poets, on the other millionaire communist singer-songwriters. On one side Freudian Marxist structuralists, on the other those for whom style is an ethical imperative and a national duty. Anyone who writes in a smokescreen style (i.e. the avant-garde) soon goes on to wearing the handkerchief over the face (Cavallero)[6] and planting bombs (Valpreda).[7] In the same issue, a penetrating semiotic article on the 'Effects and power of the comma' is followed by a piece in which Federico Lanzalone again emphasizes the differences between the cultural cabals and the healthy forces of literature, while Giuseppe Lega denounces television's unseemly and blasphemous decision to broadcast Pasolini's *The Gospel According to St Matthew* at Easter ('and the patriarch Urbani received the blaspheming author!')

In this way, the literary fourth dimension, from its economic to its ideological aspects, has a certain consistency, though it also comprises the freest of outlooks and the most ideologically innocent of authors. Yet there are other things that characterize the fourth dimension besides its deliberate or unconscious conservatism: an arrogant assertion of its own values, an eclectic editorial multivalency (several magazines are published by the same person, authors are also publishers, etc.), a tireless pro-lificacy, and great (and often unwitting) daring in the choice of titles and authors' names.

The literary fourth dimension is also characterized, however, by a strong sense of cohesion and mutual assistance which is totally lacking for instance in the philosophical fourth dimension. For just as there are fourth-dimension poets and novelists, so there are fourth-dimensional philosophers. Rather than put himself in the hands of the FD publisher, however, the philosopher publishes his works at his own expense, reviled by all and in turn reviling all, scorning the world and conscious only of being the bearer of a truth which others refuse to recognize.

The figure who looms largest in this field is Giulio Ser-Giacomi from Offida (Ascoli Piceno), until recently the cause of much bewilderment at philosophy congresses and author of several weighty tomes, among which a *Filosofia del trascendente* [Philosophy of the Transcendent], a *Post fata resurgo* and eighteen other volumes. One of Ser-Giacomi's famous works is epistolary, running to hundreds of pages and gathering together all his letters to Pope Pius XII and Einstein (letters which unfortunately never elicited replies) and in which the philosopher refuted both Christian and relativistic metaphysics in one breath. In his concluding remarks to the seventeenth congress of philosophy (where, as in preceding congresses, Ser-Giacomi's contributions had understandably given rise to some consternation) the philosopher stated: 'Nobody has bothered to discuss the many historical questions asked then answered well ahead of their time in my *Alea jacta est*, likewise as to the ones in my *Gutta cavat lapidem* which I took the trouble to send to several scholars before the Congress . . . Philosophy is in need of new lymph, that lymph which I have been giving it for so long . . .'

Ser-Giacomi's adversaries are Professor Ugo Spirito ('How is it that some "big names" find it so difficult to acknowledge the superiority of my thought above any other?') and Professor Cleto Carbonara. Ser-Giacomi winds up his speech to the congress with an appeal to readers to help him find a patron 'for the reprinting, by the thousand, of all my writings'. Between Ser-Giacomo and the aforementioned Tummolo a bitter polemic is running, with the latter defending his Mystic Atheism, which all goes to show that, unlike the poet, the philosopher finds an audience but not affection and understanding.

Another little understood figure engaged in a tragic battle against the world of knowledge is Eulogo D'Armi of Cagliari. After warring with contemporary Italian thought, D'Armi recounts in his *Teismo e monismo di fronte* [Theism and Monism Compared] how at the 1958 philosophy congress the 'lackey' secretariat had 'employed a series of frivolous and false pretexts to dissuade me from making an address.' But D'Armi had noticed that the head of the Soviet delegation, Mitin, was exceeding his allotted time ('the advantage of being backed by a great power!') and had rebelled against this blatant tryanny. To the mocked and misunderstood philosopher, the congress rules appear as manoeuvres deliberately contrived to prevent him from making any contribution. And this cannot be attributed to a persecution complex, for it is true that one of the major preoccupations of all philosophy congresses or journals is indeed to prevent the often uncontrollable participation of eccentrics.

The suffering endured by these thinkers could lead me to end this account of the fourth dimension on too pathetic a note. Yet the fourth dimension is vast. Here, everything is possible. Things and people can sometimes, by accident, emerge and leave it. Equally, the youngster destined for another dimension may, through error or inexperience, end up there instead. A study of first works by established writers might lead to some curious discoveries. Above all, the fourth dimension provides the ideal conditions for the eccentric, weighed down by intimations of his own originality and imminent greatness.

The most obvious (and least studied) example of this ambiguity at the threshold between one dimension and another is the work of the Piedmontese writer Augusto Blotto. Blotto, who apparently leads a sober and upright life as a clerk, publishes his luxury-bound volumes with Rebellato of Padua. The books are very expensive and, as far as I know, Blotto has never sold them through bookshops. Instead, he distributes them with largesse to critics and newspapers. To date he has published sixteen or seventeen volumes, and has plans to produce the same number again. Each volume contains from three to six hundred pages of poetry. The titles are, without a doubt, brilliant: *Trepide di prestigio* [Anxious from Prestige], *Autorevole e tanto disperso* [Authoritative and Ever so Lost], *Il maneggio per erti, senza sugo* [Steep Ascent, without Sauce], *Castelletti, regali, vedute* [Castles, Gifts, Views], *La forza grossa e varia* [The Great and Varied Strength], *I boli (i baldi)* [Boles and the Brave], *Nell'insieme, nel pacco d'aria* [Together, in a Parcel of Air], *Triste attentissimo informarsi* [Sad, Alert, Find out], *Svenevole a intelligenza* [Affectation to Intelligence], *Tranquillità e presto atroce* [Tranquillity and Atrocious in no time].

Unbridled linguistic invention is a feature of almost all of Blotto's poems. The objection that this inventiveness is mostly gratuitous (putting it in a different class from that of Gadda or Sanguineti) comes up against the perseverance of a poet who for thousands of pages invents his own language of demented innovation: 'The asphalt thigh, all a tiggering, a talcum powder – amidst the scaly meadows a bit of slate – a candle – detaching itself perhaps with clouding, being well absent . . . A boarded up Christ – with holes in stones, with mothy mantisisms of shoulder blades . . .' Blotto's lexicon is made up of things like: 'cabonetta evening', 'rod of vehemence of the southern abominator', 'horrible long nails', 'perhaps I'll paint wormlet of crocus', 'doubling myself to get inside us', 'tonguecrusts'. His poems are hard, stony, their syntax laborious, their comprehensibility nil (which is not to say they are meaningless), their plausibility difficult to ascertain. Yet over thousands and thousands and thousands of poems. Blotto goes on building his world on the tip of one of those forked headlands that fall steeply away to genius on one side and to monomania on the other. Anyway, it is one of those cases in which sheer output makes the reader suspect that he has unrecognized qualities.

It may be, however, that the relationship between the literary dimensions is fixed for all time. Certainly an abyss separates Blotto from those lady primary school teachers who write verses concerning mournful throbbings. Yet, for reasons that are unclear, an abyss may forever separate him from the poets of the second and third dimension. Could it be that the cabals really do exist?

1973

NOTES

INTRODUCTION

1. See David Robey's introduction to the English version, *Open Work*, trans. Anna Cancogni (London: Hutchinson Radius, 1989).

2. Umberto Eco, *Diario minimo* (Milan: Mondadori, 1963); trans. William Weaver as *Misreadings* (New York: Harcourt Brace, 1993).

3. 'The present situation is one in which it is possible to say that there is one culture (albeit with divisions in it) or several cultures (overlapping and rubbing up against each another) but no longer that there are two cultures, high and popular, divided from each other.' Geoffrey Nowell-Smith, 'Popular Culture', *New Formations*, 2, 1987, p. 75. For an analysis of the debate in the United States, see Andrew Ross, *No Respect: Intellectuals and Popular Culture* (New York and London: Routledge, 1989).

4. 'Pop goes the Artist', *Times Literary Supplement*, 17 December 1964. See also the ensuing correspondence in the 31 December issue which includes a letter beginning: 'I see your reviewer is another believer in the tiresome old cliché that the Latins, notably the French and Italians, are an especially clear-thinking race.'

5. Chapter-headings are telling: 'Invitations to a Candy-Floss World: The Newer Mass Art' or 'The Newer Mass Art: Sex in Shiny Packets'. Richard Hoggart, *The Uses of Literacy* (London: Chatto and Windus, 1957).

6. See Zygmunt Barański and Robert Lumley (eds.), *Culture and Conflict in Postwar Italy: Essays on Mass and Popular Culture* (London: Macmillan, 1990).

7. Umberto Eco, 'Verso una civiltà della visione', in *Pirelli: Rivista e informazione*, 1, January 1961. The cultural gap which Eco felt existed between different social groups is indicated by his reference to the housemaid 'who was convinced that the presenter Mike Buongiorno regarded her with particular fondness because during broadcasts he always looked in her direction.'

8. In 1984 the *New York Review of Books* asked Eco if they could reprint his 'World of Charlie Brown'. He notes that such a request would have been unthinkable when the essay was first written as the lines drawn round Literature and Art were more exclusive: 'My text hadn't changed, though; the world of Charles Schulz belongs to the history

of American culture, whether to the history of art or literature I don't know, but it belongs there precisely because it is able to put these distinctions in doubt.' Eco's introduction to Charles M. Schulz, *40 anni di vita e di arte*, ed. Giovanni Trimboli (Milan: Rizzoli, 1990).

9. Notably Eco's 'Cogitus interruptus' in *Travels in Hyperreality*, trans. William Weaver (New York: Harcourt Brace Jovanovich, 1986); also towards the end of the essay 'Political Language' in this volume.

10. Eco's first job at Bompiani was to edit a series entitled 'Idee nuove' (New Ideas), which had originated with the purpose of 'introducing those currents of contemporary philosophy that Benedetto Croce ignored, i.e. excluded'. Valentino Bompiani, *Il mestiere dell'editore* (Milan: Longanesi, 1988). It should be noted, however, that the openness of Italian culture, especially its propensity for translation, has also been seen as a sign of weakness; for Edgar Morin, for example, 'It is the victim of its own richness, given that for all its assimilation it doesn't digest or recreate anything.' Quoted in Enzo Golino, *La distanza culturale* (Bologna: Cappelli, 1980).

11. See Christopher Wagstaff, 'The Neo-Avantgarde', in Michael Caesar and Peter Hainsworth (eds.), *Writers and Society in Contemporary Italy* (Leamington Spa: Berg Publishers, 1984).

12. Umberto Eco, 'The Death of Gruppo 63', in *Open Work*, pp. 238–9. On the subsequent success of members of this avant-garde, Omar Calabrese notes: 'The Italians who are enjoying success today often come from the experimental circles of the 1950s and 1960s. One could say that it is a certain Italianness of the avant-garde that is getting international recognition.' Omar Calabrese, 'Che effetto fa?', *Panorama*, 21 April 1985, p. 141.

13. For Eco's reflections on book titles, see *Notes on the Name of the Rose* (London: Secker & Warburg, 1985).

14. Raymond Queneau, *Esercizi di stile*, trans. Umberto Eco (Turin: Einaudi, 1983); English version: *Exercises in Style*, trans. Barbara Wright (London: John Calder, 1981).

15. Teresa De Lauretis, *Eco* (Florence: La nuova Italia, 1981), p. 85.

16. Umberto Eco, *Come si fa una tesi di laurea* (Milan: Bompiani, 1977). The figure of Casaubon in *Foucault's Pendulum*, described as a 'Sam Spade' of cultural information, embodies this kind of DIY approach to culture.

17. For an extended discussion of the relationship of intellectuals and social movements, see Robert Lumley, *States of Emergency: Cultures of Revolt in Italy, 1968–78* (London: Verso, 1990), especially chapter 10, 'Dreaming of a Cultural Revolution'.

18. Scott Sullivan, 'Master of the Signs', *Newsweek*, 22 December 1986, p. 49.

19. See, for instance, Eco's illuminating reading of workers' and students'

slogans during the 1977 protest, as discussed in Meagan Morris, 'Euro-communism versus semiological delinquency', in M. Morris (ed.), *Language, Sexuality and Subversion* (Darlington, Australia, 1978), pp. 66–8.

20. Jean Chesneaux, Umberto Eco and Gino Nebiolo (eds.), *I fumetti di Mao* (Bari: Laterza, 1971).

21. David Robey, 'The centre cannot hold', *Times Higher Education Supplement*, 20 January 1989. For fuller analyses of Eco's work see Robey's essays 'Umberto Eco', in M. Caesar and P. Hainsworth, *Writers and Society in Contemporary Italy* and 'Umberto Eco and the Analysis of the Media' in Barański and Lumley (eds.), *Culture and Conflict in Postwar Italy*.

22. Contrast, for example, the sympathetic yet detached analysis of 'On Chinese Comic Strips' with the statements of fellow semioticians of Maoist persuasion: 'The Cultural Revolution has been practically bloodless, although combative; this was because the political power always remained socialist, thanks to the People's Army'. Ugo Volli, 'Contre-information et communication de masse', *V.S.*, 1, 1971, p. 107.

23. Carlo Ginzburg, *Il giudice e lo storico* (Turin: Einaudi, 1991), p. 57.

24. Umberto Eco, 'A Guide to the Neo-Television of the 1980s', in Barański and Lumley (eds.), *Culture and Conflict in Postwar Italy*. See also the essays on the Italian television system by Philip Schlesinger, Beppe Richeri, Chris Wagstaff and Mauro Wolf. For a fascinating analysis of television criticism in the Italian press from 1956 to 1990, see Elena Dagrada, *A parer nostro* (Rome: RAI ERI, 1992).

25. Umberto Eco and Stuart Hall, 'Crisis? What crisis?', in Bill Bourne, Udi Eichler and David Herman (eds.), *Writers and Politics* (Northampton: Spokesman/Hobb Press, 1987), p. 18.

26. De Lauretis, *Eco*, p. 90.

27. Omar Calabrese, 'Ma che effetto fa?', *Panorama*, 21 April 1985, p. 143.

28. Hans Magnus Enzensberger, *Europe, Europe* (London: Hutchinson Radius, 1989).

29. Enrico Castelnuovo and Carlo Ginzburg, 'Centro e periferia', in Giovanni Previtali (ed.), *Storia dell'Arte Italiana. 1: Questioni e metodi* (Turin: Einaudi, 1979), p. 287.

30. Tullio De Mauro, *L'Italia delle Italie* (Rome: Editori Riuniti, 1987), p. xvii.

PART ONE
CHAPTER 1

1. Heraclitus, *Fragments*, trans. T. M. Robinson (Toronto: Toronto University Press, 1987).

2. Antonio Gramsci, 'Popular Origin of the "Superman"' in D. Forgacs and G. Nowell-Smith (eds.), *Gramsci: Selections from Cultural Writings*, trans. W. Boelhower (London: Lawrence and Wishart, 1985), pp. 355–9.

3. For Eco in Eugène Sue, see 'Rhetoric and Ideology in Sue's *Les Mystères de Paris*' in *The Role of the Reader* (Bloomington: Indiana University Press, 1979); for Poe on Sue, see Edgar Allan Poe, *Essays and Reviews* (New York: Library of America, 1984), pp. 1404–7; for Marx and Engels, see K. Marx and F. Engels, *On Literature and Art* (Moscow: Progress Publishers, 1976), pp. 296–313.

4. *Revolt of the Masses:* José Ortega y Gasset's celebrated attack on mass culture published in Madrid in 1930; two works, *Esquema de la crisis: Historia como sistema* and *El Espectador*, were published in Italy by Bompiani in 1946 and 1949 respectively.

5. On the Young Hegelians, see D. McLellan, *The Young Hegelians and Karl Marx* (London: Macmillan, 1969).

6. 'The Frankfurt School' is shorthand for Institut für Sozialforschung, the Institute for Social Research based in Frankfurt until the rise of Nazism drove its members into exile. For a standard account, see Martin Jay, *The Dialectical Imagination* (London: Heinemann, 1973).

7. Max Horkheimer: founder member of Frankfurt School. Works in translation include *Critique of Instrumental Reason* (1967) and, with Theodor Adorno, *Dialectic of the Enlightenment* (1947).

8. Renato Solmi: a key figure in persuading the publisher Giulio Einaudi to introduce the Frankfurt School to an Italian readership; responsible for Italian editions of Adorno's *Minima Moralia* and Benjamin's *Angelus novus*.

9. Theodor Adorno, *Minima Moralia*, trans. E. F. N. Jephcott (London: New Left Books, 1974), p. 247.

10. 'The material doctrine that men are products of circumstances . . . forgets that it is men that change circumstances.' K. Marx, 'Theses on Feuerbach', in K. Marx and F. Engels, *Selected Works* (London: Lawrence and Wishart, 1968), p. 28.

11. Karl Markus Michel: New Left intellectual and editor of the cultural review *Kursbuch*.

12. Günther Anders: pacifist and campaigner against the Bomb and the Vietnam War; an exile from Nazi Germany, 'his ruthless abandonment of philosophy's systems, doctrines and institutionalized self-importance, and unerring commitment to practical intervention mark his philosophical work' (obituary in the *Guardian*, 9 January 1993).

13. Jorge Luis Borges, 'Tlön, Uqbar, Orbis Tertius', in *Labyrinths*, trans. J. Irby (London: Penguin, 1981).

14. *The Works of Bernard of Clairvaux*, vol. I, *Treatises* (Shannon: Irish University Press, 1970), p. 64.

15. Ibid., p. 66.
16. Eco is referring to the various essays that make up *Apocalittici e integrati*, not to this volume. It seemed better not to edit out these remarks because of their intrinsic interest. References are given to those essays available in translation.
17. Umberto Eco, 'The Structure of Bad Taste', in *Open Work*, trans. A. Cancogni (London: Hutchinson Radius, 1989).
18. Umberto Eco, 'A Reading of Steve Canyon', *Twentieth Century Studies*, December 1976; reprinted in catalogue accompanying the Institute of Contemporary Art's exhibition *Comic Iconoclasm* (London, 1987).
19. 'The World of Charlie Brown' in this collection comes from section two of *Apocalittici e integrati*.
20. *The Notebooks of Leonardo da Vinci*, selected and edited by Irma A. Richter (Oxford: Oxford University Press, 1980), p. 283.

CHAPTER 3

1. The title of *Opera aperta* has been given in English (*Open Work*). However, the versions in Italian contain a number of essays not included in translation, whereas *Open Work* includes writings from other books.
2. Elémire Zolla's opinions remain largely antithetical to those of Eco: 'For two centuries, from all the avant-garde groups one has heard go up the old cry of the witches in *Macbeth*: "Fair is foul and foul is fair." The artefacts they produce are like the ingredients the witches throw into the cauldron, and the bubbling broth is the flow of cultural commodities issued by the mass media – what the avant-garde boils down to in time.' *The Uses of the Imagination and the Decline of the West* (Ipswich: Golgonooza Press, 1978), p. 30.
3. ARCI: cultural and recreational organization closely associated with the Communist Party.
4. *Linus*: A review dedicated to comic strips launched in April 1965 and unlike any other of its kind because of philological rigour, footnotes and debates accompanying the presentation.
5. Umberto Eco, *Diario minimo* (Milan: Mondadori, 1963); trans. William Weaver as *Misreadings* (New York: Harcourt Brace, 1993).

CHAPTER 4

1. Umberto Eco, *La struttura assente* (Milan: Bompiani, 1968).
2. Edgar Morin, *L'Esprit du temps* (Paris: Grasset, 1962).

3. Umberto Eco, 'Verso una civiltà della visione', in *Pirelli: Rivista di informazione e di tecnica*, 1 January 1961.

4. 'Phenomenology of Mike Buongiorno': essay included in *Diario minimo* (Milan: Mondadori, 1963), trans. William Weaver as *Misreadings* (New York: Harcourt Brace, 1993).

5. Guido Viale: subsequently a leader of the 1968 student movement.

6. Valentino Bompiani: 'the most influential as well as the oldest of literary publishers when he died aged 93 in February 1992 . . . His first two books in 1929 were the biography of a would-be saint, written by a priest, and *Mein Kampf*, translated by a Jew, who wanted people to be aware of what Hitler was up to . . . In the postwar period he was equally alert to the new trends of European and American thought. After all, Umberto Eco had his training as an editor of Bompiani for many years' (*Guardian* obituary, 25 February 1992).

7. Umberto Eco, 'Narrative Structures in Fleming', in *The Role of the Reader* (Bloomington: Indiana University Press, 1979).

8. Umberto Eco, 'Rhetoric and Ideology in Sue's *Les Mystères de Paris*', in *The Role of the Reader*.

9. Umberto Eco, *Le forme del contenuto* (Milan: Bompiani, 1971). Neither this book nor *La struttura assente* have been translated in their entirety. However, Eco noted that *A Theory of Semiotics* (Bloomington: Indiana University Press, 1976) was 'halfway' between the two.

10. See the essays included here under the section 'The Rise and Fall of Countercultures', notably 'The New Forms of Expression'.

11. Herbert Marcuse: an 'apocalyptic intellectual' according to Eco's definition; a member of the Frankfurt School whose works became very influential among radicals in the 1960s, especially *Eros and Civilization* (Boston, 1955), and *One-Dimensional Man* (Boston, 1964).

12. Marshall McLuhan: an 'integrated intellectual'; author of best-selling *Understanding Media* (New York: McGraw Hill, 1964). Subject of a sharp critique in Eco's 'Cogitus interruptus' in *Travels in Hyperreality* (New York: Harcourt Brace Jovanovich, 1986).

13. See the essay 'Independent Radio in Italy' in this collection.

14. A reference to Horkheimer's rift in the 1960s with the more left-wing currents, such as that represented by Marcuse.

15. For a discussion of the comic strip as 'alternative information', see the essay in this collection, 'On Chinese Comic Strips'.

16. Eco, 'The Myth of Superman' in *The Role of the Reader*.

CHAPTER 5

1. M. Foucault, *Discipline and Punish: The Birth of the Prison* (London: Penguin, 1977).

CHAPTER 6

1. *Imago mundi*: a compendium of cosmology and geography popular throughout the Middle Ages and translated into various vernaculars.

PART TWO
CHAPTER 1

1. See U. Eco, *La struttura assente* (Milan: Bompiani, 1968), especially section A4 ('The Persuasive Message') and A5 ('Rhetoric and Ideology'), not to mention the analysis of advertising posters in B5.

2. The most wide-ranging and comprehensive reinstatement of rhetoric in a contemporary perspective is C. Perelman and L. Olbrechts-Tyteca, *The New Rhetoric: A Treatise on Argumentation* (trans. J. Wilkinson and P. Weaver; London: University of Notre Dame Press, 1969). Many of the observations I make here, especially concerning the affinities between persuasive rhetoric and undogmatic philosophical discourse, are inspired by this work.

3. It is easy to point out how the three arguments concerning property and theft condense three different ideological positions. The first harks back to the argumentation of Catholic casuistry, notably the principle of 'hidden compensation' according to which a badly paid employee, having heard the advice of his confessor and in the absence of other means of redress, is able to compensate himself in some way in order to restore the proportion of the 'just wage' wrongly denied him. The second argument is that of currently established law: in order to restore what someone has wrongly taken possession of I must have recourse to the courts so that the possession is declared wrongful. Otherwise it is property that the law recognizes and I cannot reappropriate it through an arbitrary individual act. The third argument is, broadly speaking, that of communists. One should note, however, that the first and third argument could well coincide; but for the fact that, by common agreement, the casuistic argument is clearly limited to the ethical sphere (personal relations and matters on a small scale), while the communist argument extends to the political sphere (collective relations and planetary scale). However, the fact is that with the communist set of premises there is no difference between political and ethical spheres, with the former subsuming the latter. Instead, the casuistic argument, if it is to work, needs to assume as implicit the premises that establish the difference between politics and ethics. For argument number two, by contrast, both spheres are neutralized by that of the law, which rules supreme. The fact that all three

arguments are rhetorical in nature is shown by the following: they all cease to be valid if the system of implicit premises underpinning them is changed.

4. For two exemplary repertories, see the nimble 'L'ancienne rhétorique' (*Communications*, 8, 1965), by R. Barthes, and the denser H. Lausberg, *Elementi di retorica* (Bologna: Mulino, 1972). For the definitive manual, see H. Lausberg, *Handbuch der literarischen Rhetorik* (Munich: Hueber, 1960).

5. The graffiti of the Sorbonne of May 1968 are all excellent examples of fresh and effective rhetorical formulations. Take some of the best known: 'Popularize the struggles of the Divine Marquis' (*paradox*); 'Patriotism is mass egoism' (*oxymoron*); 'CRS-Assassins' (*alliteration*); 'Power to the Imagination' (*personification*); 'Society is a carnivorous flower' (*similitude*); 'At Nanterre you enter' (*paronomasia*); 'It is prohibited to prohibit' (*derivatio* + *antithesis*); 'Leave fear of the reds to animals with horns' (*metonym* + *periphrasis* + *metaphor*).

6. See Paolo Fabbri, 'Prospettive di analisi del lingauggio politico', in *Il Telecomizio – Aspetti semiologici e sociologici del messaggio televisivo* (Urbino: Editrice Montefeltro, 1971).

7. See 'Risultati di una indagine sulla comprensione del linguaggio politico', RAI, *Appunti del Servizio Opinioni*, 37.

8. The polemic on technological language, launched by Pasolini's intervention at a conference, took place in late 1964/early 1965; for an initial résumé, see Andrea Barbato, 'Da Dante a Granzotto', *L'Espresso*, 24 January 1965.

9. In this sense the dominant rhetorical figure when politicians communicate with the public at large is *euphemism*. See the chapter entitled 'Political Interdiction' in Nora Galli de' Paratesi, *Semantica dell'eufemismo* (Turin: Giappichelli, 1964), later published by Mondadori under the title *Le brutte parole*.

CHAPTER 2

1. Marisa Borroni was one of the first TV presenters in Italy.

2. *Lascia o raddoppia* (*The 64,000 Dollar Question* in the United States and *Double Your Money* in the UK) was an immensely popular quiz programme whose presenter became the subject of a celebrated essay, 'Phenomenology of Mike Buongiorno', in *Diario minimo*.

3. *Carosello* was a daily programme in prime-time composed of advertisements.

4. San Remo was (and is) the annual song festival held in the seaside resort of that name; *Canzonissima* was a 1960s TV song contest.

5. *Campanile Sera*: a talk, quiz and game show which included an outside broadcast from a village or town in Italy.

6. Col. Bernacca: a pedantic weather forecaster with a taste for quotations and anecdotes who became a personality in his own right.

7. *Tribuna politica*: a pre-election current affairs programme in which politicians were questioned by journalists.

8. Father Mariano: a benevolent bearded figure who provided a five-minute 'thought for the day'.

9. An allusion to the infamous German Protestant mercenaries who watered their horses in St Peter's during the 1527 sack of Rome.

10. *Cronache italiane*: a parish-pump current affairs programme; *Tv degli agricoltori*: farming programme; *Giocagiò*: children's programme.

11. U. Eco, P. Fabbri, P. P. Giglioli, F. Lumachi, T. Seppilli and G. Tinacci Manelli, 'Towards a Semiotic Inquiry into the Television Message', *Working Papers in Cultural Studies*, 3, Autumn 1972 (translation by Paola Splendore of original 1965 paper).

12. The concept 'opinion leader' was first developed in the study by P. Lazarfeld, B. Berelson and H. Gaudet, *The People's Choice: How the Voter Makes Up His Mind in a Presidential Campaign* (New York: Columbia University Press, 1944).

13. Orietta Berti: a singer of traditional Italian songs.

14. P. Fabbri, 'Le comunicazioni di massa in Italia: sguardo semiotico e malocchio della sociologia', *Versus*, 5, 1973.

15. E. Garroni, *Progetto di semiotica* (Bari: Laterza, 1973).

16. C. S. Peirce, *1931–58 Collected Papers* (Cambridge: Harvard University Press, 8 vols., 1931–58); see also Eco's discussion of interpretants in *Theory of Semiotics* (Bloomington: Indiana University Press, 1976).

17. L. Hjelmslev, *Prolegomena to a Theory of Language* (Madison: University of Wisconsin, 1961).

18. 'Lascia che io vadi': the 'grammatically correct' version would be 'lascia che io vada'. An equivalent in English for the verb 'to do' might be: Standard English: 'You did it', non-standard dialect: 'You done it.'

19. 'Grammar-oriented' and 'text-oriented': concepts developed from J. Lotman and B. Uspenskij, *Tipologia della cultura* (1973); see also Lotman, *Universe of the Mind: Semiotic Theory of Culture* (London: Tauris, 1990), with introduction by Eco.

20. Published by Gollancz in 1935 and by Bompiani in Italy after the war, A. J. Cronin's *The Stars Look Down* was a best-seller serialized for television; described on the blurb of the English 1965 paperback as 'A book about PEOPLE, the story of miners – their land, their lives, their loves, their fights, their scars'.

21. W. Benjamin, *Illuminations* (trans. Harry Zohn, London: Jonathan Cape, 1970).

CHAPTER 3

1. G. F. Bettetini, *Produzione del senso e messa in scena* (Milan: Bompiani, 1975).
2. 'Il caso e l'intreccio': an essay unfortunately not incuded in *Open Work*; a title translatable as 'Chance and Plot'.
3. Vermicino: a place in central Italy associated with the tragic episode of the small boy who fell down a well. Attempts to rescue him over several days galvanized the attention of the nation.

CHAPTER 4

1. Surrounded by enemy troops at Waterloo, the French general Cambronne shouted the five-letter word thereafter known as *le mot de Cambronne*.
2. Paleotelevision: a term first used by Eco in an article for *L'Espresso* (30 January 1983), reprinted in translation as 'A Guide to the Neo-Television of the 1980s' in Z. Barański and R. Lumley (eds.), *Culture and Conflict in Postwar Italy* (London: Macmillan, 1990).
3. Famous quiz show originating in the USA and hosted by the ever-green presenter of Italian television, Mike Buongiorno.
4. TV critic of the newspaper *La Repubblica*.
5. A late-night 'post-modern' TV show of the mid-1980s.
6. A Neapolitan comedy actor, star of numerous films in the pre- and postwar periods.

PART THREE
CHAPTER 1

1. L. Wittgenstein, *Philosophical Investigations* (trans. G. E. M. Anscombe; Oxford: Basil Blackwell, 1968), sections 66–75.
2. See essay in this collection, 'Apocalyptic and Integrated Intellectuals'.
3. Carl von Clausewitz: author of famous treatise *On War* (1932), best remembered for his pronouncement that war is the continuation of politics by other means.
4. Reference to the protest characteristic of the 'Movement of 1977' involving mass absenteeism from work, 'self-reduction' of bus and cinema tickets, and cultural transgression; themes discussed elsewhere in Eco's *Sette anni di desiderio* (Milan: Bompiani, 1983).
5. The P.38 magnum became the symbol of the violent wing of the 1977 protest.
6. Edward Burnett Tylor: Victorian anthropologist and author of

Researches into the Early History of Mankind (1865), *Primitive Culture* (1871), and *Anthropology* (1881).

7. Benedetto Croce: philosopher and historian in the idealist tradition whose ideas were pursued in the field of anthropology by Ernesto de Martino; for his conceptions of historical explanation, see *The Theory and History of Historiography* (trans. D. Ainslie; London: Harrap, 1921), and *History as the Story of Liberty* (trans. S. Sprigge; London, 1941).

8. *Cane sciolto*: 'unloosed dog'; a term used in the 1970s for ex-members of revolutionary organizations.

9. A Gramscian definition of those who perform tasks of intellectual leadership in relation to the dominant or subordinate class.

10. Replying to the Communist Party leader Togliatti's idea that intellectuals should subordinate themselves to the cause, Elio Vittorini, the writer, declared that one shouldn't play the piper to either the state or the party.

11. An allusion to Julien Benda's *Trahison des clercs* (1927), which criticizes intellectuals who prostitute their talents for the achievement of political ends.

CHAPTER 2

1. Clement Greenberg, 'Avant-Garde and Kitsch' (1939) in B. Rosenberg and D. Manning White (eds.), *Mass Culture: The Popular Arts in America* (New York: Free Press, 1957).

2. *Linea lombarda*: a current of poetry spanning the period from the late 1930s to the early 1960s, including such figures as Attilio Bertolucci and Vittorio Sereni; characterized by lyricism, a feeling for the countryside and a register more colloquial than that of contemporary Tuscan poets.

3. Gruppo Ufo: 'Doing architecture became an activity of free expression, just as making love means not just producing children but communicating through sex' (Andrea Branzi, *The Hot House: Italian New Wave Design*, London: Thames and Hudson, 1984), p. 60.

4. *The Encomium of Helen* by the Greek sophist Gorgias.

5. Tommaso Grossi (1790–1853) and Cesare Cantù (1804–95) were writers in the Romantic tradition and vehemently anti-Austrian.

6. For Eco's reflections on the Italian neo-avant-garde, see 'The Death of Gruppo 63' in *Open Work*, and 'Il Gruppo 63, lo sperimentalismo e l'avanguardia' in *Sugli specchi* (Milan: Bompiani, 1985).

7. Novissimi: the title given to an anthology edited by Alfredo Giuliani and subsequently applied to the poets themselves (Giuliani, Elio Pagliarani, Antonio Porta, Edoardo Sanguineti and Nanni Balestrini) in a conscious assertion of avant-garde ambition.

8. An allusion to the opening line of *Sant'Ambrogio*, a poem by Giuseppe Giusti (1809–50) in which the poet addresses the Austrian Emperor, head of the army of occupation, in markedly ironic tones. He recounts how, although identified as a rebel for his writings, the sight of the enemy soldiers at prayer in the cathedral still moved him greatly.

9. Gruppo 70: 'formed in Florence in 1963 and led by Lamberto Pignotti, it pressed its theories on the necessity of incorporating scientific and technical language into contemporary poetry . . . it also stressed inter-disciplinary cooperation between the visual arts and literature; *poesia visiva* became the focus of their work.' Laurence R. Smith (ed.), *The New Italian Poetry* (Berkeley and Los Angeles: University of California Press, 1981), p. 36.

10. Nanni Balestrini: one of the linguistically most inventive of the Novis-simi poets; for parallel text translation of some of his work from the 1960s, see Smith (ed.), *The New Italian Poetry*. Balestrini has also written 'novels', including *Vogliamo tutto* (Milan: Feltrinelli, 1971) and *Gli invisibili* (1987), the latter in translation as *The Unseen* (trans. L. Heron; London: Verso, 1989).

11. Roman Jacobson, 'Linguistics and Poetics', in Thomas A. Sebeok (ed.), *Style in Language* (Cambridge, Mass: The Technology Press/ MIT, 1960).

CHAPTER 3

1. E. Panofsky, 'The History of the Theory of Human Proportions as a Reflection on the History of Styles', in *Meaning in the Visual Arts* (London: Penguin, 1970).

CHAPTER 4

1. For A/traverso and the Bologna movement of 1977, see R. Lumley, *States of Emergency: Cultures of Revolt in Italy, 1968–78* (London: Verso, 1990).

CHAPTER 5

1. In the mid-1970s the Italian Communist Party, under the leadership of Enrico Berlinguer, formally recognized the impossibility of making further progress with the policies of an alliance of socialist forces which it had espoused since 1943, and opted instead for what it called the 'historical compromise' (*compromesso storico*) between the socialist forces and Italy's ruling Christian Democrats.

2. The reference is to a phrase from Brecht's *Galileo:* 'Unhappy the land that has need of heroes' ('Unheil das Land das Helden braucht').

PART FOUR
CHAPTER 2

1. 'La Cicciolina' was elected in the 1987 elections. However, she failed to get re-elected, for the Party of Love, in April 1992.
2. Lilly Niagara's act at the Crazy Horse in Paris is described in an essay on striptease in *Diario minimo*.
3. An allusion to Mario Praz's *La carne, la morte e il diavolo*, whose title in English is *The Romantic Agony*.
4. Pippo Franco: a third-rate comedian, a regular on Saturday night variety shows who trades in sexual innuendo and popular Roman slang.
5. Reference to a celebrated incident of the Sardinian regional elections of 1957 when voters for Achille Lauro candidates received one shoe before voting and the other afterwards. 'It is well-known that the Lauro electoral campaigns of the fifties were based on the distribution of packets of macaroni and five thousand lire notes.' P. A. Allum, *Politics and Society in Post-War Naples* (Cambridge University Press, 1973), p. 105.
6. Paolo Villaggio: genial Genoese comic and inventor of 'Fracchia', a character in a TV show later transferred to the big screen, a servile and terrified clerk who always loses out.
7. To fully appreciate this passage one needs to know that Craxi has a huge head, Fanfani is diminutive, De Mita cannot pronounce his r's, Occhetto has a thick moustache, and Andreotti a hunchback.

CHAPTER 3

1. A witty allusion to Giosuè Carducci's poem *Inno a Satana* (1863). 'The title comes from Baudelaire, but the poem is outside the line of Baudelaire or Praga, and Carducci's Satan stands for the sunshine of life in opposition to the must of asceticism. Amongst the symbols recurrent in his poetry are the train and the fulling-mill; both stand graphically for adherence to a world of activity.' J. H. Whitfield, *A Short History of Italian Literature* (London: Penguin, 1969), p. 241.

CHAPTER 4

1. An allusion to Giorgio Bassani's famous novel *Il giardino dei Finzi-Contini* (1962).
2. On 25 July 1943, Mussolini was first asked for his resignation by the King and then placed under arrest: a 'coup' in the eyes of Mussolini's loyal followers.
3. The original text of *I promessi sposi* is over 500 pages long. Cetti's final sentence replaces the whole of the last two chapters.
4. *Finti* means false.
5. An organization of the extreme Left active in the early 1970s.
6. Piero Cavallero was a self-proclaimed Robin Hood of the Left, active in the 1960s.
7. Pietro Valpreda was an anarchist (wrongfully) accused of planting a bomb in a Milan bank in 1969.

INDEX